# The Chosen Ground

# The
# Chosen
# Ground

*Essays on the Contemporary Poetry
of Northern Ireland*

## Edited by Neil Corcoran

SEREN BOOKS

Dufour

Published in the United Kingdom by Seren Books
the book imprint of Poetry Wales Press Ltd
Andmar House, Tondu Road, Bridgend, Mid Glamorgan

Selection, editorial matter and Introduction © Neil Corcoran, 1992
Content of essays © The Essayists, 1992

**British Library Cataloguing in Publication Data**
The Chosen ground: essays on the contemporary poetry of Northern Ireland.
1. Northern Ireland. English poetry
I. Corcoran, Neil
821.914
UK ISBN 1-85411-024-1
ISBN 1-85411-028-4 paperback

Published with the financial support of the
Welsh Arts Council

First Published in the United States of America, 1992, by Dufour Editions Inc
Chester Springs, Pennsylvania 19425

**Library of Congress Cataloguing-in-Publication Data**
The Chosen ground : essays on the contemporary poetry of Northern Ireland /
edited and introduced by Neil Corcoran
    p. cm.
Includes bibliographical references (p. ) and index.
ISBN 0-8023-1291-8 : $35.00
    1. English poetry – Irish authors – Northern Ireland – History and criticism.
    2. English poetry – 20th century – History and criticism. 3. Northern Ireland –
Intellectual life – 20th century. 4. Northern Ireland in literature. I. Corcoran,
Neil.
PR8761.C47 1991
821'.914099416–dc20                                    90-24815
                                                        CIP

Typeset in 10½ point Plantin by Megaron, Cardiff
Printed by Billings & Sons Ltd, Worcester

# Contents

# Acknowledgements

The publisher acknowledges permission to make quotations from the following poets:

John Montague: quotations from *The Rough Field* (1972) and *Mount Eagle* (1988) by permission of Gallery Press, Ireland and Wake Forest University Press

Michael Longley: quotations from *Poems 1963-1983* (1991) by permission of Martin Secker and Warburg, and Peters Fraser & Dunlop Ltd.

Derek Mahon: quotations from *Poems 1962-1978* (1979) and *The Hunt by Night* (1982) by permission of Oxford University Press; from *Selected Poems* (1991) by permission of Gallery Press and Wake Forest University Press.

Tom Paulin: prose quotation reprinted by permission of Bloodaxe Books Ltd from: *Ireland and the English Crisis* by Tom Paulin (Bloodaxe Books, 1984); quotations from *The Strange Museum* (1981) by permission of Faber & Faber Publishers Ltd.

Paul Muldoon: quotations by permission of Faber & Faber Publishers Ltd.

Ciaran Carson: quotations from *The Irish for No* (1987) by permission of Gallery Press and Wake Forest University Press.

# Introduction

Some recent and influential anthologists would have it that the subject of this collection of essays hardly exists. Thomas Kinsella, in *The New Oxford Book of Irish Verse*, regards the idea of a "Northern Ireland Renaissance" (he holds the term in the sterilised tongs of quotation marks) as "largely a journalistic entity";[1] and Peter Fallon and Derek Mahon in their *Penguin Book of Contemporary Irish Poetry* repeat Kinsella's charge and explicitly devote their anthology to the "polemical" task of "correct[ing] imbalances", attempting to define "a national body of work which, in its turn, belongs to a global community".[2] Mahon is, of course, one of the poets discussed in the present book and so is John Montague, who has put the case even more emphatically (or intemperately): the "northern thing", he says, is "depressingly close to *Ulsterkampf*, when our giant forebears, Yeats and Joyce, have given us the freedom of the world".[3] The Penguin anthology, although not explicitly, is presumably reacting to Paul Muldoon's *Faber Book of Contemporary Irish Poetry* which notoriously limits its selection to the work of ten poets; six of them are contemporary Northerners; another is Louis MacNeice, who has become the lost father in some persuasive accounts of Northern poetry; and yet another is Patrick Kavanagh who, coming from Co. Monaghan, and figuring so significantly in Seamus Heaney's criticism, may be regarded as a kind of honorary Ulsterman.

The danger in the all-Ireland anthologies is that of reducing the significance of the Northern work. In the face of the evidence it seems unlikely that the polemic will succeed all that well, and merely unexamined to talk about a 'journalistic entity': the quality of the work produced in Northern Ireland since the mid-1960s constitutes one of the most remarkable facts in contemporary literary history. (And what, by the way, does 'journalistic' mean here? If it means an entity created by *literary* journalism, then perhaps this is the place—since several contributors to this volume are notable reviewers of new verse—to say that the reviewing of contemporary poetry, when disciplined by scholarship and concerned to formulate difficult judgement, is as good a place as any for such categories to be constructed.) The danger in the Muldoon anthology, on the other hand, is that the word 'Irish' is being all too easily commandeered by a *parti-pris*, a danger in no way mitigated by the book's 'prologue' which (in the least excusable disappearing trick in Muldoon's extensive repertoire) sets F. R. Higgins up as fall guy to MacNeice in an anthology that finds no room for Austin Clarke. This is to tell a distinctly skewed story about contemporary 'Irish' poetry.

These accounts all ignore the other, British history of which the contemporary poetry of Northern Ireland has also, long since, been an inevitable part. Its assimilation into this history is clear enough from the fact that most of the work has had English publication, but it is made strikingly apparent in the introduction to the *Penguin Book of Contemporary British Poetry* edited by Blake Morrison and Andrew Motion in 1982. They argue bluntly that "the new spirit in British poetry began to make itself felt in Northern Ireland during the late 1960s and early 1970s"; and Seamus Heaney's role in this story is recognised by his being placed first in the anthology.[4] The story is complicated by Heaney's well-known demurral at his incorporation in an anthology of 'British' poetry in the poem 'An Open Letter', published as the second Field Day pamphlet in Derry (although, as Richard Brown points out below, nobody has seen fit to remove him from subsequent reprints).[5] Rejecting the national identity, Heaney was also possibly rejecting a certain aestheticising of his work in the Morrison/Motion introduction. They read his Ovidian/Mandel-stamian self-description in 'Exposure' from *North*, for instance—"an inner émigré"—as the origin of an *ostranenie* surfacing in contemporary British poetry as varieties of Martianism, new narrative and so on, in which poets become "not inhabitants of their own lives so much as intrigued observers".[6] This is probably the accurate tracing of an influence, but it tends to elide the fact that the phrase 'inner émigré', when used by a poet as, in part, a figure for his move from the North to the South of Ireland, reminds us that, as John Kerrigan says below, "Ireland is not integral", that in Ireland you can be literally an 'inner' or internal émigré by crossing a national border.

If it seems to fit completely successfully into neither an exclusivist Irish account nor an exclusivist British account, then, this is one clear reason why the contemporary poetry of Northern Ireland earns its place as a special case. In the essays collected here, many of them written by critics (and poet-critics) whose personal and/or professional lives have frequently crossed the Irish Sea, there is a fundamental awareness of hybrid heritage and influence, of what John Kerrigan calls the "state of between-states", which is the characteristic state of much of this poetry. Gerald Dawe's essay on John Montague analyses his use of the rhetoric of "romantic nationalism" in the different contexts which challenge and question it, discovering an analogue in Stephen Spender's study of another hyphenation, *Love-Hate Relations: A Study of Anglo-American Sensibilities*. Stan Smith explores Seamus Heaney's work by regarding attentively his uses of that preposition of balanced position, 'between', and newly applying Heaney's own critically descriptive terms, "place and displacement", to the poet himself; he reveals *en route* an unsuspected and suggestive relation between Heaney and Donald Davie, meeting in the 'between' of Dante. Peter McDonald analyses the various resonances of the word 'home' in Michael Longley, differentiating it from uses in English poems and pointing to the relationship between a Northern home and a 'home-from-home' in the West in Longley's verse, a relationship in which the word is purged of those territorial claims it often carries in Irish writing. Hugh Haughton relates the categories of 'place and displacement' to the work of Derek Mahon, insisting (against the grain) that the concept 'Irish poet' is still a necessary definition of this poet in whom the whole concept of place is called into question, but one that must be made with a wholly new subtlety and precision. Bernard O'Donoghue examines in Tom Paulin another kind of between-state: that of the poet bent on making a poetry from a language "unflinchingly drawn from the public domain", and writing a verse coincident with a developing critical and cultural analysis. John Kerrigan draws a number of poets—in particular Heaney, Muldoon and Mahon—into his Ovidian net, exploring the extraordinary variety of figures cut by this 'Latin Ulsterman', poet of metamorphosis and exile (those twin between-states), in contemporary Northern verse, and eventually discovering in Derek Mahon the most exemplary Northern Ovidian imagination.

It is notable that many of these essays propose new connections and inter-relationships: Dawe's use of Spender and Smith's of Davie, for instance; Hugh Haughton's tracing of Mahon's affinities with Camus to a point where his Northern displacement comes to seem a paradigm for the condition of the modern intellectual; and Kerrigan's reading of Mahon through the lens of the sociologist Michael Thompson's *Rubbish Theory*. Other essays foreground another juncture or alliance: that between Northern poetry and the discourses of postmodernism. Clair Wills brings Paul Muldoon's obliquity into focus via Barthès's reflections on the "staging of violence" in *Writing Degree Zero* and finds Bakhtin usefully apposite in charting the way the nature of responsibility is moved by Muldoon into a debate between linguistic arbitrariness and stability. Richard Brown, noting that "naturalness and literariness jostle for ascendancy" in readings of Heaney, focuses on the latter in an exploration of the pun and the "punning identity" in Heaney himself and in Muldoon; he proposes a postmodernism in both poets which calls into question some characteristic but ana-chronistic readerly assumptions. Thomas Docherty uncovers a postmodern writing in Medbh McGuckian, relating her, among much else, to Jean-François Lyotard's concept of 'untimeliness' and Luce Irigaray's opposition between the specular and the tactile; suggesting her affinities with nineteenth-century French decadence and early twentieth-century surrealism rather than any Irish models, he offers a reading of her work as "a call to a critical historicism". My own essay on Ciaran Carson attempts a more tentative combination of close reading and some theories of the postmodern with a view to discovering in Carson's digressive narratives, in his playing of the oral against the literary, in his central tropes, in his preoccupation with advertising and commodity, and in his intertextuality a postmodern poetry of the city of Belfast, worked out in contradistinction to some received literary forms.

The combination in this collection of essays of some long-sanctioned critical and scholarly practices with some more theor-etically-based ones witnesses, I hope, to a pluralism not weakly unresisting but considered and self-challenging. That seems to me entirely appropriate to a volume whose essays describe, again and again, a poetry in which categories are (with whatever difficulty and resistance) unsettled, in which positions are located at the preposition 'between', in which stasis is perturbed into movement. Yet many of these essays are also sensitive to the self-doubt, scepticism, scruple and fear of presumption in this poetry, its tactful withdrawals and refusals. Which is why I have entitled the collection with a phrase from Tom Paulin's long poem 'The Caravans at Lüneberg Heath' which closes his *Fivemiletown* (1987). As Bernard O'Donoghue demonstrates below, the poem intricately draws together different historical periods in its complex meditation/dialogue. At one point Paulin addresses Simon Dach, author of a poem written during the Thirty Years War but first published in 1936 (during the rise of German Fascism with which, in the figure of Heidegger, Paulin's poem is also concerned). The word "chosen" has of course its vibrant resonances with the European Protestant history and sensibility revealed in the poem:

> Simon I sometimes believe it's us poor saps
> give each of these places its strange and exact presence
> as if we're part of the action though the whole bloody mess
> it doesn't depend on our minds just
> for the chosen ground is always packed
> with skulls in section norns some end result

That combines a proper temerity and vaunt—poetry is, after all, what will name the event when the event has gone—with a properly self-correcting and self-punishing humility: the poetic intelligence is chastised by the action from which it always remains apart, the action which always exceeds all contemplation of it, whether in a Thirty Years War or a (now, in 1991) 23-years war in Northern Ireland. The chosen ground of the poet's writing is always already the given ground of violence and *realpolitik*, a burial-ground.

I am grateful to all the contributors to this volume for making an editor's job as agreeable and intellectually stimulating as it may be; and to the Research Fund of Sheffield University for a helpful grant.

NOTES

1.  Thomas Kinsella (ed.), *The New Oxford Book of Irish Verse* (Oxford: Oxford University Press, 1986), p. xxx.
2.  Peter Fallon and Derek Mahon (eds.), *The Penguin Book of Contemporary Irish Poetry* (Harmondsworth: Penguin Books, 1990), p. xx.
3.  John Montague, *The Figure in the Cave and Other Essays* (Dublin: Lilliput Press, 1989), p. 15.
4.  Blake Morrison and Andrew Motion (eds.), *The Penguin Book of Contemporary British Poetry* (Harmondsworth: Penguin Books, 1982), p. 12.
5.  Seamus Heaney, *An Open Letter* (Derry: Field Day Theatre Company Ltd., 1983); reprinted in Field Day Theatre Company (ed.), *Ireland's Field Day* (London: Hutchinson, 1985), pp. 23-30.
6.  Morrison and Motion, p. 12.

# Gerald Dawe
## Invocation of Powers: John Montague

# Invocation of Powers

## 1 The Lost Childhood

In the title essay of his collection, *The Figure in the Cave and other Essays*,[1] John Montague reveals the extent to which his adult life and work have been directed towards creating for himself a central place in the Irish literary canon. It is an ambition, as the essay outlines, deeply influenced by the experiences Montague underwent as a child, first uprooted from his family in New York, and subsequently returned to Northern Ireland as a foster-child in the care of elderly aunts in Co. Tyrone. The sense of dislocation that pervades Montague's poetry, and the self-conscious search for both a real (emotional) and imagined (cultural) home represent the twin areas which I plan to discuss. What the bond proves to be in John Montague's poetry between these two preoccupations is the presentation of his own 'self' as it responds to, and anticipates, various elements in Irish literary and political history.

The essay to which I have referred is important in this particular regard for as the editor of his essays, Antoinette Quinn, has pointed out, Montague is "primarily an autobiographical poet for whom the provincial and local unrest and violence, whether historical or contemporary, are extensions of ancestral, familial and personal traumas".[2]

In 'The Figure in the Cave', Montague relates his personal life-story to his artistic life. At several points they intersect and are made to take on an historical significance of self-mythologising:

> . . . Brooklyn-born, Tyrone-reared, Dublin-educated, constituted a tangle, a turmoil of contradictory allegiance it would take a lifetime to

unravel. And the chaos within contrasted with the false calm without: Ireland, both North and South, then seemed to me 'a fen of stagnant waters'. And there was no tradition for someone of my background to work in; except for the ahistorical genius of Kavanagh just across the border, there had not been a poet of Ulster Catholic background since the Gaelic poets of the eighteenth century. So when I describe myself as 'the missing link of Ulster poetry' I am not only joking, for, hard as it may be to understand today, there was no Northern dimension to Irish literature then . . . [3]

The 'then' is the late 1950s and early 1960s. What Montague is clearly seeking to establish here is his own place in Irish literature, notwithstanding the "ahistorical genius of Kavanagh". Throughout the essay, Montague informs us of the role he played in restoring to print such poets as John Hewitt and Patrick Kavanagh;[4] how he simultaneously promoted the notion of what he calls "the French idea of a fertile literary community" since he "would not wish anyone to go through what [he] endured as a young writer". Montague goes on to list his work in this regard—*The Dolmen Miscellany of Irish Writing* (1961) *The Faber Book of Irish Verse* (1974) and *Bitter Harvest* (1989).[5]

Having therefore outlined his making available a tradition that was either historical (the Gaelic poets of the eighteenth century) or otherwise obscured (like Kavanagh or Hewitt), Montague traces the wider net of his ambition by revealing his "veneration for older writers of genius" such as Ezra Pound, Wallace Stevens, Hugh MacDiarmid, Robert Graves, David Jones, Samuel Beckett and Austin Clarke:

> Graves was also writing in a tradition of love poetry going back to the *amour courtois* which began . . . in the valley of the Dordogne, a tradition in which I also inscribe myself, with modern hesitations. But I was always fond of my literary fathers, in verse and prose, and they usually returned the compliment.[6]

As earlier in the essay, when Montague writes of his own name and its changing from Tague to Montague ("I have played upon our change of name and am delighted that in the original Irish *taidgh* means 'Son of philosopher, poet or fool': I claim all three")[7] so too in the above extract the important point of note for present purposes is the identification with other writers as "my literary fathers" and the implicit sense of approval-seeking. This form of self-vindication is furthered by the preoccupied manner in which Montague relates himself to "several interlocking groups of writers" outside Ireland, from Gary Snyder, Robert Duncan, Charles Tomlinson and Ted Hughes, to poets writing in languages other than English, such as Octavio Paz. The tradition-making which such listing implies bears down directly upon one of the concluding motifs from 'The Figure in the Cave' as essay and as collection.

For Montague meditates on the way "destiny seems to have decided to give me back my lost childhood in America" with the honour of a first US honorary doctorate and a reception from both houses of the New York legislature while "my Tyrone background is being destroyed by bulldozer and bomb. Ballygawley is now as black a name as South Bronx or Brooklyn":

> It is like a fairytale, the little child who was sent away being received back with open arms. But while awed at the reappearance of this golden cradle to rock my dotage, I am grateful to have explored Ireland so intimately. Standing-stones and streams are not part of Brooklyn, nor are *cailleachs*. To judge by my contemporaries I would probably have been a writer, certainly a journalist, had I stayed in America. But who cut the long wound of poetry into my youth? Was it my mother who chose for her own good reasons to cast me off?[8]

## 2  The Long Wound

Now in his early sixties, John Montague has published ten collections of poetry between *Forms of Exile* (1958) and, thirty years later, *Mount Eagle* (1988). Alongside these volumes, two works of fiction have appeared: *Death of a Chieftain* (1964) and *The Lost Notebook* (1988). In an essay of this length, it would be impractical to deal with Montague's work in its entirety, including the editorial and critical writing. I intend focusing instead upon a cluster of poems which form, in my own mind at least, an imaginative counterweight to my introduction.

It will be recalled that in the last quotation from 'The Figure in the Cave' Montague directly associated poetry with "the long wound" and his sense of being "cast off". Poetry is both an affliction and, by implication, a mode of consolation and compensation. The individual 'self' is repatriated to the lost homeland through poetry and held up as a focus of (predominantly inherited) social, political, literary and cultural experiences. The overriding impression this figure presents in Montague's poetry is that of a 'victim'.

There are, for instance, the portraits of womanhood such as the *cailleach* (Ir. *old woman, hag*) from 'The Wild Dog Rose'[9] who suffers rape and loneliness; the "old bitch, with a warm mouthful of game" in 'Dowager',[10] representative of the Anglo-Irish caste, "humming with satisfaction in the sun". More convincingly, there is Nurse Mullen from 'Herbert Street Revisited'[11] who "knelt by her bedside/to pray for her lost Mayo hills,/the bruised bodies of Easter Volunteers" before her own death, "upright/in her chair, facing a window/warm with the blue slopes of Nephin".

The characteristic gesture is passive acceptance: "treading the pattern/of one time and place into history" as Montague remarks in 'Herbert Street Revisited'. Resignation or acceptance is a typical note in the poetry as memories are fixed upon family items like a locket or silver flask.[12] In the face of Nature too, the dominant note is elegiac as the landscape represents "a manuscript./ We had lost the skill to read,/A part of our past disinherited".[13]

The landscape becomes impregnated with historical signs and symbols which the poet decodes as best he can, knowing, all the while, of the "severed head" which "chokes to/speak another tongue":

> To slur and stumble
>
> In shame
> the altered syllables
> of your own name;
> to stray sadly home
>
> and find
> the turf cured width
> of your parent's hearth
> growing slowly alien:
>
> . . . .
> To grow
> a second tongue, as
> harsh a humiliation
> as twice to be born.
>
> Decades later
> that child's grandchild's
> speech stumbles over lost
> syllables of an old order.[14]

From figures of the victim, to a sense of resignation and the very "humiliation" of finding his ancestral language suppressed, the poet seeks an understanding of his own 'speech' in the 'Sound of a Wound':

> Scar tissue
> can rend, the old hurt
> tear open as
> the torso of the fiddle
> groans to
> carry the tune, to carry
> the pain of
> a lost (slow herds of cattle
> roving over
> soft meadow, dark bogland)
> pastoral rhythm.[15]

Yet out of this loss, "the old hurt", Montague summons "in my bloodstream", bitterness inherited

> from my father
> the swarm of blood
> to the brain, the vomit surge
> of race hatred,
> the victim seeing the oppressor,
> bold Jacobean planter, or gadget laden marine,
> who has scatter-
> ed his household gods, used
> his people
> as servants, flushed his women
> like game.

The recurrence of this image of the wound and its association with loss is unmistakable in Montague's poetry. His father, "a traditional Irishman" in 'The Cage',[16] is re-imagined: "his bald head behind/the bars of the small booth; the mark of an old car/accident beating on his/ ghostly forehead" while in the uncollected poem, 'Sands', about the IRA hunger-striker who died, the reconciliation of wound as metaphor with loss is subsumed into the absolute mark of sacrifice as an historical birthright:

> This is a sign of silence.
> This is the sound of the bone

> breaking through skin
> of a slowly wasting man.
> This is the sound of his death:
> but also of his living on.[17]

This is quite close in tone to the famous rhetoric of Padraig Pearse and his vision of sacrifice, a belief that sustained the hunger-strikers in the 1980s as much as beforehand: the rhetoric which other Irish writers, like O'Casey, have questioned and exposed. Indeed, discussing this very point in relation to Irish drama, Philip Edwards commented upon "the intoxicating power of the language of romantic nationalism, a *damnosa hereditas*, that cannot be shaken off. If modern Irish drama is a drama of victims, they are chiefly victims of language".[18] In this way too Montague is making poetry from the assimilation of the 'victim' with 'language' and his own recreated sense of his 'self' as constituted by these same forces.

As Nadine Gordimer has remarked in another context, "There is no moral authority like that of sacrifice".[19] This has obviously influenced, to put it at its mildest, the critical and historical terms of reference (and expectation) by which much, if not all, of contemporary Irish poetry has been received by readers and critics alike, particularly in the U.S. but also in Britain and Ireland. The important point to stress is that Montague's role in establishing these terms, both imaginatively and critically, anticipates[20] the poetic negotiations a writer such as Seamus Heaney was to make in, for example, *Wintering Out* (1973) and *North* (1975).

In his early experiences as an 'exile' of sorts, who returns on a voyage of rediscovery, his country origins framed by the colonizer's tongue, in a political state not of his or his family's making or choosing, Montague *represents* an identifiable pattern in his life and art. One consolidates the other in recognisable, even predictable, ways. So that the creative triangle (poetry as wound, victim of language, and the *inherited* sense of self seen as essential characteristics of Irish literature and history) forms an almost archetypal mandatory ritual, irresistible in its appeal to writer and audience alike:

> Grounded for the second time
> my tongue became a rusted hinge
> until the sweet oils of poetry
>
> eased it and light flooded in.[21]

In the background of Montague's poetry there is that much-quoted passage from Joyce's *A Portrait of the Artist as a Young Man* when, facing the Dean of Studies, Stephen thinks:

> The language which we are speaking is his before it is mine. How different are the words *home, Christ, ale, master*, on his lips and on mine! I cannot speak or write these words without unrest of spirit. His language, so familiar and so foreign, will always be for me an acquired speech. I have not made or accepted its words. My voice holds them at bay. My soul frets in the shadow of his language.[22]

The seventy and more years which separate Joyce's fictional character and Joyce's own obsessive and unique relationship with the English language can still aesthetically sustain a contemporary poet like Montague and one need only turn to Seamus Heaney's *Station Island* (1984) for further illustration of this resilient theme. So dominant is it in effect that, unlike the 'Big House/Ascendancy' motif in Irish writing, little discussion has taken place about how relevant Stephen Dedalus's words actually are *now* to Irish experience and the social and political realities of the island, notwithstanding the powerful universal appeal of Joyce's story.

# 3 *Damnosa Hereditas?*

In John Bayley's *The Uses of Division*, the chapter which deals with the poetry of John Berryman, Robert Lowell and Philip Larkin contains the following remark:

> The public status and recognition of poets in Russia, in the smaller European countries or in Spanish America, puts them in a different class: to be a national poetic rhetorician, like Mayakovsky or Neruda, is to be in some sense naive, to achieve power through naiveté. And not to be *taken in*, not to be thus socially and nationally innocent, is vital to the working of the poetry we are discussing.[23]

The section of the chapter from which this quotation comes is called 'The Self as Available Reality' (after R.P. Blackmur) and it represents the kind of tension that characterizes the poetry of John Montague. For his work, it seems to me, is caught between two poles of attraction: the "national poetic rhetoric" and "naiveté" of an acquired outrage and bitterness as exhibited in *The Rough Field* ranged against the later

Lowellesque self-dramatisations of *The Dead Kingdom*. As Bayley remarks in the second section, 'The Importance of Elsewhere':

> . . . it is difficult not to conclude that the dynamic of today's [1976] best poetry is a setting up in it of the poet, which, when accomplished, constitutes an aesthetic goal. The poet has arrived in our midst, his newness defined by the personal reality of the self his art has brought to us.[24]

In Montague the aesthetic goal *is* the personal reality, of making an imaginative home for himself out of a powerful, monolithic and conservative literary and cultural tradition. This means that, like a divining rod, his imagination wavers from the assembled sequences of love lyrics and recollections in *The Great Cloak* and *The Dead Kingdom* to the epical aspiration of attempting a poetry that will be shaped through (and in turn shape?) an entire province's history, torn by moral, political and cultural division, such as he finds in the North of Ireland:

> Lines of leaving
>      lines of returning
> the long estuary
>      of Lough Foyle, a
> ship motionless
>      in wet darkness
> mournfully hooting
>      as a tender creeps
> to carry passengers
>      back to Ireland
> a child of four
>      this sad sea city
> the landing place
>      the loneliness of
> Lir's white daughters
>      ice-crusted wings
> forever spread
>      at the harbour mouth.[25]

Personal reality here assumes historical proportions and *vice versa*. The poet inherits the past *a priori* and the poetry conveys, again compliantly, an already given identity for the self: "a child of four/this sad sea city/my landing place".

Ironically, perhaps, when glossing this poem, Montague advocated "a deliberate programme of denationalisation" but went on to say that "all true experiments and exchanges only serve to illuminate the self, a rediscovery of the oldest laws of the psyche".[26] Yet it is true to say that much of Montague's own poetry is totally bound up with the nation-place and nationalism, with what he has called "our racial drama of conscience".[27] Irish mythology, such as Lir's daughters, is never far from the surface and many of his poems deal with Irish cultural icons, for example the Irish landscape or the 'loss' of the Irish language. Furthermore, an elegy like 'O Riada's Farewell' —"pride of music/ pride of race"—concerning the premature death of the contemporary musician and composer Sean O Riada, carries an almost talismanic significance in recent Irish poetry.[28] It is in this poem that one sees clearly enough Montague's intention of restoring to life what he had earlier called, in 'The Road's End', the "shards/of a lost culture"[29] since 'O Riada's Farewell' bears Ezra Pound's flourish, "To have gathered from the air a live tradition".[30] The poem provides us with a useful text in more ways than one since it shows how, in the characteristic gesture of a lament, memorialising the past and life of one man goes beyond the celebration of the solely human:

> And a nation mourns:
> The blind horseman with his harp carrying servant,
> Hurrying through darkness to a great house
> Where a lordly welcome waits, as here:
>
> Fingernail spikes in candlelight recall
> A ripple & rush of upland streams,
> The slant of rain on void eye sockets,
> The shrill of snipe over mountains
> Where a few stragglers nest in bracken —
> After Kinsale, after Limerick, after Aughrim,
> After another defeat, to be redeemed
> By the curlew sorrow of an aisling.[31]

What is more, the poem itself is an act of redeeming what has gone or is lost: for "defeat" read "aisling"; the imagination lodged in the heroic past converts its failures (Kinsale, Limerick, Aughrim) to compensatory images of acceptance, the "curlew sorrow" of the impoverished present. However, this process, of "a lost pastoral rhythm", begs a central question of Montague's own imaginative priorities and the extent to which he has created, in John Bayley's words again, "supreme beauty out of ugliness, emptiness and contingency, the trapped and the doomed . . . (while keeping) us continuously interested in himself, always wanting to hear more about him". This is the real *aesthetic* risk a prolific autobiographical poet such as John Montague takes, given as well the cultural agenda he has set for himself:

> *Dia dhuit/*
> *Dia agus Muire dhuit/*
>     *Dia agus Muire*
> *agus Padraig dhuit*
>      invocation of powers
> to cleanse the mind.
>      Then the question
> and answer.
>     'What did she say?'
> I was asked when I came back to the car
> but could only point the way
> over the hill to where
>       obscured in sea
> mist, the small, grey stones of the oratory
> held in the Atlantic for a thousand years.[32]

## 4  Illuminating the Self

It is the "thousand years" which stands as a metaphorical *locus* to most of John Montague's poetry; the ancestral haunting of the present as much as the present obscuring the past.[33] Montague attempts to embody this duality and the most revealing aspect of his work is its sense of foreboding, an anticipation of closure and completion. For his poems deal in half-light, dawns or dusks, elusive moments of recollection, when the *frisson* of political or sexual tension has passed and the poet draws attention to their significance. This narrative urge to resolve his poems can falter, however, and lead into the clichéd rhetoric of, for instance, his poem in memory of Hugh MacDiarmid, 'Scotia' from *Mount Eagle*:

> Nourishing a lonely dream of how
> this desolate country might have been!
> The rightful arrogance of MacDiarmid's
> calling together of Clann Albann,
> or the surging lamentations of MacLean,

> the sound of his echoing Gaelic
> a fierce pibroch crying on the wind.[34]

Whereas in 'Discords', also from *Mount Eagle*, the rhetorical question that closes the first section of the poem carries a personally-charged vindication clearly absent from the ceremonial poems such as 'Scotia':

> There is a white light in the room.
> It is anger. He is angry, or
> She is angry, or both are angry.
> To them it is absolute, total,
> It is everything; but to the visitor,
> The onlooker, the outsider,
> It is the usual, the absurd;
> For if they did not love each other
> Why should they heed a single word?[35]

These two persistent directions of Montague's writing—one auto-biographical, the other explicitly cultural—can find themselves insufficiently sustained by a distinct imaginative *raison d'être*. This lack means that some of Montague's poetry has a conventional air of being written to a prefabricated formula, with certain stock images and characters guaranteeing the 'Irish' authenticity of his work.[36] This may be linked to an awareness of what Stephen Spender outlined in the introduction to his study of Anglo-American sensibilities, *Love-Hate Relations*.

When describing the contrasting attractions of the American writer for Europe (and England) as against the establishing of a 'native' literature (Williams *v* Eliot), Spender comments on the "connection between their separate existence [autobiography] and their country, in its history, landscape and people". He goes on:

> This awareness is of a life which is that of an ideal United States or England which the writer, if he is in a correct relation to it, releases in his work. Unless he does have such a relation, his work will be peripheral to that centre or turned inward on himself. It follows that if the nation itself presents conditions which prevent the writer identifying it with the ideal of the country of the mind, then he will find himself opposed to the official nation. His work will find its centre in a patriotism against which he measures the surrounding public nation. To simplify my argument, let me call the idea of a true nation, 'the patria'.[37]

In Ireland, the modern "idea of a nation" has of course been efficiently repossessed and institutionalised by the political course of nationalism and poets were (*are?*) generally seen as guardians of that sacred,[38] rather than civic, duty. There are many questions at issue here, too many to be discussed in an essay such as the present one. One thinks, for example, of the complicated relationship between 'old' and 'new' cultures and of how, paradoxically, a *nation* like Ireland's is both simultaneously. There is also the sense in which 'the patria' in Spender's terms can be viewed autobiographically as the individual's generalised search for a father-figure; the nation, his or her home; the idealised community, the family. Or, more specifically, the manner in which a poet like John Montague sees himself self-consciously as a bridge between these divides of American, European and Irish cultures in his own life and through his own writing. Thus, when he states the following in 'The Impact of International Modern Poetry on Irish Writing' (1973) one senses the ground being cleared for his own role:

> . . . the only literary art in which we have not made our presence felt is the one in which we are supposed to excel: that is, poetry. Yeats apart, few Irish poets have been accepted as international figures in the way that Pablo Neruda is, or Octavio Paz, or Ungaretti.[39]

The essential point I take from Stephen Spender's introduction concerns 'patria', the national ground out of which "international figures" emerge, set alongside the "ideal United States or England [or Ireland] which the writer, if he is in correct relation to it, releases in his work". Whatever qualifications one may have about that phrase "correct relation", the ideal Ireland that has been released in John Montague's poetry is effectively *now* the official version. One can go a step further and even suggest that a possible reading of Montague's poetry is that it completes and concludes the cultural (and I stress, *cultural*) agenda Yeats set down by redefining that movement of Irish literary nationalism from a northern republican point of view. For at various stages Montague has insisted upon the non-English but 'European' dimension of Irish literature. His comments on exile in 'The Impact of International Modern Poetry on Irish Writings' are a case in point, as are his remarks on Louis MacNeice whose work Montague sees "very much in the non-experimental tradition of English modern poetry, and, as such, nearly unexportable".[40]

Matters of trade apart, somewhat later in the same broadcast, when describing Denis Devlin and Austin Clarke in terms of "our racial drama of conscience", Montague proclaims that while "difficult to define (perhaps the imperial habit dies hard, and the British Council is a more subtle version of the *Pax Britannica*) an Irish writer has a better chance of being a European than has an Englishman".[41] Yet such potentiality is qualified in Montague's mind by the injunction that "if one is going to be influenced by contemporary poetry outside Ireland, it should be at first hand and not by hearsay, years after the event".[42]

The imperative sense here of the contemporaneity of poetry and the necessarily *positive* value of 'influences' *per se* is recalled in Montague's follow-on comment to the effect that having "participated in one of the early readings of *Howl*, I found it depressing when the Ginsberg wave broke over Ireland a decade later, drowning many potential young poets".[43]

The subjective reading assumes an impersonal critical status, yet who these "young poets" were is left out of the account. Shakespearian fish or not, they represent an audience of failure somewhat remote ('hearsay') from where the poet himself is, at the heart of things. "We move in a world which is increasingly both local *and* international and in poetry, as in science, there is nothing so irrelevant as repeating someone else's experiments".[44]

Montague includes in his talk an admonition of "the majority of Irish poets" who write "as though Pound, Lawrence, Williams, had not brought a new music into English poetry, as though the iambic line still registered the curve of modern speech".[45] Against this "majority" failure on most sides, Montague requests, in characteristic flourish, that "an Irish poet should be familiar with the finest work of his contemporaries, not just the increasingly narrow English version of modern poetry, or the extensive American one, but in other languages as well". He concludes:

> I would say that my contemporaries are not just the Irish poets I admire but those with whom I feel an affinity elsewhere, Ponge in France, Octavio Paz in Mexico, Gary Snyder and Robert Duncan in San Francisco. I seem to be advocating a deliberate programme of de-nationalization, but all true experiments and exchanges only serve to illuminate the self, a rediscovery of the oldest laws of the psyche.[46]

So we are back at that intersection of "a thousand years" with the added presence of nominated contemporary international figures at the crossroads. It is important to remind ourselves of the date for this broadcast—1973—and of how it was around this time, the late 1960s and early 1970s, that other voices, indisputably Irish in experience and accent, confidently familiar with developments in European and American poetry and trained in English literature, were establishing themselves in the forefront of the public mind and critical press. Names like Seamus Heaney, Derek Mahon, Seamus Deane and Michael Longley. Freed from any need to prove themselves or the ground of their being poets (Northern or otherwise), they moved with self-determination, absorbing in the main the artistic legacy of W.B. Yeats rather than the left-overs of his cultural programme, such as it was.

'Denationalization' applied to the poetry of any one of these poets sounds incongruous and out of place and as dated as Montague's exhortation that his fellow Irish poets must look beyond their own immediate borders. Such transcendence is imaginatively assumed in the work of these and other poets and is also one of the central intellectual preoccupations in the critical writing of Seamus Heaney and Seamus Deane.[47]

In this sense John Montague has been vindicated by the example of his younger peers whose very difference challenges any deterministic or inherited formulation of what a poet should or should not do, read or write about. The only exigency is the recognition of individual talent and the limits of tradition.

There is the unimpeachable wisdom of Philip Larkin's comment to bear in mind in this regard. When responding to a request from D.J. Enright for a brief statement of his views on poetry, Larkin replied:

> I find it hard to give any abstract views on poetry and its present condition as I find theorizing on the subject no help to me as a writer. In fact it would be true to say that I make a point of not knowing what poetry is or how to read a page or about the function of myth. It is fatal to decide, intellectually, what good poetry is because you are then in honour bound to try and write it, instead of the poems that only you can write.[48]

It is an early example (1955) of Larkin-speak, deceitfully sharp-witted *and* intuitive, preserving the private, almost secretive sources of his own imagination, and bluntly refusing to budge or reveal anything of himself. With certain changes in register this could be Cavafy speaking, but the stabilising force and composure of the English tradition in poetry acts like a rudder behind the concluding phrase, "the poems that only you can write". For the sense of who "you" are as a writer strikes me as being one of, if not *the*, most important themes in John Montague's writing. His poetry and criticism (and fiction, for that matter) believes in the rhetorical weight of showing what *should* be done, read, claimed, written about, in order that a local field, like Garvaghey, can enjoy as much imaginative light as will also illuminate the amenable profiles of one's self. This is the insistently moral ambience of John Montague's work which sees the autobiographical and cultural as one and the same recurrent imaginative project: the poet as oracle; invoker of powers. In this regard Montague is very much more a traditionalist than he would have us believe from his comments on experimentalism, international writing and so forth. His poetry is lodged firmly in the custodianship of generous images of good[49] rather than in the quicksand of a modernism either fiercely introverted or aggressively peripheral.[50] In establishing, or re-establishing this ancient territorial rite, Montague probably made it possible for a poet like Seamus Heaney to speak out of his own experience without loss of face, or for that matter, of faith in the mythic possibilities of poetry.

Yet throughout Montague's poetry there is a stylisation of experience which is essentially literary; and that works against its epic grain. It is as if the poet were self-consciously setting out to prove something—about his past and its potency as a poetic theme. This side to Montague's poetry is characteristic of quite a lot of contemporary Irish writing in the 1970s and 1980s. As critics rarely fail to remind us, it has a direct bearing upon the colonised basis of English as a language spoken and written in Ireland. Certainly, the bardic strain associated with the tradition of Irish poetry in Gaelic breaks through Montague's poems and reveals a world strangely subsumed in the highly-polished and achieved form of its expression, as in some of Montague's best-known lyrics, 'The Wild Dog Rose', 'The Sean Bhean Bhocht' and 'A Lost Tradition'.

John Montague stands as the epitome of that dominant view of Irish poetry which derives from the national ideas, heritage and messianic ideals forged as the cultural foundation of the Irish state[51] and rehearsed in the mind and experience of one of its prodigal sons. As 'Knockmany' from his most recent collection, *Mount Eagle*, underlines, Montague sees his work as an artist strictly and reverentially as the sexual, political and cultural communion of his life with its natural homeland, the creation of an internationally recognisable identity called 'Irish Poet':

You do not forget
and I always come back.
Stepping from the car
outside Clogher, I sàw
a brilliant rainbow
lifting its prismatic arch
across Knockmany Hill
as in a healing dream
in savage Chicago. It
shone both a secret
and a sacrament, a promise
and its fulfillment.
I still live by it.[52]

NOTES

1. John Montague, *The Figure in the Cave and other Essays* (Dublin: The Lilliput Press, 1989).
2. Antoinette Quinn, 'The Well-Beloved": Montague and the Muse' in *Irish University Review* (Vol. 19, No. 1, Spring 1989). Ms. Quinn's essay elaborates upon these themes and in particular, Montague's sense of being "a virtual orphan . . . continually seeking to compensate for the maternal bonding of which he was deprived in infancy". The present writer will not pursue the psychological dimensions of such a quest but rather concentrate upon the nature of their transformation into art.
3. *The Figure in the Cave*, pp.8–9. The blurb on the cover of Montague's most recent collection, *Mount Eagle* (Meath: The Gallery Press, 1988) states: "John Montague commands a pivotal place in contemporary Irish writing. His achievement . . . may be seen as a vital link between Patrick Kavanagh's instruction and a number of important younger poets".
4. *The Figure in the Cave*, p.10 ". . . I was editing the poetry of Patrick Kavanagh in the background . . ."; "In helping to get Kavanagh and Hewitt back into print . . ." p.15.
5. *ibid.*, p.15.
6. *ibid.*, It is interesting to note Montague's 'Introduction' to *Poisoned Lands* (new ed. Dublin: The Dolmen Press, 1977): "An editor-poet I studiously avoided was T.S. Eliot but when the volume was being considered for American publication, it crossed his desk. Old Possum risked a friendly pat: 'I have, indeed, found Mr. Montague's poems worthy of study", p.10.
7. *The Figure in the Cave*, p.11.
8. *ibid.*, pp.17–18.
9. *The Rough Field* (Meath: The Gallery Press, 1989), pp.78–80.
10. *A Slow Dance* (Dublin: The Dolmen Press, 1975), p.23.
11. *The Great Cloak* (Dublin: The Dolmen Press, 1978), pp.40–42.
12. 'The Locket' and 'The Silver Flask' in *The Dead Kingdom* (Portlaoise: The Dolmen Press, 1984), p.92, 72.
13. *The Rough Field*, p.35.
14. *ibid.*, p.39.
15. *ibid.*, pp.44–45.

16. *ibid.*, p.46. Titled 'Cage' but subsequently reprinted in *Selected Poems* (London: Oxford University Press, 1982) and *New Selected Poems* (Meath: The Gallery Press, 1989) as 'The Cage'.

17. *Aquarius* (15/16, 1983/84), p.80.

18. Philip Edwards, *Threshold of a Nation: A Study in English and Irish Drama* (Cambridge: Cambridge University Press, 1979), p. 232.

19. Nadine Gordimer, *The Essential Gesture: Writing, Politics and Places* (London: Jonathan Cape, 1988), p.294.

20. Montague says as much himself in 'Dennis O'Driscoll: An Interview with John Montague', *Irish University Review*, vol. 19, no. 1 (Spring 1989), ". . . I ante-date this new emphasis on Ulster writing. I mean I had done *Poisoned Lands*, *Death of a Chieftain* and I was working on *The Rough Field*. I have described myself as the missing link of Ulster poetry" p.60.

21. John Montague, 'A Flowering Absence'. *The Dead Kingdom*, p.91.

22. James Joyce, *A Portrait of the Artist as a Young Man* (London: Jonathan Cape, 1920), p.215.

23. John Bayley, *The Uses of Division: Unity & Disharmony in Literature* (London: Chatto & Windus, 1976), p.165.

24. *ibid.*, p.177.

25. *The Rough Field*, p.73.

26. 'The Impact of International Modern Poetry on Irish Writing', *The Figure in the Cave and other Essays*, p.219.

27. *ibid.*, p.213.

28. *cf.* Thomas Kinsella, 'A Selected Life & Vertical Man', *Fifteen Dead* (Dublin: The Dolmen Press, 1979); Seamus Heaney, 'In Memorium Sean O Riada', *Field Work* (London: Faber & Faber, 1979) and Sean Lucy, 'Unfinished Sequence for Sean O Riada', *Unfinished Sequence* (Dublin: Wolfhound Press, 1979).

29. *A Chosen Light* (London: MacGibbon & Kee, 1967), p.32.

30. *A Slow Dance*, p.57.

31. *ibid.*, p.62.

32. *A Chosen Light*, p.37.

33. Thus the three-faced stone-head (c.3rd–2nd B.C.) that adorns the cover of *New Selected Poems* (1989).

34. *Mount Eagle*, p.61.

35. *ibid.*, p.45.

36. *cf.* Richard J. Loftus, *Nationalism in Modern Anglo-Irish Poetry* (Madison and Milwaukee: The University of Wisconsin Press, 1964), pp.16–17. One of the more critical readings of modern Irish poetry available.

37. Stephen Spender, *Love-Hate Relations: A Study of Anglo-American Sensibilities* (London: Hamish Hamilton, 1974), p.xiii. It is remarkable that no equivalent study has been undertaken in Anglo-Irish literary and cultural sensibilities.

38. In Seamus Heaney's terms: "The landscape was sacramental, instinct with signs, implying a system of reality beyond the visible realities". 'The Sense of Place' (1974) in *Preoccupations: Selected Prose 1968–1978* (London: Faber & Faber, 1980), p.132.

39. *The Figure in the Cave*, p.210. 'The Impact of International Modern Poetry on Irish Writing' was originally broadcast on RTE radio as part of a series of talks, *Irish Poets in English*, and subsequently published under that title in a collection edited by Sean Lucy (Cork: The Mercier Press, 1973).

40. *ibid.*, p.211.

41. *ibid.*

42.  *ibid.*, p.213.
43.  *ibid.*, p.216.
44.  *ibid.*.
45.  *ibid.*, p.218.
46.  *ibid.*, p.219.
47.  *cf*. Seamus Heaney, *The Government of the Tongue* (London: Faber & Faber, 1988) and Seamus Deane, *Celtic Revivals* (London: Faber & Faber, 1985).
48.  Philip Larkin, *Required Reading: Miscellaneous Pieces 1955–1982* (London: Faber and Faber, 1983), p.79. It is interesting to compare Larkin's remark with Seamus Heaney's similar comment in 'Feeling into Words' (1974): " . . . it is dangerous for a writer to become too self-conscious about his own processes: to name them too defininitively may have the effect of confining them to what is named". *Preoccupations*, p.52.
49.  From Montague's poem, 'Waiting': "some/Generous natural image of the good" in *The Great Cloak*, p.56.
50.  To pick up again on Spender's terms of reference in *Love-Hate Relations*, p.xiii.
51.  See Loftus, *Nationalism in Modern Anglo-Irish Poetry*, in particular chapters 1,2,3 and 6.
52.  *Mount Eagle*, p.71.

**Stan Smith**
The Distance Between: Seamus Heaney

# The Distance Between

## 1  A Place to Come From

Perhaps Seamus Heaney's commonest critical mannerism is the teasing out of innuendoes and ambiguities in some ordinary locution, as for example in his comments in *The Government of the Tongue*[1] on Robert Lowell, whose poetic "resources proved themselves capable of taking new strains, in both the musical and stressful sense of that word." Heaney's device doesn't always take the strain, sometimes seeming more a tic of rhetorical routine than a necessary complication: "that strain again, it had a dying fall." As with his recurrent arguing from etymology, too much of the argument's strain can be taken up in a verbal play which substitutes for logic and demonstration. Most notorious perhaps is the schoolboy *double entendre* of that lecture given at the Royal Society of Literature in 1974, 'Feeling into Words', which effectively exposed Leavisite pieties by touching up their lower parts as a discourse of sexual displacement. But it is apparent even in such apparently innocuous items as his 1977 lecture at the Ulster Museum, 'The Sense of Place', a phrase which he glosses as "our sense, or—better still—our *sensing* of place."

Nevertheless, the linguistic strategy is deeply symptomatic. It effects a kind of destabilisation on the ground of language itself, unsettling what he calls the "sovereign diction"[2] with alternative, subversive voices. This is apparent in the slant light cast on the 1977 lecture by a later one given at the Wordsworth Summer Conference at Dove Cottage. 'Place and Displacement: Recent Poetry of Northern Ireland' makes it clear, in terms of a Saussurean binary, that place is impossible to define without displacement. Displacement, one might say, is the necessary ground upon which to find or found one's place.

> 'I hate how quick I was to know my place.
> I hate where I was born, hate everything
> That made me biddable and unforthcoming',

the poet mouths at his "half-composed face/In the shaving mirror" (Joyce's "cracked looking-glass of the servant") in a moment of confessional self-loathing in 'Station Island'. But really knowing your place means refusing to settle for being put in your place, whether it is your own people or an occupying presence (Joyce's Haines) which is doing the placing—means learning, in the ghostly ventriloquism of 'Station Island', "that what I thought was chosen was convention". The subtitle of this lecture significantly speaks of poetry *of* Northern Ireland, not *from* it, and a whole world of difference can hang on such a preposition. In *The Haw Lantern*, four parables give a precise twist to this topographic insistence: 'From the Frontier of Writing', 'From the Republic of Conscience', 'From the Land of the Unspoken', 'From the Canton of Expectation'. The preposition in one sense simply indicates the place of origin of the missive (as in 'A Postcard from Iceland'). But that 'from' carries more weight than this. In the first poem he *writes from* the frontier; but as the last three stanzas indicate he also experiences a sense of release at having *come away from*, escaped across it:

> And suddenly you're through, arraigned yet freed,
> as if you'd passed from behind a waterfall . . .
>
> past armour-plated vehicles, out between
> the posted soldiers flowing and receding
> like tree shadows into the polished windscreen.

The prepositions do much here in effecting the sense of relief in passage, "passed from behind . . . past . . . out between . . . receding . . . into". That "through", a preposition turned adverb and then colloquially a verb complement, takes on a heavy freight of meaning. If it "concentrates an identity in a heave of renewal" it also "disperses it in a blast of evacuation", a process which in *The Government of the Tongue*[3] Heaney finds "morbid" in Sylvia Plath's 'Daddy'—where, though he does not remark on it, the word acquires a similar duplicity:

> So daddy, I'm finally through.
> The black telephone's off at the root,

> The voices just can't worm through . . . .
> Daddy, daddy, you bastard, I'm through.

Working it through, getting through, may mean saying you're through with it for ever. This poem Heaney disapproves of (though he nevertheless calls it a "brilliant . . . *tour de force*"), is highly apposite to the frontier of writing. Heaney too is not only through the roadblock. He is also through with that country: with its exposed positions, with having to justify himself, with perpetual interrogation. In the light of Plath's usage, "through" picks up the resonance of that "spent" applied to the self earlier—spent, that is, like a used cartridge, or a life "spent" by an over-itchy trigger finger:

> the sergeant with his on-off mike repeating
>
> data about you, waiting for the squawk
> of clearance; the marksman training down
> out of the sun upon you like a hawk.

The prepositions themselves relentlessly train *down out of upon* the "subjugated, yes, and obedient" self held in its place down the sights of "cradled" guns.

That the preposition is a key resource in Heaney's poetic armoury is confirmed by his remarks, in 'The Sense of Place', on a line of Kavanagh's:

> And the same vigour comes out in another little word that is like a capillary root leading down into the whole sensibility of Kavanagh's place. In the first line, 'the bicycles go by in twos and threes'. They do not 'pass by' or 'go past', as they would in a more standard English voice or place, and in that little touch Kavanagh touches what I am circling. He is letting the very life blood of the place in that one minute incision.[4]

"Pass by" may be a sly dig at Yeats's horseman. Heaney, *at* the frontier, we note, is *suddenly through*, as if by magic without any apparent act of transit, only in a simile *passing from behind, passing out between*. The 'From' of the poem's title takes up but also takes on the title of W.H. Auden's play *On the Frontier*. In 'Sounding Auden', the second lecture of *The Government of the Tongue*, Heaney remarks on the oddity of the preposition 'between' at another frontier of decision in Auden's verse:

> Who stands, the crux left of the watershed,
> On the wet road between the chafing grass
> Below him sees . . .[5]

Similarly, in analysing the effect of "chafing"[6] he tunes in, finely, on its inbetweenness: "disturbed by a lurking middle voice" between active and passive, it "occupies" (a loaded word before the Popean noun phrase) "a middle state between being transitive and intransitive, and altogether functions like a pass made swiftly, a sleight of semantic hand which unnerves and suspends the reader above a valley of uncertainty." When he writes of "this deferral of a sense of syntactical direction" Heaney is indicating some of the preoccupations of his own poems in *Station Island* and *The Haw Lantern*, which also, like early Auden, turn upon "the necessity of a break, of an escape from habit, an escape from the given . . . only to expose their ultimate illusory promise".[7]

If Auden's poems 'sound back' to earlier ones, Heaney's own poem here resounds with this earlier source in Auden, coming out "from behind a waterfall/on the black current of a tarmac road." Auden's advice to the stranger, "frustrate and vexed", is to "Go home", or find himself equally emptied and subjugated by a land which "cut off, will not communicate." Heaney's poem inhabits an occupied "middle state" and "middle voice" full of spoken and unspoken communications (the "intent" of the rifles, the atmosphere of "pure interrogation"), of knowledges of the self withheld from it, and of the silent messages of fear, obedience and power that grow from the barrel of a gun. In 'The Mud Vision' this is identified as that state of Irish paralysis in which, once, "We sleepwalked/The line between panic and formulae", unable to "dive to a future." 'Terminus', recalling his variously divided childhood, takes a more balanced position—between rural and urban, agrarian and industrial, active and passive, transitive and intransitive, weighing pros and cons. If "Baronies, parishes met where I was born", so that he grew up "Suffering the limit of each claim", these 'limits' are not only passively borne (suffered) as limitations on the self but also tolerated, in a learnt and active sufferance, as limited claims, which can be put in their place *because* they are limited. Coming to understand such limits can then offer insight:

> Two buckets were easier carried than one.
> I grew up in between.

"Second thoughts" thus become the first fruits of thinking itself, and the poem's second thoughts, moving out from between, end at a watery margin which is also a crossing point, a place of negotiation between opposing forces which figures the stance of one whose end is peace, "in midstream/Still parleying, in earshot of his peers."

Whereas the early Auden stands repeatedly transfixed "Upon this line between adventure", caught "Between attention and attention", ordered to "Turn back" before he reaches any frontier by a man with a gun, because "There is no change of place"[8], Heaney's prepositional space is a different one, not transfixed but moving "with guarded unconcerned acceleration" from "out between". In 'Station Island' the ghost of William Carleton speaks of his own hardness in a hard time as maybe containing a lesson for the poet, " 'whoever you are, wherever you come out of' ". Freedom may be found in displacing oneself. But, as Heaney observes in 'The Sense of Place', citing Carson McCullers, "to know who you are, you have to have a place to come from".

## 2  Sounding Out Through

For such "an earnest of the power of place" this essay returns to the world of Heaney's own childhood:

> The landscape was sacramental, instinct with signs, implying a system of reality beyond the visible realities. Only thirty years ago, and thirty miles from Belfast, I think I experienced this kind of world vestigially and as a result may have retained some vestigial sense of place as it was experienced in the older dispensation.[9]

The Celtic Twilight, for all its naiveties, was "the beginning of a discovery of confidence in our own ground, in our place, in our speech, English and Irish", a discourse "that would bind the people of the Irish place to the body of their world." This bodiliness of a world "instinct with signs", I shall suggest, is important. Heaney's model here is Patrick Kavanagh's assertion that "Parochialism is universal; it deals with fundamentals . . . now that I analyse myself I realize that throughout everything I write, there is this constantly recurring motif of the need to go back". Kavanagh's "sense of his place involves detachment", for it is only when one is fully *in* and *of* a place that one

can feel fully Kavanagh's need to be "detached, remote . . . take part
but . . . not belong". As with Wordsworth, these native places are
"influential in the strict sense of the word 'influential'—things flowed
in from them". As Heaney elaborates the argument, the prepositions
once again pre-position the preoccupied subject, in this "middle
state" where things *flow in from* and *flow out to*.

Etymology is summoned to explain this relation at the beginning of
the Plath lecture, speaking of a Yeats

> less concerned in his criticism to speak about the actual tones and strains
> of poetic language than to evoke the impersonal, impersonating, mask-
> like utterance which he takes all poetry to be. We are reminded how
> *persona* derives from *personare*, meaning 'to sound out through', how the
> animation of the verb lives in the mask's noun-like impassiveness. For
> Yeats, the poet is somebody who is spoken through.[10]

"Sounding back" in the discussion of Auden has its corollary in this
"sounding out through". "Through", as we have seen, is "another
little word" fraught with ambivalence. "Poetry makes nothing
happen", Auden said famously, in what is clearly a direct response to
Yeats's fretful questions about poetic responsibilities in 'The Man
and the Echo'. But it is nevertheless, in a less frequently cited line, "A
way of happening, a mouth." This is what Heaney argues in the
opening, title lecture of *The Government of the Tongue*, quoting the
Polish poet Anna Swir on the poet as "an antenna capturing the voices
of the world, a medium expressing his own subconscious and the
collective subconscious":

> Poetry's special status among the literary arts derives from the
> audience's readiness to concede to it a similar efficacy and resource. The
> poet is credited with a power to open unexpected and unedited
> communications between our nature and the reality we inhabit. [11]

Heaney's habit of ringing all the possible changes on an equivocal
word or phrase comes from a refusal to be pinned down prematurely
in a fixed place, a wish to keep open those channels of communication
which allow all the ambivalences of his Northern Irish provenance to
sound through. As 'From the Republic of Conscience' indicates, dual
citizenship as an Irishman and an Ulster Catholic has its poetic
equivalents. To *come back from* is to carry no baggage of duty-free
allowance; but, as the comic circumlocution makes clear, it does carry

the duty to be oneself, and to speak conscientiously, and without relief, as an ambassador of this freedom:

> I came back from that frugal republic
> with my two arms the one length, the customs woman
> having insisted my allowance was myself

and the old man at immigration

> therefore desired me when I got home
> to consider myself a representative
> and to speak on their behalf in my own tongue.

In the Republic of Conscience, "You carried your own burden and . . ./your symptoms of creeping privilege disappeared". But if this is a place where the salt has not lost its savour, it is also a place where everything has to be taken with a pinch of salt. For speaking in your own tongue means avoiding the folly of "the fork-tongued natives" of 'Parable Island', who "keep repeating/prophecies they pretend not to believe", and who, in some perpetually deferred future, are going to start mining for truth beneath the mountain where, it is said, "all the names converge", and all the conflicting narratives are reconciled.

In 'Station Island', the ghost of Carleton laments being made by Ribbonmen and Orange bigots "into the old fork-tongued turncoat/ who mucked the byre of their politics". In 'Whatever You Say Say Nothing' (*North*) it is difficult not to be "fork-tongued on the border bit" in a world "Where tongues lie coiled, as under flames lie wicks" and " 'You know them by their eyes,' and hold your tongue." It is in the context of these locutions and locations that we must understand the title of *The Government of the Tongue*. It is a characteristically tricksy phrase, and its tricks lie in that multiple-choice preposition: government of the tongue, by the tongue, for the tongue? The book itself offers the first two possibilities:

> what I had in mind was this aspect of poetry as its own vindicating force. In this dispensation, the tongue (representing both a poet's personal gift of utterance and the common resources of language itself) has been granted the right to govern. The poetic art is credited with an authority of its own. As readers, we submit to the jurisdiction of achieved form, even though that form is achieved not by dint of the moral and ethical exercise of mind but by the self-validating operations of what we call inspiration.[12]

However, such a jurisdiction may be that of a poetic Diplock Court, and a poet who has inscribed in a poem's title the homespun political wisdom of the Irishism 'Whatever You Say Say Nothing' (almost a performative injunction, self-exemplifying, nullifying itself in a paradox in which nothing is said, twice), knows that utterance is never quite so undemanding. I am not myself sure whether Heaney picked up this phrase from an existing political slogan, or whether the Provisional IRA got it from Heaney. In either case, the poetry accrues legitimacy to the political slogan, putting the poem in the same compromised place as those writings Yeats fretted over in 'The Man and the Echo', opening up a whole new area in the relations between poetry and politics. The poem refers to "The famous/Northern reticence, the tight gag of place". If, in *The Government of the Tongue*, Heaney claims that "I have, on the whole, been inclined to give the tongue its freedom"[13], the poem defines the constraints of a freedom which "Still leaves us fork-tongued on the border bit". The border may be the bit that is between the teeth, but the poem leaves us with the biter bit, and biting his own tongue. *The Government of the Tongue* likewise speaks with a forked tongue, immediately qualifying its grandiose reiteration of Romantic clichés with a word to the wise:

> All the same, as I warm to this theme, a voice from another part of me speaks in rebuke. 'Govern your tongue,' it says, compelling me to remember that my title can also imply a *denial* of the tongue's autonomy and permission. In this reading, 'the government of the tongue' is full of monastic and ascetic strictness. One remembers Hopkins's 'Habit of Perfection', with its command to the eyes to be 'shelled', the ears to attend to silence and the tongue to know its place.[14]

Its place here is firmly in the cheek. It's noticeable that Heaney nominates an equally Romantic, inspirational source for this countervailing instruction: "a voice from another part of me . . . compelling me". Yet it is an impersonal "one" who remembers, not from the poet's original place, but from a position where the voice assumes, not the vatic authority of the bard, but that of a well-placed member of the literary ascendancy, languidly calling up fellow members of the club. Just which place is it that Heaney is knowing about, here?

A moment in *The Haw Lantern* sneakily qualifies this authority, reminding us from what part of himself that voice may in fact have spoken, as well as *what* he may know better, in the fourth of his sonnet elegies for his mother:

> With more challenge than pride she'd tell me, 'You
> Know all them things.' So I governed my tongue
> In front of her, a genuinely well-
> Adjusted adequate betrayal
> Of what I knew better.

The maternal reproach arises from her own "Fear of affectation", her mispronunciation of words "beyond her" expressing—possibly— fear of betraying "The hampered and inadequate by too/Well- adjusted a vocabulary". The already readjusted poet, condescend- ingly relapsing into "the wrong/Grammar which kept us allied and at bay", only obliquely questions how this community's demotic is somehow ruled "wrong" in the discourse of polite society. Although the poet is instructed to govern his tongue, it seems that it is the mother's tongue—the mother tongue—which is put in its place, and that place is *in the wrong*. However, the poem's tongue is subtle and diverse here, as I will argue later.

There is another moment in *The Haw Lantern* where the poet governs his tongue, self-consciously submitting, not to the voice of inspiration, but to a formal tradition of occasional verse which has 'English' written all over it. 'A Peacock's Feather' is a poem written for the christening of an "English niece" (as the text designates her), and it squirms with polite embarrassment at so bridling its tongue as to utter something alien but in keeping with the pastoral "mellow- ness" of a Gloucestershire landscape. Even here the poem still knows where it comes from:

> I come from scraggy farm and moss,
> Old patchworks that the pitch and toss
> Of history have left dishevelled.
> But here, for your sake, I have levelled
> My cart-track voice to garden tones,
> Cobbled the bog with Cotswold stones.

But it's not so sure of where it's going. Compelled by occasion, status, loyalty, to write a light celebratory poem, one thinks of Yeats, that earlier voice which spoke with Ascendancy accents in a good cause:

> While I, a guest in your green court,
> At a west window sat and wrote
> Self-consciously in gathering dark.
> I might as well be in Coole Park.

Slyly coiled in the "in-law maze" of the tongue, in the poem's absolving "touch of love", the voices wait to speak out through the mask: "Couldn't you do the Yeats touch?" One thinks too, that is, of Joyce, deflating Yeats's flattery of Lady Gregory: "The most beautiful book that has come out of our country in my time. One thinks of Homer."[15]

The tone is very different from Yeats's, a 'billet-doux', a nursery rhyme, quiet, casual, governed, wishing no harm, its blushful whimsy calling up the de la Mare of *Peacock Pie*. But there is an altogether more strident resonance to the bird, recalling that peacock which screamed among a rich man's flowering lawns in Yeats's 'Ancestral Houses', betokening the end of a civilisation, adding a deeper darkness to the gathering dark. "The future's not our own". But neither is the past. This levelled landscape requires a prayer for its future precisely because of that past:

> May tilth and loam
> Darkened with Celts' and Saxons' blood
> Breastfeed your love of house and wood.

That "blood/Breastfeed" is a dark enjambement, in which the mother's milk runs with blood.[16] The slate of the opening may not, after all, be wiped clean, for all our pious hopes. The poem sounds out through the persona it assumes against the place to which it is quite sincerely addressed—a place identified in an essay in *Preoccupations* as 'In the Country of Convention: English Pastoral Verse'. Pastoral is a conventionally innocent realm, certainly; but England is a country governed by the false naiveties, the feigned ingenuousness, of pastoral.

## 3 Thinking In and Back Into

Kavanagh's landscapes, Heaney says, are "hallowed by associations that come from growing up and thinking oneself in and back into the place".[17] Heaney's own most Kavanaghish poem is probably 'The Old Team' in *The Haw Lantern*, but even here the real places "Have, in your absence, grown historical", part of a history which is a repertoire of antagonistic stories. The title of *Field Work* had pointed the way to these later developments, poised equivocally between the local—the real fields and hedges of this sequence, from which the particular poetic talent emerged—and the larger field of meanings within which that life now finds itself, which, as indicated in a poem such as 'A Postcard from North Antrim', is always *elsewhere*. 'A Postcard from Iceland' in *The Haw Lantern* reads like an ironic postscript to Auden's and MacNeice's *Letters from Iceland*. Auden may have had his Ulster travelling companion in mind when he wrote, in the opening poem to that volume, "North means to all: reject!". Certainly Heaney seemed to be recalling this when, in the title poem of his own *North*, he "faced the unmagical/invitations of Iceland", foremost of which is the invitation to encompass by going beyond, rejecting his native culture as Auden did in casting from Iceland a cold anthropologist's eye on Englishness. Heaney's island parables (including 'Station Island' and 'Parable Island' itself), all test and transcend the limits of Irish insularity, the better to return to and interpret it—to rediscover, thinking in and back into the place, "How usual that waft and pressure felt/When the inner palm of water found my palm."

It is from outside the field that the pattern of forces can best be understood, rather than simply suffered. That identity is best found in displacement, in both the literal and the psychoanalytic sense, is the point of the important lecture on *Place and Displacement* Heaney delivered at Dove Cottage in 1984, seeing in the uprootedness of the returning native Wordsworth, a displaced person, *persona non grata* in his own country, a model for all subsequent poetic displacements:

> The good place where Wordsworth's nurture happened and to which his habitual feelings are most naturally attuned has become . . . the wrong place. He is displaced from his own affections by a vision of the good that is located elsewhere. His political, utopian aspirations deracinate him from the beloved actuality of his surroundings so that his instinctive being and his appetitive intelligence are knocked out of alignment. He feels like a traitor among those he knows and loves.[18]

Recent Northern Irish poetry, he says, reveals the same double displacement. The way to cope with "the strain of being in two places at once, of needing to accommodate two opposing conditions of truthfulness simultaneously"[19] is not despair, however, but Jung's strategy of finding a "displaced perspective" in which the suffering individual can outgrow particularist allegiance while managing to "keep faith with . . . origins", "stretched between politics and transcendence . . . displaced from a confidence in a single position by his disposition to be affected by all positions, negatively rather than positively capable".[20]

The echo of Keats's "negative capability" as an answer to Wordsworth's "egotistical sublime" indicates the way out Heaney was to find from the Northern Irish deadlock from *Field Work* onwards. It is in the "lyric stance", in language as itself a site of displacement, "the whispering gallery of absence", "the voice from beyond"[21], that the writer can seek the hopeful imaginary resolution of real conflicts. Heaney's poetry has pursued language as political metaphor and metonymy through to its source, to a recognition of language as both place of necessary exile and site of a perpetual return home. *Station Island* is the product of such a recognition, a volume full of departures and returns. Displacement is here seen not as exile but as freedom, whether in the wide-blue-yonder of America or the poetically licensed otherworlds of Dante's *Divine Comedy*. The loving fidelity of the émigré who, like Wordsworth, is necessarily now just 'visiting' that which he's left behind provides the motive force for the volume, and a poem such as the ironically entitled 'Away from it All' catches some of the complexities of such a position. In *The Haw Lantern* Heaney goes a step further, beyond the margins altogether, to deconstruct those blarney-laden tales of nativity, decentring and redefining a self-regarding Irishness. In the words of the title poem, it is not enough to bask in "a small light for small people". The modest wish to "keep/the wick of self-respect from dying out,/not having to blind them with illumination" is too limited, too easy an ambition. Now "it takes the roaming shape of Diogenes/with his lantern, seeking one just man" to be the true measure of this field, scrutinising with a gaze which makes "you flinch . . ./its blood-prick that you wish would test and clear you." The terror of being tested, assessed, and the anxious yearning for clearance, run through most of the poems in the volume. The gaze that "scans you, then moves on" here brings to bear both a moral and a poetic measure. 'Parable Island' tells us that there are no authenticating origins, only a plethora of story-tellings which push the origin further back into an original emptiness, scrawled over with too much meaning. It is in this area of dense secondary signification, where script dissembles an original emptiness, that Ireland 'begins'.


# 4 Drawing a Line Through

'Whatever You Say Say Nothing' speaks of the ends of art:

> To lure the tribal shoals
> To epigram and order. I believe any of us

> Could draw the line through bigotry and sham
> Given the right line, *aere perennius*.

The word "order" crosses its customary frontiers here, negotiating familiar transactions between political and literary structures, as that pun on "line" as boundary demarcation, poetic line and, possibly, ideological narrative indicates. The further, suppressed meaning of "line" (taking up "gaff and bait") adds a rather more dubious resonance, for the fisher of men may lure the tribal shoals into those Joycean nets which ensnare the soul, though purification, in the echo of Mallarmé mediated by Eliot, is clearly the poet's aim. In 'The Sense of Place', Heaney writes *en passant* of Synge "whom Yeats sent west to express the life of Aran, in the language of the tribe", thereby creating "a new country of the mind"[22] and, although he sees this here as positive, in 'A Tale of Two Islands: reflections on the Irish Literary Revival' he speaks rather more warily of Synge's enterprise, invoking in support not only Kavanagh but, most potently, Stephen Dedalus's intense and satiric rejection, at the end of *Portrait*, of the old man of the west whose mountain cabin is "hung with the nets of nationality, religion, family, the arresting abstractions." But, Heaney adds, though Stephen fears, he will not destroy him:

> The old man is as much a victim as the writer. His illiterate fidelities are the object of Stephen's scepticism, the substance of what Stephen rejects; and yet they are a part of Stephen himself. Stephen is angry that all his culture can offer him for veneration is this peasant oracle, yet understanding the ruination that he and the old man share, he is not prepared to struggle to the death.[23]

There is a poetic course to be charted here between the demands of 'native' orality and 'universal' writing. But if the siren voices of an illiterate oracle are not to run the project aground on populist mudbanks it must take on board those instructions to "purify the dialect of the tribe" from 'Little Gidding' which resonate in Heaney's own ghostly Dantean sequence, 'Station Island'. And indeed, Eliot, Dante and Jung rub shoulders in the last displacing moments of the essay. However, the fullest account of Dante as role-model in this later poetry is given in Heaney's 1985 article, 'Envies and Identifications: Dante and the Modern Poet':

> The way in which Dante could place himself in an historical world yet submit that world to scrutiny from a perspective beyond history, the

way he could accommodate the political and the transcendent, this too
encouraged my attempt at a sequence of poems which would explore the
typical strains which the consciousness labours under in this country.
The main tension is between two often contradictory commands: to be
faithful to the collective historical experience and to be true to the
recognitions of the emerging self.[24]

Heaney's use of the phrase "the language of the tribe" in 'The
Sense of Place' is suggestive, for it reproduces the mis-citation of Eliot
Donald Davie deploys throughout *Purity of Diction in English Verse*[25]
a book not unrelated in theme and argument to Heaney's recurrent
concerns. (Davie speaks of " 'Mr Eliot's phrase, to purify the
language of the tribe' "[26] and uses this formula for the title of his
crucial chapter.) Davie's book, written while he was a lecturer in
Dublin, also deploys Synge as an example of a suspect linguistic
populism which exploits the "bathetic" and "brutal"; while in an
important chapter he sets up Dante as an antithetical model of how
poetry should relate to "the vulgar tongue". Davie's introduction
raises questions of diction as political and moral touchstones in terms
which are strikingly consonant with Heaney's:

[T]he poet who uses a diction must be very sure of the audience which he
addresses. He dare not be merely the spokesman of their sentiments
and habits, for he must purify the one and correct the other. Yet he
dare not be quite at odds with his age, but must share with his readers
certain assumptions. . . . At this point, discussion of diction becomes
discussion of the poet's place in the national community, or, under
modern conditions (where true community exists only in pockets), his
place in the state. This aspect of the matter will become clearer when
we ask how the poet, in his choice of language, should be governed, if at
all, by principles of taste. And this is inseparable from the question of
what Goldsmith and others understood by chastity and propriety in
language.[27]

Dante's treatise *De Vulgari Eloquentia* is a key item in Davie's
argument[28], and the terms in which Dante negotiates the relation
between the vernacular ('The Vulgar Tongue') and 'Grammar'
(Latin) are cast in a language suggestively similar to that Heaney
deploys in *The Haw Lantern*. This is specifically a question of the
relations between "the language of the tribe" and its many dialects,
and the distinction, in many ways corresponding to the Saussurean
one between *langue* and *parole*, explains why both Davie and Heaney
misquote Eliot's formula.

Davie observes: "Dante remarks that no one of the dialects can be considered the most illustrious, since the best poets have always departed from their own dialect for the purposes of their poetry". What Dante calls the "Illustrious Vulgar Tongue" is "the perfection of a common language", "intelligible to all . . . but peculiar to none". And, in words which recall the figure of the lantern-bearing Diogenes in the title poem of *The Haw Lantern*, "our Illustrious Language wanders about like a wayfarer and is welcomed in humble shelters' " and "shines forth illuminating and illuminated". It recognises no local princely court or court of justice, because it is itself "courtly" and "curial", carrying within itself "the justly balanced rule of things which have to be done", itself the final court of linguistic appeal, "though, as a body, it is scattered"[29]. This is, in fact, language as that "frugal republic" with "embassies . . . everywhere" of which the poet is required to be "a representative/and to speak on their behalf in my own tongue", in 'From the Republic of Conscience'.

Dante's discourse on the "Illustrious Language", and Davie's commentary on it, call up many of the preoccupations of *Station Island* and *The Haw Lantern*. In particular, they go some way to explaining that complex, multiply punning play on "clear" and "clearance" in the latter volume, linking the "blood-prick" of the haw lantern "that you wish would test and clear you", "the squawk of clearance" of 'From the Frontier' to the running motif of the elegiac sequence 'Clearances', where his mother's death effects a clarification of meanings and clears a space which is momentarily common:

> And we all knew one thing by being there.
> The space we stood around had been emptied
> Into us to keep, it penetrated
> Clearances that suddenly stood open.
> High cries were felled and a pure change happened.

The inconspicuous metaphor "felled" then leads on to the final clearance of the sequence, and the poet's sense of his own mortality in the image of the chestnut tree, coeval with him, now long gone from the hedge where it was planted, no more than "a space/Utterly empty, utterly a source", having "lost its place", "become a bright nowhere,/ A soul ramifying and forever/Silent, beyond silence listened for". The motif here is not finally personal life and death, but the sources and ends of poetry, calling up both that line quoted in *The Government of the Tongue* as evidence of Larkin's unlikely affinity with Dante,

"Such attics cleared of me, such absences"[30], and Auden's elegy for
Yeats, who "became his admirers", "scattered among a hundred
cities/And wholly given over to unfamiliar affections".

Heaney's prose gloss of this anecdote in 'The Placeless Heaven:
Another Look at Kavanagh' makes it clear that it is a parable about the
relation between the poet's actual and his verbal universe. As a child,
he says, he identified with the tree; now he identifies with the
"luminous emptiness" its absence creates:

> Except that this time it was not so much a matter of attaching oneself to a
> living symbol of being rooted in the native ground; it was more a matter
> of preparing to be unrooted, to be spirited away into some transparent,
> yet indigenous afterlife. The new place was all idea, if you like; it was
> generated out of my experience of the old place but it was not a
> topographical location. It was and remains an imagined realm, even if it
> can be located at an earthly spot, a placeless heaven rather than a
> heavenly place.[31]

Dante offers an authority for effecting such a clearance of the linguistic
ground, asking, of the "Illustrious Vulgar Tongue" in a metaphor
Heaney seems to pick up, "Does it not daily root out the thorny
bushes from the Italian wood? Does it not daily insert cuttings or
plant young trees? What else have its foresters to do but to bring in
and take away as has been said?" with the result that writing is
"brought to such a degree of excellence, clearness, completeness, and
polish". Heaney, however, in a poem such as 'The Mud Vision',
knows how easy it is to forfeit such clarification (a poem "ends in a
clarification of life", says *The Government of the Tongue*, echoing
Frost), to let the truly vulgar overwhelm the possible "new place",
"transparent, yet indigenous", of the illustrious language:

> Just like that, we forgot that the vision was ours,
> Our one chance to know the incomparable
> And dive to a future. What might have been origin
> We dissipated in news. The clarified place
> Had retrieved neither us nor itself.

For this project of clarifying and clearance Davie's polemic offers
ample precedents. His exposition of Owen Barfield's analogy between
"metaphor: language: meaning:: legal fiction: law: civil life" runs
parallel with Heaney's own recurrent analogy between poetic form
and political jurisdiction:

> For just as law is consistent, inflexible and determinate, yet must, to keep
> pace with social changes, have recourse to fictions; so language is fixed
> and determinate, to satisfy needs of logic, yet must, to keep pace with
> changes in thought and life, evolve new meanings by way of metaphor.[32]

But of singular application to this volume is Davie's account of how diction can be purified when "the dead metaphors of poetry are brought to life by the tang of common usage; and vice versa". This revivification of dead metaphors has itself a social and political implication: "For if the poet who coins new metaphors *enlarges* the language the poet who enlivens dead metaphors can be said to *purify* the language". Heaney exposes the artifice of language throughout *The Haw Lantern* by showing both these processes at work. He foregrounds language, not by thickening it into the opacities of his earlier work, reinforcing that "sensation of opaque fidelity" which is the history of "a dispersed people" in 'From the Land of the Unspoken', but by insisting instead on a classical austerity and bareness of diction. The more transparent it is, "a bare wire" after all that "textured stuff"[33] the more, paradoxically, it manifests its status as language, a medium.

Heaney in fact does a remarkable thing in this volume. He inverts the traditional critical argument that language is inflected either towards its signifieds or to its signifiers, either self-effacingly presents its meanings or self-importantly calls attention to itself as a medium. In the empiricist ideology, language should ideally efface itself, act as a clear window through which its meanings are immediately and unmediatedly visible. In the radical, Modernist assault on this, language is distrusted as a suborner of meanings, and has to be fractured, dislocated, foregrounded in order to expose its ideological predisposings. Baring the device alerts us to the fact that language is not innocent but complicit, distorting or transforming that which it communicates. Heaney in these later poems demonstrates the opposite. The clearer, the more transparent the language, the more we become aware of its artifice. For in this apparent bareness it becomes clear that *no* language is free of metaphor, every word may double its meaning, and all discourse can turn back on itself in coy or brazen self-consciousness. If the clogged, sedimented streams of his earlier poetry here run clear, free of mud visions, they are still (in the words of 'The Summer of Lost Rachel') "thick-webbed currents", and, in an image from 'Grotus and Coventina' which recalls analogies in Mandelstam and Pasternak, this clear flowing can bring

Jubilation at the tap's full force, the sheer
Given fact of water, how you felt you'd never
Waste one drop but know its worth better always.

Moving towards an eighteenth-century clarity of utterance, Heaney
in such parables as 'From the Land of the Unspoken' and 'From the
Canton of Expectation' is able to write of his condition in cool,
generalising narratives which imply a view of relation and order in the
universe, and in Davie's words, "turn their back upon sense-
experience and appeal beyond it, logically, to known truths deduced
from it"[34]. Personified concepts like "Conscience", Davie says,
"specify only to the extent that they place a thing in its appropriate
class, or assign it its appropriate function",[35] in a system of
classification like that of Linnaeus. This verse, as Heaney says of
Elizabeth Bishop, "establishes reliable, unassertive relations with
the world by steady attention to detail, by equable classification and
level-toned enumeration".[36] Of personification Davie observes, "an
abstraction is personified to some extent as soon as it can govern an
active verb". Heaney turns this to good effect when in 'Alphabets', he
depicts language taking precedence over the subjects who utter and
are uttered by it: "Declensions sang on air like a *hosanna*", rising up
like columns of cherubim and seraphim in the young boy. 'The Song
of the Bullets' is even more explicitly classical in its personifications
("As justice stands aghast and stares") though it marries these with a
Hardyesque bitter whimsy. Such techniques combine with peri-
phrasis and circumlocution to make us see things in a new way, draw
new lines through experience, in parables about the dangers of
confusing story-telling with reality such as 'Parable Island' and
'From the Canton of Expectation', or fables about fable-making like
'A Daylight Art'.

# 5 Standing In and Standing For

*The Haw Lantern* shows a remarkable retreat from the linguistic
density of metaphor which characterised Heaney's earlier volumes.
Metaphor overrides all the differences between tenor and vehicle,
concentrating them into some fused and compacted unity of meaning.
Instead, these poems demonstrate language's incessantly metaphoric
power by foregrounding it in the cooler, more explicit procedures of
simile, where likeness is established between two items which

nevertheless remain discrete, unfused. These poems abound in the quasi-prepositional connective 'like', from the very first analogical moment in 'Alphabets', where the child is initiated into the human world of comparisons, shadows and reflections that become substances, similes that overwhelm their referents, as the father's hands make on the wall a shadow "like a rabbit's head". Throughout the poem, the child grows up by learning to recognise and make analogies for himself, acquiring that simile-making process which maps a world of general categories, constructing more and more elaborate systems out of comparisons between the discrete phenomena of the world, learning to seek out "the figure of the universe/And 'not just single things' ". 'The Spoonbait' reveals the secret of this analogical habit at the heart of language. Inflected into archaism by its preposition, the process takes on an odd and artificial character. We cannot slide unselfconsciously from tenor to vehicle as if this were the most natural thing in the world:

> So a new similitude is given us
> And we say: The soul may be compared
>
> Unto a spoonbait that a child discovers . . .

As the analogy is developed, metaphor crowds out the original similitude until the narrative generates its own new simile ("Like the single drop that Dives implored"). But the poem then disrupts this naturalising of simile into metaphor by offering two equally unexpected alternative endings, foregrounding the fact that we are dealing here with analogies, not literal acts. One is a fanciful metaphor achieved simply by omitting the 'like'; the other stresses its 'alternative' status, and insists once again on the gratuitousness of the simile, "spooling out of nowhere" and "snagging on nothing".

By calling our attention to the process of analogy-making, these poems emphasise that meaning is a linguistic act, subject to choice and capriciousness, and not a natural event. 'Parable Island' is the clearest exploration of such a process. Stressing in the idea of parable the gratuitous and deliberate drawing of analogies between one narrative and another, it offers a metanarrative in the parable-making act itself. Even Heaney's own recurrent argument from etymology is here satirised, in deriving 'Island' from 'eye' and 'land', in this parable of visions and revisions. The dilemma of 'Parable Island' is that the competing narratives that dominate this terrain, so close and so far from 'Ire-land', do not know they are metaphoric, and so condemn themselves to beating their heads against stone. As so often, Heaney's precedent here is Joyce. Not, this time, the much-quoted encounter between Dedalus and the old English Dean but that earlier episode in which the infant Stephen naively tries to resolve the political and religious squabbles of the Christmas dinner by dissolving them into problems of metaphor and metonymy: "Tower of Ivory", "House of Gold". Purifying the dialect of the tribe is then not just an act of linguistic reclamation. It also clarifies moral and political confusions generated by the opacities of language itself, melting down and reforging in the smithy of the soul those clanking narratives 'From the Canton of Expectation' calls "songs they had learned by rote in the old language".

The poems in *The Haw Lantern* illustrate the ways in which the dead political and religious metaphors of everyday language can come alive in unexpected clarifications of meaning. There is 'The Wishing Tree', for example, "lifted, root and branch, to heaven". In the sequence 'Clearances', "Cold comforts *set* between us" sees the ordinary past participle of place turn into a verb which sets (seals and solidifies) a covenant of comfort between mother and son. The dead metaphor of "bring us to our senses" in the same poem is renewed by being taken literally, just as the priest going "hammer and tongs at the prayers for the dying" comes alive in the echo back to the coal hammer of the opening, the household implements of the previous poem and the soldering iron, bucket and "fluent dipping knives" of this. In another poem in the sequence the simple chore of folding sheets "hand to hand" and "touch and go" opens up these dead metaphors by figuring them forth in real space as enacted moments in a complicated relation:

> So we'd stretch and fold and end up hand to hand
> For a split second . . .
> Beforehand, day by day, just touch and go,
> Coming close again by holding back.

An implied pun in 'Parable Island' says it all, speaking of archaeologists who variously interpret stone circles as "pure symbol" or "assembly spots or hut foundations":

> One school thinks a post-hole in an ancient floor
> stands first of all for a pupil in an iris.
> The other thinks a post-hole is a post-hole.

The exasperation of that last bald statement restores the dead metaphor of 'stands for' back to an original literalness, in which a post-hole *stands for* the post which *stood in* it. A change of preposition converts literal into metaphoric and back again. By insisting on such clarifications of experience in language the poet can, in the words of 'The Sense of Place', define "where he stands and he can also watch himself taking his stand."

It is perhaps in the Latinate pun that Heaney most clearly fulfils Davie's prescription for purity of diction. "The clarified place" of 'The Mud Vision' refers to both a physical and an intellectual process. The soul "ramifying" in 'Clearances' extends the analogy with the chestnut tree. 'Clearances' is particularly rich in the device. Religious and everyday meanings of "incensation" are brought out by juxta-position with "the psalmist's outcry taken up with pride". A scarcely noticed series of these in the fourth sonnet plays on a range of etymologies to suggest the complex negotiations of mother and son. The mutual jostlings of "affectation" and "affect" (to put to, aspire to something beyond, put on), "adequate" (made level with, equal to) and "adjusted" (put next to) open up the central ambiguity of the clause "whenever it came to/Pronouncing words 'beyond her' ". The relation of the here and now ("came to") to a "beyond" is in fact the subtext of the whole sequence, even at the level of its prepositions. "Adjusted" (actually from *adjuxtare*) according to the *OED* was early confused with the idea of an equalizing 'justice' (*ad justus*) which put things in their proper place, thus establishing a kind of punning relation with "adequate"; and the poet enacts this adequation by juxtaposing them in his own "genuinely well-/adjusted adequate betrayal". "Pronouncing words 'beyond her' " thus overlays the simple speech act with the pronouncement of an edict of expulsion by and from the tongue's seat of government. This in turn opens up the politic adjustments of "manage": in "affecting" incompetence (all she could manage) she adroitly manoeuvres the son to fall fittingly back into his place ("decently relapse").

The Latinate pun is most brilliantly affected, however, in the conclusion of the poem:

> I'd *naw* and *aye*
> And decently relapse into the wrong
> Grammar which kept us allied and at bay.

"Allied" (from *alligare*) can mean bound together either by kinship or treaty, and so keeps open the nature of the truce negotiated between them. "At bay", however, is a dead metaphor which ramifies into remarkable life when its etymology is considered. According to the *OED* (p. 712):

> Two different words seem to be here inextricably confused. Originally the phrase *to hold at bay* seems ad. OF *tenir a bay* (Godefroy) It. *tenere a bada*, where *bay*, *bada*, means the state of suspense, expectation, or unfulfilled desire, indicated by the open mouth (late L. *badare* to open the mouth); but *to stand at bay*, *be brought to bay*, correspond to mod. Fr. *être aux abois*, meaning to be at close quarters with the barking dogs, and *bay* is here aphetically formed from ABAY, a. OF *abai* barking.

"Allied and at bay" is itself a state of suspension between decency and lapse, wrong grammar and right place. The poem's open-mouthed closure, a fork-tongued moment of unfulfilled desire in the government of the tongue, speaks from the central reticences of Heaney's verse. What 'Grammar' (Greek *gramma*, a written mark) and "at bay" (open-mouthed) set up at either end of this line is the same antithesis uttered in the Latinate pun of the prefatory poem of the sequence, which speaks of a "co-opted and obliterated echo" struck off the real world, which may "teach me now to listen/To strike it rich behind the linear black" of a written text. "Obliterated", literally, means *erased from writing*: in a Derridean sense, the voice's echo or trace erased and yet co-opted in the lines of writing. It is by making such clearings in the undergrowth of language that the bewildered self can find a place to stand, a place to make a stand.

## 6  The Distance Between

The relation between mother and son, "allied and at bay", is also a relation between two moments of language – between writing and speech, and between *langue*, 'Grammar', and *parole*, voice. It is a relation of kinship and treaty, not hostility. It reproduces, therefore, a more condign version of that stand-off Stephen Dedalus effects in relation to the "illiterate fidelities" of a "peasant oracle". An alternative relation in *Portrait* is figured in a passage to which Heaney has adverted more than once, Stephen's encounter with the old English Dean. "Stephen, in that famous passage," Heaney says in the lecture 'Among Schoolchildren', "feels inadequate when he hears the English Jesuit speaking English". The differences between them, differences according to Heaney of "cultural and geographic placing", are the oral register, "on his lips and mine", of a *différance* within a shared "language, so familiar and so foreign" ("allied and at bay"). Heaney first drew on this passage for the epigraph to 'The Wool Trade' (*Wintering Out*), where the words are finally left to "hang/ Fading, in the gallery of the tongue". In the lecture, however, he moves on, calling our attention to Stephen's less frequently remarked comeback, in which, brooding on his linguistic displacement, he looks up the word 'tundish' in the dictionary only to "find it English and good old blunt English too". Heaney's comment is significant:

> What had seemed disabling and provincial is suddenly found to be corroborating and fundamental and potentially universal. To belong to Ireland, to speak its dialect, is not necessarily to be cut off from the world's banquet because that banquet is eaten at the table of one's own life, savoured by the tongue one speaks. Stephen now trusts what he calls 'our own language' and in that trust he will go to encounter what he calls 'the reality of experience'. But it will be his own specific Dublin experience, with all its religious and historical freight, so different from the English experience to which he had heretofore stood in a subservient relationship.[37]

In his encounter with the ghost of Joyce at the end of 'Station Island', the poet returns to this episode, referring to it jokily as "The Feast of the Holy Tundish", canonizing it among his stars as Stephen had turned it into a governing myth in his diary.

I take these three writing events to be crucial for Heaney. Stephen recuperates the event by writing it up, and he turns to the higher authority of the dictionary to find the true lineage of the word restored in the authentic history on the printed page, rather than in the unreliable local narratives of the oral order. He thus delivers the rationale for Heaney's own compulsive resort to etymology, not as a search for lost origins, but so as to restore language to a living, changing history, to underwrite (I use the metaphor deliberately) the written synchronic *langue* and the diachronic spoken *parole* with the print that establishes authentic historic relation between them. Joyce refuses to be displaced by linguistic nationalism, English or Irish, because, as Heaney notes in a Latinate pun, he "is against all such alibis". In refusing to claim he was somewhere else, "he is also intent on deconstructing the prescriptive myth of Irishness which was burgeoning in his youth and which survives in various sympathetic and unsympathetic forms to this day."

Rewriting this episode in 'Station Island', Heaney attempts a similar deconstruction, putting words into the mouth of a dead man which turn in the mouth itself into a highly material simile of *writing*:

> His voice eddying with the vowels of all rivers
> came back to me, though he did not speak yet,
> a voice like a prosecutor's or a singer's,
>
> cunning, narcotic, mimic, definite
> as a steel nib's downstroke, quick and clean.

Joyce's peroration likewise homes in on writing as a physical act, something effected by that hand which grasps the ash plant, which grips that of the younger writer, and which Joyce once joked no-one would ever want to kiss who knew what other things it had done besides writing *Ulysses*:

> . . . The main thing is to write
> for the joy of it. Cultivate a work-lust
> that imagines its haven like your hands at night
>
> dreaming the sun in the sunspot of a breast.

A final ironic transformation turns the broadcast voice into a metaphor of that writing which most intimately defines the unique, autonomous self:

> swim
> out on your own and fill the element
> with signatures on your own frequency.

Heaney here gives a subtle, original twist to the cliché of the poet finding his own voice. It is no accident, then, that the poem which follows this and opens the next sequence, 'The First Gloss', should instruct the poet to hold his pen like a spade ("Take hold of the shaft of the pen"), in an intensely physical act of writing which recalls the resolution in the first poem of his first collection:

> Between my finger and my thumb
> The squat pen rests.
> I'll dig with it.

"Subscription", in 'The First Gloss', means paying one's dues, accepting a lineage and an authority, even as the first step is "taken/ from a justified line/into the margin". 'Alphabets', the opening poem of *The Haw Lantern*, spells out this subscription in the most literal of terms, exploring the child's conscription to his culture through the succession of writings he acquires. Writing here is a manual labour, acquired with difficulty: "there is a right/Way to hold the pen and a wrong way". We are reminded that words themselves, no matter how seamlessly interwoven in utterance, are really made up of more primary units, represented by written signs (*gramma*) which arbitrarily and artificially stand in for consonants and vowels. The poem plays games with its own origin, starting with the alphabetic Greek of the Harvard 'Phi Beta Kappa' poem, to reconstruct a whole series of other signs the child has lived through, from his father's shadow-drawing, through modes of writing pictographically only a step away from this—the letter Y seen as a forked stick, 2 as a swan's neck and back, A as "Two rafters and a cross-tie on the slate", O a schoolroom globe, the teacher's tick "a little leaning hoe"—through the joined-up writing of "new calligraphy that felt like home", the Ogham whose letters were trees, "The lines of script like briars", the bare Merovingian style, the Latin capitals of the sky-writing IN HOC SIGNO which converted Constantine, until it returns abstract signs to material reality in the balers dropping bales "like printouts where stooked sheaves/Made lambdas", the potato pit with a "delta face", and omega as the shape of a horseshoe over the door.

Such analogies between arbitrary signs and the referents they invoke are not just accidental but, as this aetiology of writing suggests, grow out of an incorrigible tendency to see correspondences in the world itself, to draw similitudes, deploying that little word "like" which runs through the poem to construct "the figure of the universe/ And 'not just single things' ". The astronaut is the first human whose O is not a figure of the world but the great globe itself, seen unprecedentedly not as an emblem but as

> all he has sprung from,
> The risen, aqueous, singular, lucent O
> Like a magnified and buoyant ovum.

Going back to the origins, this poem proposes, means rediscovering in one's own prehistory (before writing) the origin of the species as a sign-making, tool-making animal; means recovering a state where

writing is seen to be as material as that "buoyant ovum", and as
manual a labour as plastering a wall:

> Or like my own wide pre-reflective stare
> All agog at the plasterer on his ladder
> Skimming our gable and writing our name there
> With his trowel point, letter by strange letter.

This estrangement is simultaneously a homecoming—not a return to
origins but to a new "*sensing* of place" in a landscape "instinct with
signs." In his interview with Randy Brandes published in *Salmagundi*
Heaney explained the origin of the poem as a commission:

> I had a real problem: Write a poem for the Phi Beta Kappa at Harvard
> that had to be spoken aloud, and be concerned with learning. And that
> poem is precisely about the distance that intervenes between the person
> standing up in Sanders' Theatre, being the donnish orator, and the
> child, pre-reflective and in its pre-writing odd state.

That "pre-writing odd state" is not in any sense *innocent*, prior to
discourse, the poem makes clear, since the child is already captured in
the nets of language, and the whole poem explores the succession of
discourses, as of alphabets, through which he learns to construct, not
just a writing, but a self. And it is in some Popean "middle state" that
both poem and speaker find themselves, in that intercalated "distance
. . . between" of which Heaney speaks in the interview:

> there is a bemused, abstracted distance intervening between the
> sweetening energy of the original place and the consciousness that's
> getting back to it, looking for sweetness.

Contemplating a prehistoric "dried-up source" in the last poem of
*Station Island*, Heaney speaks of keeping a stone-faced vigil "For my
book of changes",

> until the long dumbfounded
> spirit broke cover
> to raise a dust
> in the font of exhaustion.

Neil Corcoran[38] sees this as a holy water font, and so it is. But it is also
the font of print itself, which is where all new texts find their origins.

Here, in the punning metaphoric overlaying of particular life and printed page, Heaney figures forth that relation between place and displacement which is the very ground of his writing.

NOTES

1. Seamus Heaney, *The Government of the Tongue* (London: Faber & Faber, 1988), p. 132.
2. *ibid.*, p. 137.
3. *ibid.*, p. 168.
4. Seamus Heaney, *Preoccupations* (London: Faber & Faber, 1980), p. 138.
5. 'Sounding Auden', *The Government of the Tongue*, p. 118.
6. *ibid.*, p. 123.
7. *ibid.*, p. 110.
8. *ibid.*
9. *Preoccupations*, pp. 131–49.
10. *The Government of the Tongue* p. 149.
11. *ibid.*, p. 93.
12. *ibid.*, p. 92.
13. *ibid.*, p. 166.
14. *ibid.*, p. 96.
15. James Joyce, *Ulysses* (1937 text), pp. 204–05.
16. W. B. Yeats, 'Ancestral Houses', in *The Tower*, 1928.
17. *Preoccupations*, p. 145.
18. Seamus Heaney, *Place and Displacement* (Grasmere: Trustees of Dove Cottage, 1984), p. 3.
19. *ibid.*, p. 4.
20. *ibid.*, p. 8.
21. Seamus Heaney, *Field Work* (London: Faber & Faber, 1979) p. 7, 9, 10.
22. *Preoccupations*, p. 135.
23. Seamus Heaney, 'A Tale of Two Islands', *Irish Studies 1*, ed. P. J. Drudy, (Cambridge, 1980), pp. 1–20.
24. Seamus Heaney, 'Envies and Identifications: Dante and the Modern Poet', *Irish University Review* (Spring, 1985), pp. 15–19.
25. Donald Davie, *Purity of Diction in English Verse* (London: Chatto, 1952).
26. *ibid.*, p. 31.
27. *ibid.*, pp. 16–17.
28. *ibid.*, pp. 82–90.
29. *ibid.*, pp. 86–89.
30. *The Government of the Tongue*, p. 22.
31. *ibid.*, pp. 3–4.
32. *ibid.*, pp. 29ff.
33. Neil Corcoran, *Seamus Heaney* (London: Faber & Faber, 1986) p. 153.
34. *Purity of Diction in English Verse*, p. 48.
35. *ibid.*, p. 52.
36. *The Government of the Tongue*, p. 102.
37. Seamus Heaney, *"Among Schoolchildren"* (Belfast: John Malone Memorial Committee, 1983), pp. 10–11.
38. *op. cit.*, p. 179.

**Peter McDonald**
Michael Longley's Homes

# Michael Longley's Homes

"Home is where one starts from": the phrase, from T.S. Eliot's *East Coker*,[1] combines directness with difficulty. 'Home' means a place of origin, or the concrete site in which a poetic voice is located, and in this sense is as intimate a word as poetry can use. But 'home' is also a statement arising from intimacy: to say that a place is 'home' is to imprint the place with a personal meaning. Indeed, Eliot's poem builds upon the fact that its discussion of an ancestral 'home' is read in the context of the Home Front during the Second World War; its privacies are charged with the energy of a public meaning. The very selfconsciousness of the process does perhaps mark Eliot as a poet from outside the place he is naming, and it is rare in fact to find many twentieth-century English poets writing about England in this way. 'Home', as a word simultaneously private and public in its connotations, belongs properly to the poetry of exile or displacement. W.H. Auden's 'Thanksgiving for a Habitat', or poems by Philip Larkin such as 'Here', are English poems with a secure sense of placing and physical context, untroubled by the need to name their homes. In Irish poetry, however, things are (and possibly have always been) rather different. The resonance of 'home' in Irish poetry is due partly to its potency in the discourses of sentiment and nostalgia, its emotional pull on the individual back to something larger than his personal identity. In W.B. Yeats's 'Under Saturn', for example, 'home' resonates at the end of the poem:

> 'You have come again,
> And surely after twenty years it was time to come.'
> I am thinking of a child's vow sworn in vain
> Never to leave that valley his fathers called their home.[2]

The rhyme "come"/"home" voices a command which the poet cannot obey. 'Home' here is a place and a state left behind, one to which access is possible, but only at the price of selfconsciousness. The figure brooding alone at the end of Louis MacNeice's 'The Left-Behind' finds that the location of 'home' is diminishing in significance:

> My glass is low and I lack money to fill it.
> I gaze on the black dregs and the yellow scum,
> And the night is old and a nightbird calls me away
> To what now is merely mine, and soon will be no one's
> home.[3]

Here, as in Yeats's 'Under Saturn', 'home' is functioning as a problematic and alluring word, one which eludes the attempts of the poetic voice to possess it. In neither poem are the poets fully, or simply, 'at home'.

Poetry from Northern Ireland over the last twenty-five years has been understandably haunted by the attractions, and the liabilities, of 'home'. Often, the word occurs at moments of rhetorical intensity, such as the close of Seamus Heaney's 'The Tollund Man' where "I will feel lost,/Unhappy and at home",[4] or Derek Mahon's 'Afterlives', where a conscience-stricken poet comes back to Belfast:

> Perhaps if I'd stayed behind
> And lived it bomb by bomb
> I might have grown up at last,
> And learnt what is meant by home.[5]

If there is a basic integrity here, there is also perhaps a certain element of posturing; both Heaney and Mahon cut rather dramatic figures when they learn about 'home', as Yeats did before them. In the poems of Michael Longley, this tendency is undercut, and the scope of 'home' is widened. While still a word with its double-edge of the private and the public, in Longley's work it becomes an enabling concept, a source of both comfort and possibility, which expands the poetic voice rather than dramatizing its predicament. In doing this, Longley makes use of both the physical aspects of possible home grounds (and in particular that of the West of Ireland), and the familial element in the concept of 'home', a place for love of the living and remembrance of the dead. In this sense, Longley's 'love'-poetry and his 'nature'-poetry tend towards a common point of origin and destination.

A short poem, 'The West', shows how Longley complicates the idea of 'home' by forcing it into simple, physically precise expression:

> Beneath a gas-mantle that the moths bombard,
> Light that powders at a touch, dusty wings,
> I listen for news through the atmospherics,
> A crackle of sea-wrack, spinning driftwood,
> Waves like distant traffic, news from home,
>
> Or watch myself, as through a sandy lens,
> Materialising out of the heat-shimmers
> And finding my way for ever along
> The path to this cottage, its windows,
> Walls, sun and moon dials, home from home.[6]

The selfconsciousness of this is the opposite of self-importance; the significant activities here are listening and watching, accumulating evidence of two homes, one distant and the other immediately present. "News from home" and a "home from home" are balanced at the end of each stanza, but both of these "materialise", whether from "atmospherics" or "heat-shimmers", to become components of the speaking voice. Like much of Longley's poetry, this manages to combine the standpoints of the resident and the holidaymaker, by means of precise description. It is just this element of description, and its development in the process of naming, which is crucial for the success of Longley's poetry. At the same time, it is also one of the principal risks taken by the poet, for much of the ground onto which he ventures is not unqualifiedly 'his own' until made so by the poetry. Indeed, the poet does seem to be often a figure "materialising" in the landscape of the West of Ireland from another point of origin, a home in the North, to which the poetry itself obliquely relates. It is in the light of this that Longley's poems need to be read: their pastoral serenity, their sure-footed excursions into natural history or folklore, and their pervasive feeling for the buoyancy of love and the gravity of death, all rely on the exploration of a "home from home" where origins and destinations meet. "News from home" is thus refracted to become news *for* home.

As a place to "watch myself", Longley's West always unsettles and expands the self that has come to visit. This perhaps accounts for the prominence of the first-person voice in so much of the poetry, which speaks, not for a settled and rooted identity, but for a self in the process of being absorbed by its surroundings. In 'Landscape', where "my imagination/Tangles through a turfstack", the first-person loses its stability:

> I am clothed, unclothed
> By racing cloud shadows,
> Or else disintegrate
> Like a hillside neighbour
> Erased by sea mist.[7]

In this "place of dispersals", the voice, and the observing self behind it, are drawn closer and closer to the landscape which "rips thought to tatters". By the end of the poem, the distance between observer and observed is reduced almost to nothing:

> Melting into water
> Where a minnow flashes:
> A mouth drawn to a mouth
> Digests the glass between
> Me and my reflection.

How far this is a poem about landscape, and how far it is a poem about "me", is difficult to determine. However, the process here is not one of quasi-romantic projection of the self into nature, but of an incursion of the natural world into the stable, self-recognising perspective of identity. The nature poet, or the poet of place, is usually a kind of celebrant: in recent Irish poetry the earlier work of Seamus Heaney might come to mind as a good example of how exploration and celebration of 'home' can contribute to a solidly-defined sense of identity. Yet for Longley, the "home from home" of the West offers a way of *undoing* the settled nature of an identity rooted in its own place of origin.

Here the question of the relation between this process and Longley's origins in the Protestant community of Northern Ireland inevitably arises. In the terms of such a question, the seemingly uprooted, homeless poetry of Mahon, or perhaps even that of MacNeice, makes for a neater solution than does Longley's neutral, precise and faithful approach to the West. However, the question itself may be mistaken in its implicit assumption that a secure sense of 'home' necessarily follows from, or gives rise to, a stable feeling of 'identity'. Longley's work almost never addresses this problem of the supposed crisis of identity of the Protestant writer in the North, but this is not a sign of evasion on his part. Rather, Longley helps to provide angles from which 'home' can be reapproached without the encoding of tribal claims to certain territories. In this, admittedly, it can indeed be seen to diverge widely from the approaches to place in the work of poets like Heaney or John Montague, and widely also from the example of John Hewitt, whose attempts to write a poetry answering to the particular landscape and history of Ulster lacked the atavistic force of the work of his younger, Catholic, successors amongst Ulster poets.

The element that is, at first sight at least, missing from Longley's different home is community. The landscapes of the West are sparsely populated at best, while the Northern 'home' tends to be restricted to the poet's immediate family. Typically, Longley is drawn to what MacNeice called "island truancies":[8] islands in the West, or places on the very edge of the ocean, are the counterparts to a family origin islanded in history. In the poem 'The Island', Longley creates a place where "Visitors are few", and "we" (for a change, the first person plural) build up a place to live from bric-a-brac arriving by chance:

> One ship continues to rust on the rocks.
> We stripped it completely of wash-hand basins,
> Toilet fitments, its cargo of linoleum
> And have set up house in our own fashion.[9]

This community is on the edge of everything, self-marginalizing and finally slipping out of view altogether:

> We count ourselves historians of sorts
> And chronicle all such comings and goings.
> We can walk in a day around the island.
> We shall reach the horizon and disappear.

The reader of 'The Island' is put in the visitor's position, unable to enter the community that is observed, and in the end unable to share the home. The attempted objectivity of "Linguists occasionally, and sociologists" is defeated because it asks the wrong questions, and takes up the wrong angle of approach. Longley is in fact not very concerned with entering the West on such terms, preferring to let the places he describes provide him with the physical material from which a personal—and lonely—environment can be put together.

Such communities as Longley does allow himself to inhabit are made up as much of concrete bits and pieces as of people. In 'Detour',[10] the poet's imagined funeral "Down the single street of a small market town" takes him past shops with "such names/ As Philbin, O'Malley, McNamara, Keane", but the non-human inhabitants are also listed:

> A reverent pause to let a herd of milkers pass
> Will bring me face to face with grubby parsnips,
> Cauliflowers that glitter after a sunshower,
> Then hay rakes, broom handles, gas cylinders.
> Reflected in the slow sequence of shop windows
> I shall be part of the action . . .

The poet makes little or no impression on this community, moving through its streets "Behind the only locked door for miles around". Again, the relation between the poet and this other home is an oblique one, which does not express itself directly in any statement of place or 'belonging'. An earlier poem, 'Ghost Town', takes a more interventionist approach to the "place of interminable afternoons,/Sad cottages, scythes rusting in the thatch":[11]

> Since no one has got around to it yet
> I shall restore the sign which reads CINEMA,
> Rescue from the verge of invisibility
> The faded stills of the last silent feature –
> I shall become the local eccentric . . .

Again, however, the first-person voice is subject to irony here, exposing its own determination to use this place for its own purposes ("Already I have retired there to fill/Several gaps in my education"). The poem ends with the voice plotting a course for itself which relies on separation from its origins in the familial 'home':

> Indeed, with so much on my hands, family
> And friends are definitely not welcome –
> Although by the time I am accepted there
> (A reputation and my own half-acre)
> I shall have written another letter home.

In striving to impose itself on a community, the voice in this poem in
fact ensures its own isolation. The difficulty lies perhaps in the desire
to be accepted rather than the ability to accept, in imagining that
"family and friends" have to be left somewhere else to wait for news of
the poet's experiment in self-education.

Longley's poetry is engaged in "writing home" in a richer sense
than that suggested at the end of 'The Island'. Writing often serves to
articulate careful observation, listening and watching, by providing
the names proper to the environment. The creation of a "home from
home" is for Longley an act of naming, and it is this act, in turn, which
reshapes the vocabulary and tone of the poetic voice. There are certain
significant precedents here, such as Edward Thomas's 'Adlestrop',
which allows a place-name to expand in meaning until it encompasses
an entire countryside, "all the birds/Of Oxfordshire and Gloucestershire".[12] Closer to Longley's own favoured landscapes, Patrick
Kavanagh's 'Kerr's Ass' allows the particularity of a name to resonate,
with "The God of imagination waking/In a Mucker fog".[13] In
Longley's poetry, the voice in solitude is left to list the names that are,
in fact, the real community in the midst of which it must exist. In the
sequence of short poems entitled 'Fleadh', for example, different
musical instruments are taken on board by the poet as parts of a rural
environment. The pipes, the last items on Longley's list, do not just
sound *like* the natural world, but are in fact parts of it:[14]

> One stool for the fireside
> And the field, for windbag
> And udder: milk and rain
> Singing into a bucket
> At the same angle: cries
> Of waterbirds homing:
> Ripples and undertow –
> The chanter, the drones.

Longley's device of letting nouns drop free at the end of a poem can be
seen here to be an act of naming, or rather of allowing the voice to
*accept* names as adequate to the full range of its observations. Another
sequence, 'Carrigskeewaun' (itself named for the place which has
served increasingly as the poet's particular "home from home" in the
West) begins by bringing one home into contact with another through
naming the elements that are missing. Here, it is the family 'home'
that is named in the stern solitude of a mountain landscape:[15]

> This is ravens' territory, skulls, bones,
> The marrow of these boulders supervised
> From the upper air: I stand alone here
> And seem to gather children about me,
> A collection of picnic things, my voice
> Filling the district as I call their names.

This is the other side of Longley's naming process, one which colonises the new place with a "voice/Filling the district". The irony of a poem like 'Company', where "we are living in the country/In a far-off townland" under constant observation by the local populace, undercuts any attempts the poet might make to claim direct authority over the adopted place:

> As I sit late beside a tilley-lamp
> And try to put their district on the map
> And to name the fields for them, for you
> Who busy yourself about the cottage,
> Its thatch letting in . . .[16]

This version of pastoral, which sets out to impose something on its subject, is undermined by the slow seeping-in of rain, like a neighbour "leaning against the half-door", which provides the "Watermarks under all that we say". The attempt "to name the fields for them" is not adequate to the actual conditions: if the concerns of 'home' are to find a place, they have to be able to accommodate the "watermarks" of a different environment.

The degree to which the poet, who brings with him the elements of his own 'home', enters and affects the landscape he describes is carefully judged in Longley's work; the balance between one 'home' and another, though often delicate, is never lost. In his earlier work, Longley tends to dramatise the self in a new landscape: in 'Leaving Inishmore', for instance, he speaks for himself and a companion whose "holiday" perspective means that "we left too soon/The island awash in wave and anthem". However, the poet's stance is perhaps too secure, too confident in finding the names for its surroundings:

> Summer and solstice as the seasons turn
> Anchor our boat in a perfect standstill,
> The harbour wall of Inishmore astern
> Where the Atlantic waters overspill –
> I shall name this the point of no return . . .[17]

This remains the visitor's perspective, which approaches a place in a self-interested spirit: Inishmore, in fact, merely provides Longley with images of peace and escape, a far point on a mental horizon. Here, Longley is closer to MacNeice's West, or to the numerous points of no return to which Derek Mahon's poetry returns obsessively. The change in Longley's angle of approach informs his verse-letter to Mahon, recalling a trip to Inisheer:

> That was Good Friday years ago –
> How persistent the undertow
> Slapped by currachs ferrying stones,
> Moonlight glossing the confusions
> Of its each bilingual wave – yes,
> We would have lingered there for less . . .
> Six islanders for a ten-bob note
> Rowed us out to the anchored boat.[18]

Once the "anchored boat" has been left for actual contact with the island, for "confusions" rather than the "perfect standstill" of 'Leaving Inishmore', the self-centred perspective is no longer adequate. The poem carries its own "undertow" of reference which partly explains the lack of integration with the island, "Our ears receiving then and there/The stereophonic nightmare/Of the Shankhill and the Falls". The bringing-together of 'homes' is threatened by the hostility of one place and its concerns to those of another: the poem admits that there are no easy escapes to be made from this situation.

Of course, the point of intersection between Longley's different 'homes' is bound in part to be a violent one; it is also, however, coloured by intimacy and love. What Longley brings to the West from 'home' is "My children and my dead",[19] love and grief that expands from the family out into a whole society. 'In Mayo' is a love-poem in which the significance of the visiting lovers for the district is weighed up:

> Though the townland's all ears, all eyes
> To decipher our movements, she and I
> Appear on the scene at the oddest times:
> We follow the footprints of animals,
>
> Then vanish into the old wives' tales
> Leaving behind us landmarks to be named

> After our episodes, and the mushrooms
> That cluster where we happen to lie.[20]

Love is the act of most significance with which Longley, as visitor, associates himself: the ambition to enter folklore as "landmarks" associated with love indicates the centrality of intimacy to the poet's self-projection. Similarly, in the poem 'On Mweelrea' the lovers find themselves absorbed in the landscape, finally perhaps becoming that landscape:

> Behind my eyelids I could just make out
> In a wash of blood and light and water
> Your body colouring the mountainside
> Like uncut poppies in the stubbly fields.[21]

Love-poetry is in fact very close to the centre of Longley's concerns: in his writing, it expands to fill, not only the district, but the entire range of concerns the poet feels obliged to comprehend.

The landscape of the body is the scene of much of Longley's love-poetry, and his work is distinctive in the degree to which it allows this landscape to be coloured by both delight and grief. The processes involved in 'nature-' and 'love-' poetry are very similar in Longley, each necessitating a reverential exploration of new territory, and a consequent mingling of 'homes'. The difference between the human and the pastoral landscapes, however, is that one involves the recognition of mortality. In 'Love Poem', Longley explores "your magnetic lines,/Your longitudes, latitudes" in the hope of a complete absorption in the loved one, a total immersion, and loss, of the self.[22] But the poem is in the conditional voice:

> If my ears could hear nothing
> But the noise of your body's
> Independent processes,
> Lungs, heartbeat, intestines,
> Then I would be lulled in sleep
> That soothes for a lifetime
> The scabby knees of boyhood,
> And alters the slow descent
> Of the scrotum towards death.

The lover here becomes both enfolding landscape and enveloping mother, but the poem itself does not quite escape from the conditional

voice in which it is cast. However, the balance which Longley achieves
here does succeed in holding in equilibrium mortality and comfort,
acknowledging the relation between death and love. Like inanimate
landscape, and the creatures that populate it, the lovers embody
"processes", elements in flux, and on their way somewhere else. In
'Meniscus', Longley observes the body as moisture:

> You are made out of water mostly, spittle, tears
> And the blood that colours your cheek, red water.
> Even your ears are ripples, your knuckles, knees
> Damp stones that wear the meniscus like a skin.
> Your breasts condense and adhere, drops of water.[23]

Again, body and landscape are brought together, the mortality of the
one colouring, and being coloured by, the resilience of the other.

In achieving this balance in his love-poetry, Longley often uses
images of the loved one's breasts to combine associations of eroticism
and the maternal, both making sense only in the context of death. Two
lines in MacNeice's early poem 'Mayfly' seem to have influenced
Longley profoundly here, and have had a talismanic function in his
approach to love-poetry: "But when this summer is over let us die
together – / I want always to be near your breasts".[24] In 'No
Continuing City', the poet starts by contemplating "My hands here,
gentle, where her breasts begin", and ends by welcoming the lover's
arrival "To eat and drink me out of house and home".[25] The
injunction in 'The Linen Industry' to "be shy of your breasts in the
presence of death" develops beautifully from MacNeice's lines,
reluctant to abandon the breasts to mortality.[26] The lover/mother
combination in Longley's use of the image is made explicit in a more
recent poem, 'Icon', where the poet "on the day my mother died" is
"protected" by the lover's "shoulders and hair":

> Your tears fell from the ceiling on to my face.
> I could not believe that when you came to die
> Your breasts would die too and go underground.[27]

Going underground, entering the landscape at a more intimate level
than the visitor, takes the lover literally into the world of nature-
poetry. Sometimes, the tension between the two modes, the poetry of
nature and that of love, can be felt in Longley's work, as in 'View',
where the loved one threatens to slip away and become the shoreline:

> I have put my arms around her skeleton
> For fear that her forearms might unravel
> Like hawsers, ligaments stiffening to kelp
> That keeps ocean and boulders in their places,
> Weights on the heart, ballast for the ribcage . . .[28]

As in a great deal of Longley's love-poetry, the setting and the subject are difficult to distinguish from one another. The 'view' in question is one of mortality at the same time as a more conventional 'view' of the landscape from "the same cottage on every island".

Love-poetry, then, deepens the tone of Longley's West by bringing to it the desires and the grief associated with 'home'. This is true of two different aspects of the process, the private, familial area of memory, and the public domain of history. Of course, these aspects of Longley's approach are often combined, but both are altered by their projection onto a "home from home". Here again, Longley's principal resource lies in the candour of the first-person voice he employs: a good deal of autobiographical material is filtered through the poems, while references out to points in more public history are always particular rather than general. Whereas Longley's perspectives on the West are almost always set outdoors, the poems relating to the familial 'home' are domestic affairs, in which the house contains everything of significance. In 'The Linen Industry', the "bleach green" on which the lovers find themselves is in fact "our attic under the skylight",[29] while in the elegy 'The Third Light' the poet turns his parents' grave into a dwelling-place:

> Where I kneel to marry you again,
> My elbows in darkness as I explore
> From my draughty attic your last bedroom.
> Then I vanish into the roof space.[30]

This sense of domestic space is always open to distortion in Longley's work, and can also be seen as restricting or limiting. In the short poem 'The Lodger', a novel-writing lodger in the attic with "the run of the house" "occupies my mind as well", and threatens the freedom of the family space:

> A hundred noons and sunsets
> As we lie here whispering,
> Careful not to curtail our lives
> Or change the names he has given us.[31]

Similarly, in 'Check-up' the self as a body becomes cramped and closed, so that finally "There's no such place as home".[32] More distortion is evident in 'Second Sight', where Longley follows a course back to his father's 'home' in London, another domestic space which opens to include the Irish 'home', so that the poet's grandmother would "see right through me and the hallway/And the miles of cloud and sky to Ireland".[33] In this poem, however, the ability to see beyond "home" is also a way of perceiving nightmare:

> Flanders began at the kitchen window –
> The mangle rusting in No Man's Land, gas
> Turning the antimacassars yellow
> When it blew the wrong way from the salient.

'Home' both is and is not private in this respect: it is a place where past and present are liable to fold into one another, and into which death can enter. In the elegy for his father, 'In Memoriam', Longley remembers how "Death was a visitor who hung about/Strewing the house with pills and bandages".[34]

When Longley comes to write about the Irish troubles, the only perspectives he will allow himself are domestic ones. In 'Wounds', the bus-conductor is "shot through the head/By a shivering boy who wandered in/Before they could turn the television down/Or tidy away the supper dishes."[35] Similarly, 'The Civil Servant' ('Wreaths') "was preparing an Ulster fry for breakfast/When someone walked into the kitchen and shot him".[36] The disruption of the domestic space by death happens either violently, as here, or through more 'natural' causes; Longley, however, sometimes attempts to bring these together, as in the short 'Kindertotenlieder', where new lodgers arrive to live "unrestricted" in the family home:

> There can be no songs for dead children
> Near the crazy circle of explosions,
> The splintering tangent of the ricochet,
>
> No songs for the children who have become
> My unrestricted tenants, fingerprints
> Everywhere, teethmarks on this and that.[37]

The poem, like all of Longley's 'troubles' poems, refuses to be a statement of anything; what it is, on the other hand, is an admission that 'home' is changing, that it is open to the disruptions of loss. Once again, it is necessary to emphasise that the poet is not setting out to evade issues that sometimes appear both pressing and clear, but is instead attempting to experience them in a different way, to let them sink in to the deepest level of personal concern at 'home'.

The pastoral side of Longley's writing does not exist in isolation from such violent disruptions, any more than his love-poetry can isolate itself from the burden of mortality. The poet does not set out to establish some kind of equivalence between one 'home' and the other, but he does allow the violence of one to shadow the peace of the other. The sequence of short poems, 'Lore', records straightforwardly items of practical wisdom from the country, but certain images recur within the sequence, of binding and tying, of cutting and bleeding, and finally of healing. Gauging the resonance of the final section, 'Finding a Remedy', must be an extremely delicate business:

> Sprinkle the dust from a mushroom or chew
> The white end of a rush, apply the juice
> From fern roots, stems of burdock, dandelions,
>
> Then cover the wound with cuckoo-sorrel
> Or sphagnum moss, bringing together verse
> And herb, plant and prayer to stop the bleeding.[38]

The precision involved in the act of naming here is coming close to the more subtle sense of invocation and charm; no further meaning need be assigned than that which is already provided in the title, but 'Lore', like many of Longley's poems, seems to gesture towards an unspoken relation between its subject and the unvoiced injuries comprehended at 'home'. Naming, once again, is the soothing act, one which cannot be dramatised or overstated. 'The Greengrocer' (in 'Wreaths') provides an example of naming, or listing, giving the poet a voice to address violence which can remain uninfected by rhetoric:

> Astrologers or three wise men
> Who may shortly be setting out
> For a small house up the Shankhill
> Or the Falls, should pause on their way
> To buy gifts at Jim Gibson's shop,
> Dates and chestnuts and tangerines.[39]

The focus on the particular at the end of this poem is the very opposite of frivolous; it ensures the maintenance of Longley's characteristic *gravitas*, the seriousness of complete imaginative fidelity to the immediate. The nouns are meant to soothe, though they cannot pretend to console. Another, more recent poem, 'The Ice-Cream Man', begins with a list of flavours, but states bluntly, "That was before/They murdered the ice-cream man on the Lisburn Road".[40] Longley concludes the brief poem with a *tour de force* of botanical listing:

> I named for you all the wild flowers of the Burren
> I had seen in one day: thyme, valerian, loosestrife,
> Meadowsweet, tway blade, crowfoot, ling, angelica,
> Herb robert, marjoram, cow parsley, sundew, vetch,
> Mountain avens, wood sage, ragged robin, stitchwort,
> Yarrow, lady's bedstraw, bindweed, bog pimpernel.

The lack of affectation, and the unspoken compassion that forces this oblique angle, show Longley's style at its most mature and delicate. The basic respect for the particular in Longley's poetry is a legacy of his "home from home" and its demands on the descriptive voice and vocabulary; it is here that the poet learns to name things, not with any ulterior motive ("name the fields for them"), but as the work of humility and love.

One pattern of development in Longley's poetry centres on these issues of 'home', exile and belonging. His first book, *No Continuing City*, gestures frequently towards one literary or mythic paradigm of home and homelessness, in the Homeric figure of Odysseus, who wanders at sea in his attempts to return to Ithaca. Longley's poems 'Odyssey' and 'Circe' both concentrate on the erotic element of the wanderings, "all new areas/Of experience".[41] The imagery here, of islands and shores, of love and landscape, prefigures that of much of the poet's later work. Odysseus comes bringing both his 'home' and his dead along:

> And, going out of my way to take a rest,
> From sea sickness and the sea recuperate,
> The sad fleets of capsized skulls behind me
> And the wide garden they decorate.

Each of Odysseus' "Ladies" represents only a temporary stop on his journey, though each might also be in her way significant, "Your faces favourite landmarks always,/Your bodies comprising the long way home." Circe, one of their number, in her turn expects "Out of the night, husband after husband".[42] In fact, Odysseus' wanderings represent a series of quasi-familial relationships that foreshadow the real thing, his return to his actual wife Penelope in Ithaca. Throughout *No Continuing City* Longley uses the sea as a place of chance encounter and exile: the "ocean icebound when the year is hurt" in 'Leaving Inishmore' is part of "the curriculum/Vitae of sailors and the sick at heart".[43] The long and formally elaborate poem 'The Hebrides' negotiates a course between dizzying landscapes and a sense of identity, "My journey back from flux to poise, from poise/To attitude".[44] This journey carries overtones of Odysseus' voyage:

> For these are my sailors, these my drowned –
> In their heart of hearts,
> In their city I ran aground.
> Along my arteries
> Sluice those homewaters petroleum hurts,
> Dry dock, gantries.

There is the suggestion here that all is not well in "homewaters" that could be close to Belfast Lough as well as Ithaca.

In his most recent work, Longley revisits the Odyssey motifs of his first book, this time in a series of translations from Homer, of episodes in the actual homecoming of Odysseus. The return is interpreted by Longley primarily as a return to the family, to the father and nurse, as well as to the waiting wife; but it is also, of course, a return for revenge upon the suitors and unfaithful servants. These versions of passages in *The Odyssey* mark a deepened sense of 'home' as a place of both reunited family and the most brutal horror. Again, the moments of reconciliation are made points of lyrical intensity; Longley's translations approach Homer in search of such moments, cutting away as much as possible of the broader narrative context. Odysseus encounters his father "Laertes" "in a goatskin duncher", "So old and pathetic that all he wanted then and there/Was to kiss him and hug him and blurt out the whole story."[45] The moment of recognition comes like a gift thrown up by the sea:

> Until Laertes recognised his son and, weak at the knees,
> Dizzy, flung his arms around the neck of great Odysseus
> Who drew the old man fainting to his breast and held him there
> And cradled like driftwood the bones of his dwindling father.

In the context of the concerns of much of Longley's poetry, this episode takes on a personal charge as the father, who has always been 'buried' in the poems, is allowed to meet his returning son. Similarly, the meeting with Eurycleia, Odysseus' nurse,[46] suggests, and eventually states, a parallel with Longley's childhood nurse and 'surrogate mother' who figures prominently in the autobiographical prose-piece 'Tu'penny Stung', in which "I began by loving the wrong woman":[47]

> I began like Odysseus by loving the wrong woman
> Who has disappeared among the skyscrapers of New York
> After wandering for thousands of years from Ithaca.

The darker side of this return is faced in 'The Butchers', where Odysseus' slaughter of the suitors and the housemaids is reported in detail. Again, the parallels with Longley's own 'home' are both unstated and unmistakeable. The double consequence of imaginative return, for Longley, remains a mixture of delight and horror.

Unlike MacNeice or Mahon, Longley has not chosen to negotiate with (Northern) Irish culture from a standpoint of exile; instead, he has complicated the assumptions which are needed to give meaning to such a standpoint. Gerald Dawe, writing on Mahon and Longley together, senses that 'home' is at the heart of the matter, but fails to grasp the implications of Longley's work in this respect:[48]

> It is, one feels, a question of acceptance and rejection similar to that which MacNeice experienced. Longley, I would suggest, has accepted his past (the Protestant city, the cultural 'duality', the shaky identity) whereas Mahon has rejected his. MacNeice's spiritual sons have gone their different ways: one has remained at home, the other has left.

In fact, Longley's work makes terms like these difficult to sustain (and perhaps they are less useful for the other poets than many critics choose to believe). "Acceptance and rejection" can never be as clearcut as this, at least not at the point of writing poetry as opposed to making cultural or political statements. There is nothing uniquely "shaky" about Longley's "identity"; instead, Longley is aware of how shaky a concept "identity" is in poetry. Once terminology such as this is disowned or undermined, of course, poetry runs the risk of losing its immediate attractiveness in a critical world that needs to 'place' or identify its subjects in clear terms. Longley's poetry, though it has never gone short of respect, has yet to work its way into the

discourse of the cultural critics for whom Irish writing occupies a
central position. This is perhaps inevitable, and certainly it has done
Longley's work no harm. The cultural discussions, on the other hand,
would benefit from an understanding of this poet's complex sense of
'home', and a recognition of the breadth and significance of his
achievement. Like Edward Thomas, Longley has used his poetry to
explore "a system of vast circumferences circling round the minute
neighbouring points of home":[49] he has done so without posturing,
and without recourse to easy answers or definitions. In Ireland, the
integrity and sure-footedness of the exploration might well be seen as
exemplary.

NOTES

I am grateful to Michael Longley for allowing me, in advance of publication, to read and
quote from poems in his collection, *Gorse Fires* (London: Secker & Warburg, 1991).

1.  T.S. Eliot, *The Complete Poems and Plays of T.S. Eliot* (London: Faber & Faber,
    1969), p. 182.
2.  W.B. Yeats, *Collected Poems* (London: Macmillan, 1950), p. 202.
3.  Louis MacNeice, *Collected Poems* (London: Faber & Faber, 1979), p. 449.
4.  Seamus Heaney, *Wintering Out* (London: Faber & Faber, 1972), p. 48.
5.  Derek Mahon, *Poems 1962–1978* (Oxford: Oxford University Press, 1979), p. 58.
6.  Michael Longley, *Poems 1963–1983* (Edinburgh and Dublin: Salamander & Gallery,
    1985), p. 94.
7.  *ibid.*, p. 126.
8.  Louis MacNeice, *Collected Poems*, p. 226.
9.  Longley, *op. cit.*, p. 93.
10. Longley, *Gorse Fires*, p. 7.
11. Longley, *Poems 1963–1983*, p. 99.
12. Edward Thomas, *Collected Poems*, ed. R. George Thomas (Oxford: Oxford University
    Press, 1981), p. 25.
13. Patrick Kavanagh, *Complete Poems* (Newbridge: The Goldsmith Press, 1984), p. 254.
14. Longley, *op. cit.*, p. 125.
15. *ibid.*, p. 96.
16. *ibid.*, p. 140.
17. *ibid.*, p. 54.
18. *ibid.*, p. 83.
19. *ibid.*, p. 15.
20. *ibid.*, p. 118.
21. *ibid.*, p. 178.
22. *ibid.*, p. 115.
23. *ibid.*, p. 176.
24. MacNeice, *Collected Poems*, p. 14.
25. Longley, op. cit., p. 34–5 pp.

26.  *ibid.*, p. 179.
27.  Longley, *Gorse Fires*, p. 36.
28.  Longley, *Poems 1963–1983*, p. 187.
29.  *ibid.*, p. 179.
30.  *ibid.*, p. 200
31.  *ibid.*, p. 111.
32.  *ibid.*, p. 111.
33.  *ibid.*, p. 151.
34.  *ibid.*, p. 49.
35.  *ibid.*, p. 86.
36.  *ibid.*, p. 148.
37.  *ibid.*, p. 87.
38.  *ibid.*, pp. 158–9.
39.  *ibid.*, p. 148.
40.  Longley, *Gorse Fires*, p. 49.
41.  Longley, *Poems 1963–1983*, pp. 30–31.
42.  *ibid.*, p. 32.
43.  *ibid.*, p. 54.
44.  *ibid.*, p. 41.
45.  Longley, *Gorse Fires*, p. 33.
46.  Longley, 'Eurycleia', *Gorse Fires*, p. 31.
47.  Longley, 'Tu'penny Stung', *Poetry Review*, Vol. 74, No. 4 (Jan. 1985), p. 5; repr. in Frank Ormsby (ed.), *Northern windows: an anthology of Ulster autobiography* (Belfast: Blackstaff, 1987).
48.  Gerald Dawe, 'Icon and Lares: Derek Mahon and Michael Longley', in Gerald Dawe and Edna Longley (eds.), *Across A Roaring Hill: The Protestant imagination in modern Ireland* (Belfast: Blackstaff, 1985), p. 227.
49.  Edward Thomas, 'It's a long, long way', *The Last Sheaf* (1928), p. 111; repr. in Edna Longley (ed.) *A language not to be betrayed: Selected prose of Edward Thomas* (Manchester: Carcanet Press, 1981), p. 231.

**Hugh Haughton**
'Even now there are places where a thought might grow': Place and Displacement in the Poetry of Derek Mahon

# Place and Displacement in Derek Mahon

## 1

Cursed be he that curses his mother. I cannot be
Anyone else than what this land engendered me.

(Louis MacNeice)

L'artiste qui joue son être est de nulle part. Et il n'a pas de frères.

(Samuel Beckett)

"The time is coming fast, if it isn't already here, when the question 'Is So-and-So really an *Irish* writer?' will clear a room in seconds".[1] Mahon offered this dyspeptic observation at the opening of his short account of 'MacNeice in England and Ireland' published in 1974. Unfortunately the question hasn't gone away, however boring it was then and is now. Perhaps it won't entirely wither away until the 'Irish problem' itself does. Questions of allegiance, of cultural and tribal origins, are integral to twentieth-century Irish writing. If you are born in Ulster, you are not only born into a place, but into a place where allegiance to other places—mainland Britain or the South of Ireland—help define your place in that society. In an essay called 'Place and Displacement: Recent Poetry of Northern Ireland'—the source of my own sub-title—Seamus Heaney explores the kinds of displacement experienced by Northern Irish writers such as Mahon who "belong to a place that is patently riven between notions of belonging to other places".[2] "We are in one place and one place only", Mahon has written, yet his poetry is rarely if ever in one place. "Places as such are dead", he writes elsewhere, yet his best poems are anchored in place and place-names to an eerie degree. In this essay I wish to explore the strange place of place in the poetry of this conspicuously displaced Irish poet.

Mahon's poetry is rarely if ever concerned with definitions of the 'Irish Question', in the way that Kinsella's, Montague's or Heaney's is. Yet if the 'National' question doesn't arise in his work, the question of cultural self-definition certainly does, and as the editor of two collections of Irish poetry, Mahon has declared his hand on the matter—the *Sphere Book of Irish Poetry* and, with Peter Fallon, the invaluable *Penguin Book of Contemporary Irish Poetry* published in 1990. In the early MacNeice essay he confronts the issue of Irishness and Poetry with bracing scepticism:

> There is a belief, prevalent since the time of Thomas Davis, that Irish poetry, to be Irish, must somehow express the National Aspirations; and MacNeice's failure to do so (the National Aspirations, after all, include patriotic graft and pious baloney) is one of the reasons for his final exclusion from the charmed circle, known and feared the world over, of Irish Poets. 'A tourist in his own country', it has been said, with the implication that this is somehow discreditable. But of what sensitive person is the same not true? The phrase might stand, indeed, as an epitaph for Modern Man, beside Camus's 'He made love and read the newspapers'.[3]

Mahon's sardonic stance has something in common with MacNeice's, but its peppery polemic is also painfully conscious of the debate about the relationship between poetic and national cultural identity within the charmed circle of Irish poets. MacNeice left Ireland early and though he returned to Ireland for holidays and visits, lived his intellectual life almost exclusively within a British context. Mahon notes that 'exile', in the histrionic and approximate sense in which the word is used in Ireland, was an option available to Joyce and O'Casey, who 'belonged' to the people from whom they wished to escape', but not to MacNeice, whose background was "a mixture of Anglo-Irish and Ulster Protestant (C. of I.)". Mahon's inverted commas themselves distance him from nationalist talk of 'the people' and align him with MacNeice's expatriate and sceptical detachment. They also recognise a certain kinship with the earlier poet. Mahon was educated in Belfast and at Trinity College Dublin, but as an Ulster Protestant who has spent a substantial portion of his professional life in England, he patently feels ill at ease with monolithic nationalist assumptions about 'Irish' identity and his own cultural alignment. In the preface to a small pamphlet, *Ecclesiastes*, written soon after the appearance of his first book, *Night-Crossing*, in England, Mahon described his work as "an attempt by an uprooted Ulsterman to come to terms with his background and with something glimpsed through that back-ground".[4] If Mahon, like MacNeice, is in some measure "a tourist in his own country", this is not a kind of slur on his poetic credibility, but a mark of his inescapable modernity. It may affect his membership of the "charmed circle" of Irish poets, but it is also a sign of his kinship with "Modern Man" as viewed by writers such as Camus. There may be an element of fastidious protestant distaste in Mahon's inverted commas, but there is also a salutary impatience with the poetic passport question, and a sense of more urgent priorities elsewhere.

But Mahon himself forms part of a somewhat different "charmed circle", that of "Northern Irish poets" which he discussed in an earlier essay on 'Poetry in Northern Ireland'.[5] There he traces the emergence, from the "cultural desert" of Northern Ireland in the 1950s, of a "sense of a new Northern poetry", crystalised around Philip Hobsbaum's seminar 'known as 'The Group' from its parent body in London", and associated with the launch of *The Honest Ulsterman* initially edited by James Simmons and subsequently by Michael Foley and Frank Ormsby.[6] Mahon distinguishes between the experience and "texture" of Northern poets like Heaney, Montague, Longley, James Simmons and himself on the one hand, and their "Southern counterparts", Austin Clarke, Patrick Kavanagh, Thomas Kinsella and Michael Hartnett on the other. This has to do not only with the "struggle for political and cultural self-expression" among Northern Catholics like Heaney, but the sense in Protestant and Catholic alike of "a larger audience than Ireland provides". Those he calls "the Irish (Southern Irish) poets" have in common their "sense of what Myles na gCopaleen called the plain people of Ireland" as their "final court of appeal". In fact the Southerners, according to Mahon, are victims of something analogous to the kind of archaic Celticising that had characterised the Irish Literary Revival at the turn of the century:

> Like Ireland itself (and I intend no sneer), the 'Irish' poet is either unwilling or unable to come to terms with 'the twentieth century'. This begs at least one question, of course, and in any case one cannot prescribe for poets what they should write about or how; but to the extent that the Northern poet, surrounded as he is by the Greek gifts of modern industry and what Ferlinghetti called 'the hollering monsters of the imagination of disaster', shares an ecology with the technological societies his rulers are so anxious to imitate, he must, to be true to his imagination, insist upon a different court of appeal from that which sits in the South.[7]

Mahon's case here involves a fair amount of special pleading—the inverted commas suggest a trace of the sneer he disclaims—and his diagnosis of Southern comfort is in fact an apologia for his generation of Northern poets. More particularly it is an off-the-cuff defence of his own poetic stance—he is the only one of the poets referred to who really fits the bill in confronting the "imagination of disaster" and the "technological" society of the twentieth-century. Mahon's polemic suggests that the 'British connection', so problematic at all levels for Irish politics and art in the twentieth century, might prove potentially enabling for himself and his fellow Northern poets, whatever their background, in providing a non-nationalist and even international court of appeal. For Mahon this means confronting the "twentieth century" and Camusian Man on a wider world-stage.

The problem is whether this wide audience would substitute metropolitan English values for Irish ones, and London for Dublin. The writer's displacement might after all only be one more version of the provincial's love-affair with the capital, the nostalgia of the *colon* for the mother-country. In resisting the "pious baloney" of Ireland, the poet might be simply reproducing the 'civilised', 'urbane', 'liberal' values of the English poetic establishment, and replacing Irish literary movements by 'The Movement' with which 'The Group' was inevitably allied.[8] Though formally Mahon does indeed owe much to the lyric traditions of twentieth century English verse, it is to the tradition of early MacNeice and the expatriated middle-period Auden of *New Year's Letter* rather than the kinds of 'Movement' values associated with Donald Davie, with his attempts to promote a "tone of the centre", or Larkin and Amis with their defensive philistine armour against the wider literary and cultural world. Mahon is distinctive among contemporary Irish poets in his appetite for traditional stanzaic forms, for his brand of well-travelled and well-read wit, and for the disquieting and disquieted urbanity of his voice. He is an acutely historically sensitive writer, but he does not share the need to possess history and appropriate the uniquely Irish past that you find in Kinsella, Heaney or Montague—whose 'Like Dolmens Round My Childhood' Mahon calls "the first contemporary Ulster poem".[9] But if Mahon's work is formally and intellectually unlike the work of his Irish contemporaries, it is also profoundly unlike those of his English counterparts. I can't think of any parallels among English poets for Mahon's metaphysical unease, his sense of damage and civilisational desolation, his sense of displacement and disenchanted mobility, or indeed for the poignant elegance of his lyric music.

Though Mahon has written as vividly about Kensington and Brighton as about Portstewart and Co Cork, 'Mahon in England and Ireland' would be a dull topic. He writes of both countries with a double sense of inwardness and alienation. No doubt his unease with Unionist Belfast Protestantism and with Catholic nationalism, his distance from those he calls in *Ecclesiastes* his "people" as well as from 'the people' of Irish Catholic mythology, has something to do with this, but it would be crass to reduce it to such terms. As in the "epitaph for Modern Man" quoted previously, Mahon has frequently paired MacNeice and Camus as paradigmatic writers, and in his essay on 'Poetry in Northern Ireland' he cites the Irish critic Conor Cruise O'Brien's account of the French writer's relation to Algeria as a parallel to his own and Michael Longley's relationship to "the indigenous, Catholic-Irish culture", noting that "Camus could never have been an Algerian writer". He suggests that Northern poets from protestant backgrounds are not primarily concerned with Ireland as "a distinct cultural entity" but aware instead of "a diffuse and fortuitous assembly of Irish, British and American models". "In this", he says, quoting a displaced and anglicised American, they are "true to their dissociated sensibilities".[10] Where for Eliot "dissociated sensibility", a legacy in part of the English Civil War, was a pathological condition, for Mahon, caught in a political situation approaching that of civil war, it is a stimulus and even, I suspect, a vocation. Such a "dissociation" has taken historically violent and divisive forms in modern Northern Ireland, and Mahon's elegant lyric music operates with an exacerbated sense of cultural dissonance. In the last poem of *Antarctica*, 'Death and the Sun', he explores his sense of kinship with Camus and the affinities between his own experience of his "northern land of rain and murk", complete with its "familiar foe", and Camus's vision of a plague-ridden Algeria. He speaks of admiring in Camus "the frank composure/Of a stranger bayed by dogs" and recognising in his *La Peste* the unimaginable violence of his own country which had "never imagined the plague to come". The "frank composure" of Mahon's threatened lyricism grows out of some such vision. Yet, as 'Death and the Sun', with its elaborate sense of what Heaney calls in *Place and Displacement* "Mahon's sense of bilocation" suggests, this is not a situation peculiar to Ireland. Being caught between cultures is the common predicament of the modern intellectual—and perhaps almost everybody else too. Mahon's intense awareness of that has helped make him one of the most bracing and original poets now writing in English.

In a review of John Montague's *Faber Book of Irish Verse* of 1974
Mahon speaks of the "dramatic mutations" undergone by Irish
poetry throughout its history, the last of which was "from the English
to the Yeatsian".[11] He then goes on to suggest that "without
accelerating timescales, another is taking place now":

> In any event Irish poetry in the 20th century, like poetry everywhere,
> has been increasingly centrifugal—in Montague's phrase, 'a competing
> multiplicity of styles'.

The phrase from Montague's introduction is reminiscent of
Kinsella's now classic diagnosis of the situation of 'The Irish Writer'
as analogous to that of modern writers anywhere:

> . . . every writer in the modern world—since he can't be in all the
> literary traditions at once—is the inheritor of a gapped, discontinuous,
> polyglot tradition.[12]

Mahon's review assimilates the Northern poets to Irish poetry in
general, and dismisses as a "convenient piece of journalism" the belief
"not discouraged in the North, that the North is where the most
important Irish poetry is now being written". In fact he disclaims any
common ground between Heaney, Longley, Simmons and himself,
except the accident of their coming from the same province. Thinking
perhaps of Kinsella, he notes that Southern poets tend to look to
America or the continent "when they want to measure themselves
against a larger ground than Ireland provides, or England for that
matter"—thus disclaiming his earlier assumption that Southern poets
tended to write for "the plain people of Ireland". In the introduction
to his own anthology of contemporary Irish poetry he writes that
"poets from the North contribute to a national body of work which, in
its turn, belongs to a global community" and that Irish poets "are less
tied to particular places—or parishes—than ever before".[13]
    Like MacNeice and Auden, Mahon's work assimilates, not a
"multiplicity of styles" exactly but a multiplicity of references and
idioms within a stable but mobile mode of his own. "Centrifugal" is a
telling term, when we think of Yeats's "centre cannot hold", or
Davie's reworking of Arnold's "tone of the centre". Mahon's
brazenly "civilised" yet uncomfortably exposed verse may speak like
the troubled ghost of Arnold's "tone of the centre" but is also marked
by an acute sense of marginality—of displacement from any stable

centre. "Empire is fugitive", as at least two of Mahon's poems about England remind us ('Another Sunday Morning' and 'A Kensington Notebook'), and Mahon's verse speaks with the voice of a latecomer, a precarious and fastidious representative of an obsolescent culture, akin to that of one of his modern mentors, Cavafy, to whom he dedicates a poem in *The Snow Party*.[14] By temperament, and by cultural experience, he is obstinately attuned to what is fugitive and centrifugal.

Mahon's poetry always works with that sense of "larger ground" beyond the 'local', 'regional', and personal that he talks of in the review of Montague's anthology. His first collection was called *Night-Crossing* and nearly all his poems take an avowedly comparativist stance or are about a kind of 'crossing' between different places—between Ireland and England, England and the continent, Tomis and Rome, Ireland and America. There is no purely local world in Mahon, whose poetry reminds us that, if the world is not in Marshall MacLuhan's sense a 'global village', poetry is part of a 'global community'. 'Courtyards in Delft', for example, projects a seventeenth-century Dutch painter's view of a provincial town onto the poet's Belfast, and protestant Ulster into a painting of seventeenth-century Holland (though without mentioning William of Orange!). "The pale light of that provincial town" becomes not only a mirror of Mahon's world but a "map of the world" like that depicted in the painting. In this sense all of Mahon's poems are maps of the world, instances of a cultural frame in which particular places have no privileged part. You are always aware of an elsewhere, or a universalist's cold and rueful sense of *anywhere* in Mahon's work. Like Camus, he is a kind of unhoused universalist for whom the local detail, the detailed locality, is always an instance of a larger condition. The topographical is a topos, the graphic detail always iconographic. In this respect he takes an almost diametrically opposite stance to his close contemporary Seamus Heaney, at least in his early work. In 'Gifts of Rain', Heaney invoked the dream of "bedding the locale/in the utterance". By contrast Mahon anchors his utterance in locale, in named places, but insists on its mobility, its origins and destinations elsewhere. In fact he characteristically takes what he calls in 'The Globe in North Carolina' the "theoptic view" of things, a kind of God's eye global view, though in a world without theology. Like the seventeenth-century devotional and 'metaphysical' poets studied by Louis Martz, Mahon tends to operate with some version of Loyolan 'composition of place', but he makes of place not an end or "dream of loss and origins", such as we find in Heaney or Montague, but an ironic icon to act as a focus for our historical predicament as part of a godless technological civilisation with an "imagination of disaster".

Placing Mahon's voice and stance has in fact proved strangely difficult for critics. The ghost of urbanity, the spectre of suavity, haunts his forms and tones, with their fierce decorum and composed discomposure, but he writes without the nostalgic 'Rage for Order' of the modernists and without the glamourisation of the past characteristic of modernists like Eliot and so many Irish poets since Yeats. Seamus Deane formulates the position with provocative clarity:

> His urbanity helps him to fend off the forces of atavism, ignorance and oppression which are part of his Northern Protestant heritage. There is an ease and an elegance in his writing which can be identified with that of the world citizen, but the *urbs* from which his urbanity arises is the city

of Belfast, a bleak and ruined site—so that the wit and sophistication of the poetry is haunted by intimations of collapse, pogrom, apocalypse.[15]

Deane confines the "world citizen" too narrowly to the home territory he has defined himself against but captures something of Mahon's paradoxical stance. He is a poet with an exacerbated sense of distance—between artist and world, poet and community, poem and reality—and he writes with an uncomfortable awareness of the violence that threatens the poet's order, as in the desperately ironical portrait of the "desperate ironies" of the post in 'Rage for Order':

> Somewhere beyond the scorched gable end and the burnt-out buses
>      there is a poet indulging
>           his wretched rage for order—[16]

This rewrites Wallace Stevens' 'Idea of Order at Key West' within a threatening political landscape that compounds the Roman empire and Belfast.[17] The poet is "far from his people", which may be a measure of his experience as a disenchanted Ulster protestant, divided by his allegiances. If so, then like Beckett's or MacNeice's experiences of cultural displacement from Ireland, it stands as a figure of a more widely shared sense of disaffiliation and perplexity faced by people with very different histories. Nevertheless behind Mahon's order there is rage—and the burnt-out buses of Belfast.

## 2

> Younger
> I felt the dead
> Drag at my feet
> Like roots.
> (Seamus Deane, 'Roots')

"One part of my mind must learn to know its place", Mahon writes at the close of one of his earliest distinctive poems from *Night-Crossing*, 'In Belfast'. In this section I want to look at three early poems in which the poet attempted to know his place in the most immediate sense. The ending of 'In Belfast', heavily revised between its first appearance in 1964 and its publication in book form in 1968 in the wake of 'The Troubles', formulates Mahon's predicament with strained exactness:

> One part of my mind must learn to know its place.
> The things that happen in the kitchen houses
> And echoing back-streets of this desperate city
> Should engage more than my casual interest,
> Exact more than my casual pity.[18]

The conclusion dwells on the resonant pun between knowing the place that he comes from—his native city of Belfast—and knowing his place in the metaphorical sense—recognising his lowly status and not making too great claims for himself. Mahon's best poems are all attempts of the mind to know its place in this double sense, but the poem acknowledges his reluctance to 'know his place' on both counts. It recognises both the difficulty of conceding more than a casual interest or pity for his fellow citizens in the "desperate city"—and the danger of submissively knowing his place only too well by succumbing in bad faith to Belfast's sullen silence and "sanctimonious God". The question is how you negotiate between your necessary sense of distance and your uncomfortable sense of belonging. We remember that the mind is its own place, however, and the poet only concedes that "one part" of his mind should know its place.[19]

'In Carrowdore Churchyard' (p. 11) subtitled 'at the grave of Louis MacNeice', may be Mahon's first serious engagement with a poetic predecessor from his own place—a poet whose 'Carrickfergus' lies

behind such early poems as 'Glengormley'.[20] In it he appropriates
MacNeice's graveyard as an exemplary emblem of the role of poetry
itself in a riven culture. It is less a poem of place than a poem about the
place of poetry. In invoking the "high ground" of the earlier poet's
grave, it equates the site of the churchyard with the moral "high
ground" of MacNeice's art and then, in a comparably well-plotted
pun, calls it a "plot . . . consecrated . . . to what lies in the future
tense"—a witty conflation of the poet's grave and the plot of his
poetry. The "humane perspective" of the church and the spring
landscape are turned into embodiments of MacNeice's symbolic role
as source of renovation for "the blind writer and the bombed out
town". A vivid monument to Mahon's need for a poetic predecessor
on his native ground, the poem's own plot, with its consolatory
opposition between the traditional graveyard pastoral of the Protestant Church and the damaged city of Belfast, is all too neat.

A third early poem called 'An Irishman in London' also confronts
the relation between his poetry and his Ireland but in untidier and
more interesting form. Though it has never been collected, it
represents something of a watershed in his development as a poet.[21] It
dramatises Mahon's predicament as a genuinely displaced person in a
foreign country where, as he says, "I must find myself or founder".
The opening sets the tone:

> My draught stout sputtering in its schooner
> Is a mirocosm of this maelstrom,
> This pitching sea of nerves, this dry sargasso
> Where I must find myself or founder. Sooner
> Or later I shall have to get up and go,
> Inspect the darkness, make a course for home—

The extravagant pun on "schooner" launches the poet on a turbulent
course of linguistic intoxication and oceanic exploration "where
Odysseus and Ahab meet". It would be harsh to say the writer
founders rather than finds himself in this melodramatic quest for self-
definition, but the poem's London is a fascinating melting-pot of
other poetic voices rather than a place where he finds his own.
"Choked voices from in front/Tell of a monster", and the barely
choked voices of 'An Irishman in London' tells us less about what it
calls the "extant landmarks of the city"—contrast the wonderfully
assured later poem 'Another Sunday Morning' with its views of
London's parks—than about the extant literary landmarks and the

many-headed monster of poetic influence. Echoes of Empson, Thomas, Yeats, Auden, MacNeice rumble through the poem, intensified by the heady Atlantic music of Lowell's 'A Quaker Graveyard in Nantucket' which resounds through phrases such as "Ahab, they scour the turbulent whaling-ground". The poet's attempt to "mark the faces in the street" bears the mark of the voices of such illustrious forebears as Blake, Wordsworth and T.S. Eliot. As he admits, he is "vastly adrift", "rumour and hearsay . . . come to make/Their synthesis" upon his lines, and he cannot keep the "floodlit leviathan" of earlier poetic greatness at bay.

Nevertheless, for all its "ungoverned" magniloquence and the inflated Melvillean and Joycean terminology of its poetic quest, its swollen imagery of romantic voyaging and high tide of unconscious allusiveness, the poem successfully postpones what it calls "the course for home"—"that backward land/Which was mine once"—and confronts the imaginative realities of displacement with a certain exhilaration:

> Now I am truly rootless, having outstripped
> The streets of home. A shipyard siren
> Mourns to the stony North.

"Now I am truly rootless" swaggers with existentialist élan, but the poem remains rooted in memories of the "stony North", the "backward land" as well as in memories of the literary past and the journeys of the Ahab of Melville and Lowell and of the Odysseus of Homer and Joyce. "I must go forward to go back", the poet tells himself at the close:

> Odysseus must take
> No cheap night-crossing into Ithaca,
> But having once set out must struggle through
> With the rage of Ahab. I have imagined
> So much repose, repose is my idea.
> It is not a place that one could travel to,
> But lies in time beyond the last engagement.

Mahon must subsequently have become embarrassed by the poem's unembarrassed identifications with the archetypal literary travellers Odysseus and Ahab, but it memorably asserts the idea of ongoing poetic travel against the nostalgic "course for home". "I must go forward to go back" suggests that "the course for home" is still a goal of Mahon's travelling, even though he disdains the "cheap night-crossing into Ithaca"—the student Dublin of Joyce's *Ulysses*.

'An Irishman in London' is a flawed poem, but it sets up the terms of Mahon's work with great expressiveness—the back and forward travel of a "rootless", displaced person, between places, one of which may be 'home'. Like his later poetry, it thrives on multiple allusions to other "extant landmarks" (geographical and literary), though in his mature work the climate of well-travelled allusiveness operates with more critical wit and ironic grace. As Mahon's readers we must be grateful that what the poem calls the "fiery hunt" for repose has persisted into the work of *The Hunt by Night* and afterwards, and that his verse has been as faithful to his knowledge of being culturally "rootless" as to his fascination with the places that "one can travel to"—and from.

## 3

> Life is an affair of people not of places. But for me life is an affair of
> places and that is the trouble.
>
> Wallace Stevens.[22]

For Derek Mahon, poetry has always been largely an affair of places. Many of the landmarks of modern Irish poetry *are* literally land-marks—Yeats's 'Coole and Ballylee' and 'Under Ben Bulben', Louis MacNeice's 'Carrickfergus' and 'Carrick Revisited', Denis Devlin's 'Lough Derg' and 'Ankhor Wat', Seamus Heaney's 'Toome' and 'Glanmore Sonnets', Thomas Kinsella's 'Baggot Street Deserta' and 'Tao and Unfitness at Inistiogue on the River Nore'. Nevertheless places occupy a uniquely privileged place in Mahon's work and from 'In Belfast' in his first book to 'Antarctica' in his most recent, his poems tend to take their names from places and shape themselves around named places. His great poems of Irish dereliction, 'A Disused Shed in Co Wexford' and 'A Garage in Co Cork', like his American meditations 'A Lighthouse in Maine' and 'The Globe in North Carolina', share a style of title—for Mahon 'in' is clearly the most prepossessing of the prepositions and this titular grammar firmly places the poetic subject in a secure geographical frame. In fact Mahon's index of titles is a litany of place-names from Ireland,

England and America—'Achill' and 'Kinsale', 'Brighton Beach'
and 'Penshurst Place'. 'April on Toronto Island' and 'Mt Gabriel',
or the beautifully bilocated 'Thinking of Inis Orr in Cambridge,
Massachussets'. Even his poems about writers and artists characteristically evoke places in paint—'Courtyards in Delft'. 'Girls on the
Bridge'—or set artists in places—from the early 'De Quincey at
Grasmere' and 'Van Gogh in the Borinage' to 'Brecht in Svendborg'
and 'Ovid in Tomis'. Though they don't name individual places, the
titles of Mahon's successive books suggest travel, journeys through
negative conditions of night or snow—*Night-Crossing* (1968), *The
Snow Party* (1975), *The Hunt by Night* (1982) and *Antarctica* (1985).
As George Herbert built his art around the stable edifice of church
architecture and ritual, so Mahon, condemned to the inhospitable
freedom of what he calls, after Beckett, "the existential lyric", builds
his around the places from which he is displaced.

Yeats in his 'A Prayer for My Daughter', written in a time of
political violence and change, imagines a future for his daughter
"rooted in one dear perpetual place". Mahon as a self-declared
"rootless Ulsterman" remains fixed on the notion of the 'home' he has
left. In their introduction to *The Penguin Book of Contemporary Irish
Poetry* Mahon and Peter Fallon identify the word "home" as "the
word most frequently dwelt on" in the Irish poetry they have
selected—"as if an uncertainty exists as to where that actually is."[23]
This makes Mahon either a very typical contemporary Irish poet or
contemporary Irish poetry suspiciously Mahonian. Certainly 'home',
like 'place', is one of the most resonant words in his poetic vocabulary.
If it is not dwelt in, it is certainly 'dwelt on'.

In 'Afterlives', for example, a 'bilocated' poem about 'going home'
from London to his native Belfast "after five years of war", he says he
scarcely recognises "the places (he) grew up in" and reflects:

> But the hills are still the same
> Grey-blue over Belfast.
> Perhaps if I'd stayed behind
> And lived it bomb by bomb
> I might have grown up at last
> And learnt what is meant by home.
>> (Penguin, p.51)

The rhyme of "bomb" and "home" registers a brutal kind of
consonance while marking an ironic distance between what is usually

meant by home and his actual home-town where he no longer feels at home. In a poem called 'Going Home', which is not about Belfast but a compound of Hull and Dante's Hell, he speaks of going "home/To the blank Elysium/predicated on our/Eschewal of metaphysics" and invokes:

> A residual poetry of
> Leavetaking and homecoming,
> Of work and sentiment.[24]

In this residual poetry 'home' is the 'blank Elysium' of a post-metaphysical universe, where in a sense no-one is at home, and no one place can be privileged as 'home'.

Mahon's poetry is habitually constructed around such a "residual poetry of/Leavetaking and homecoming". In 'The Return', for example, a poem about leaving some English rural idyll for his native Ireland, the poet speaks briefly of feeling "As if I owned the place" and "as if I belonged here too", only to end with an image of a wind-battered tree in the desolate Irish landscape to which he is returning. This poet doesn't, it seems, 'belong' to or 'own' places, or own them as 'home'. 'Home' doesn't anyway necessarily represent safety for Mahon. It is intimately related to dereliction and violence. In 'A Kensington Notebook', he rhymes "home" and "the Somme" and in 'Autobiographies' speaks of his war-time childhood in Ulster as "The Homefront" where he is "A male child in a garden/Clutching the *Empire News*". "Somebody somewhere thinks of this as home", he writes of the deserted site of 'A Garage in Co Cork' and "Home is where the heart breaks" of his sea-side convalescent retreat in 'Craigvara House'. If the idea of home is allied to heartbreak, several poems speak instead of a 'home from home'. In 'Brecht in Svendborg' the exiled German poet imagines Svendborg as a 'home from home', in the grimly autobiographical 'Dawn at St Patricks' Mahon himself tries to make a 'home from home' in a Dublin hospital, while in 'The Globe in North Carolina' he calls the planet earth itself merely a "peripheral/Night-garden in the glory-hole/Of space, a home from home". Even the earth is only "a home from home", not home itself. It is wrily appropriate that 'De Quincy at Grasmere' (later 'De Quincy in Later Life') should portray De Quincey's early disorientation in London rather than his later retreat to the Lake District of the author of *Home at Grasmere*. Wordsworth—like that Irish Wordsworthian Seamus Heaney—aspired to be at home in the world, but Mahon sides more naturally with the addictive, scholastic and cosmopolite De Quincey.

'Lives' (Penguin, p.86), dedicated to Seamus Heaney, is both a tribute to his compatriot's archaeological muse and an ironic commentary upon it. In the 'Bog Poems' of *Wintering Out* and *North* Heaney explores his sense of trans-historical kinship with figures from the remote past. In 'The Tollund Man', for example, he imagines visiting a museum in Jutland and feeling "lost,/Unhappy and at home" and, for all his ambivalence in the face of the violence represented by the bodies preserved in the bog, what fascinates him is the overwhelming (or rather overwhelmed) identification of the bog people with their landscape.[25] Mahon's 'Lives', on the other hand, speaks for multiple buried lives from many places across history. Dug up as a Celtic torc in Newmarket-on-Fergus, the poem's single transmigrant speaker doesn't speak only of the Celtic past of Ireland but of its own incarnation in other artefacts—Elpenor's oar from Ithaca, a Navaho rug, a stone in Tibet, "a tongue of bark/At the heart of Africa"—and its final incarnation as an anthropologist, equipped with "a whole boatload/Of photographic equipment". "I know too much/To be anything any more", it says, and Mahon's poetry is almost too aware of its multiple and mobile anthropological alternatives to have its own identity. The anthropologist, though he may have fantasies about other people belonging, doesn't himself belong to the places he studies. Mahon's singularly plural speaker has an anthropologist's fascination with the "merely human artefact" and its "maker" but reflects its own maker's disenchanted sense of distance from the worlds to which he alludes. The mobile pluralism of the poem's speaker bespeaks a curiously privileged universalist stance but also a terrible emptiness.

'Beyond Howth Head' (Penguin, p.44), originally published in the same collection, is an autobiographical rather than pseudo-mythological poem, but it expresses something of the same disenchanted mobility. A caustic and Audenesque verse-letter from the writer in Ireland to a reader abroad, it is peppered with place-names and cultural landmarks, travelling easily "From Cararoe to Dublin Bay" and from "Denmark" to "the cool courts of Cambridge, Mass", taking in Cambodia, an Aegean prison, "in the unquiet Cyclades", Chomei at Toyama, Blackpool and Clonenacnoish. With its evocation of the poet's domestic and intellectual life in Ireland against the potentially threatening backdrop of world politics, the poem is a vivid instance of that desperate urbanity which, like the urbane desolation of 'Lives', is a mark of Mahon's best work. 'Beyond Howth Head' is a very self-conscious literary performance, a display of its author's confident familiarity with culture and society beyond Ireland, but for all its cosmopolite bravura, it is a sceptical, self-mocking and demoralised poem. If Mahon's landscapes are always *paysages moralisés*, they are characteristically written from the stance of an author who is, as here, *dépaysé* and *démoralisé* faced by what is 'beyond' him—and Howth Head.

## 4

> Elsewhere the olive grove,
> *Le déjeuner sur l'herbe,*
> Poppies and parasols,
> Blue skies and mythic love.
> Here only the stricken souls
> No spring can unperturb.
> ('North Wind, Portrush')

In the early poem 'An Irishman in London' the young poet turns his back on his "backward" land and, having certified he is "truly rootless", affirms his commitment to travel on to some notion of "repose". In 'Brighton Beach', the mature poet, "at ease along the prom", looks back on Lavery's bar in Belfast and then out towards a "Monet-monoxide dream" of Proust's Balbec, and reflects that, though "Europe thrives", the "spirit of empire is fugitive" and the "off-shore/Islanders" are in decline. This leads him to a moment of rueful expectation:

> Now, in this rancorous peace,
> Should come the spirit of place.

But the expectation is immediately dashed as the poet affirms that it is "too late" and that "already/Places as such are dead/Or nearly". Whether in Brighton or Portrush or even Tomis, Mahon is characteristically "at ease" in such resorts, despite his dispirited comparativist view of place. Nevertheless this historical angle on his imaginative geography is unusual, with its implied link between "the spirit of empire" and the nearly defunct "spirit of place". The poet, like Keats in 'Ode to Psyche', is "too late for the fond believing lyre,/

When holy were the haunted forest boughs,/Holy the air, the water, and the fire."[26] Yet the claim that places as such are dead (or nearly) is certainly paradoxical in a poet whose work depends so intimately upon them. Perhaps we should see his poems as elegies on the spirit of place?[27]

The "rancorous peace" Mahon evokes in Anglo-Irish 'Brighton Beach' does not explicitly raise the 'Irish question', but the idea of historical violence afflicts many of this poet's versions of "repose" and visions of place. The dreamy courtly English pastoral of 'Penshurst Place', for example, with its quotation from Marlowe's 'The Passionate Shepherd to his Love', is interrupted by "bad dreams" of "The Spanish ships around Kinsale/The screech-owl and the nightingale"—counterpointing the false consonance of the Tudor idyll (and Mahon's trim verse) with reminders of the nightmare of Elizabethan policy in Ireland, not least at the hands of Sir Walter Raleigh, the author of the most famous rebuff to Marlowe's pastoral, 'The Nymph's Reply to the Shepherd'. 'The Woods', (VG 154) which seems intimately related to other English idylls like 'Penshurst Place' and 'Ford Manor', is a retrospective celebration of a Marvellian "green retreat/secluded and sedate,/part of a once great estate", yet it too is ruffled by the rumour of distant battles—a clock that "expired/the night Lenin arrived in Petrograd", "a disused garden shed/where gas-masks from the war decayed". As even the cosmopolitan London of 'Another Sunday Morning' is haunted by the spears and scimitars of "so many empires come and gone", the green retreat celebrated in 'The Woods' echoes with past violence. Almost innocent words like "tocsin" and "boneshaker" stain the surface of the backwater's peace, and even the wood-anemones have "tearful metamorphic eyes". Eventually the poet recoils from a place and style that is "too creamy" for his taste and elects to ponder the darkness "in another place". This concept of "another place" or other places, like the reminders of historical violence elsewhere, is integral to Mahon's invasive (or invaded) spirit of place, and at the close of the poem he affirms his imperative to travel beyond the "pale paradise" of 'The Woods'. Like MacNeice in his poem 'Woods' about the "foreign voice" of the English woodland, Mahon finds such a world claustrophobic and alien:

> we carried on
> to chaos and confusion
> our birthright and our proper portion.

"Birthright", with its associations of inheritance and patrimony, doesn't here refer to the poet's right to any place but his right to be displaced—from the pallor of an anglicised paradise to the darkness, "chaos and confusion" (originally "doubt and speculation") associated with travel and imagination.

A high proportion of Mahon's poems recapitulates this move from an apparently enclosed touristic or aesthetic world into that of historical violence. In the touristic 'Rathlin' a trip to an island bird sanctuary tempts the poet into his recurring dream of being "through with history" only to call up a memory of "unspeakable violence" done on the island in the remote past—and return him to the historical present where "Bombs doze in the housing estates" (in Mahon no island is an island entire of itself). His poems on paintings offer comparable double visions. 'Girls on the Bridge', for example, with its crisp chiastic stanzas, evokes the sedate laundered world of Munch's 1900 painting of precarious adolescents, only to shatter it with premonitions of bad dreams and nearby violence ("a mile from where you chatter,/Somebody screams")—as if Munch's painting of 'The Scream' had infected his painting of the girls. Mahon's poem becomes a bridge between their world on the bridge and the troubling history beyond their field of vision (and the painting's). Similarly 'Courtyards in Delft' recreates the "trim composure" of a seventeenth-century Dutch painting and translates its protestant urban idyll to the Belfast of his own childhood—setting both against the "esurient seas" that will one day breach the "ruined dykes" and a vision of future violence which will discompose the "trim composure" of his own and the painter's art (and home):

> For the pale light of that provincial town
> Will spread itself, like ink or oil,
> Over the not yet accurate linen
> Map of the world which occupies one wall
> And punish nature in the name of God.
> If only, now, the Maenads, as of right,
> Came smashing crockery, with fire and sword,
> We could sleep easier in our beds at night.[28]

The violence that interrupts the provincial idyll is unexplained yet must at one level represent the punitive political violence of modern Ulster (much of which is also carried out "in the name of God"). A commentary on the sparse early and late bourgeois virtues celebrated in the painting and poem, this is also a critique of the Apollonian poet and painter with their "rage for order" which recoils from the "esurient sea" and Dionysiac crockery-smashing. It suggests a connection between the artist's rage for order and the order of rage of which it forms part, and between the poet's predilection for the "trim composure" represented by his stanza forms and his sense of unresolvable conflict elsewhere—the "esurient sea" only provisionally held back by the dykes.

'Derry Morning' is Mahon's most focused and thoroughly located representation of the Northern Irish 'Troubles', an intense vision of a city that is synonymous with "fitful revolution" and ideological contradiction ('synonymous' because even its name is controversial, Irish 'Derry', British 'Londonderry'). But Mahon characteristically uses the poem to set Derry in a broader context and in a medium which appropriates the Irish *aisling* and Gaelic 'oak-grove' into a very different kind of tradition (and vice versa, appropriating the tradition to engage with the place). For 'Derry Morning', like several other poems in *The Hunt by Night*, is written in the urbane six-line stanza Marvell uses in the very English topographical poem 'Upon Appleton House', a poem of pastoral retreat which reflects back on the civil and sectarian conflict of the seventeenth century. Mahon's Derry confronts a traditional *aisling* vision of nationalist revolution, but frames it in a much larger context—via his deployment of Marvell's cavalier puritan wit on the one hand and his acknowledgement of the journalistic 'global village' of television culture on the other:

> Hard to believe this tranquil place,
> Its desolation almost peace,
> Was recently a boom-town wild
> With expectation, each unscheduled
> Incident a measurable
> Tremor on the Richter Scale
> Of world events, each vibrant scene
> Translated to the drizzling screen.

The heartless pun "boom-town" ironically equates the boom of economic success with the horror of political violence, making us keenly aware of our linguistic distance from the realities such phrases conceal. The "Richter Scale/Of world events" and "drizzling screen" comment on the "measurable" translations of the local to the global stage—and show that the poet is aware of the way he projects such journalistic idioms, like the *aisling* of Irish poetic tradition, onto the quiet scene he actually sees before him. The desolation that is almost peace is a reminder of Tacitus's comment in the *Agricola* "Ubi solitudinem faciunt, pacem appellant" ("where they make a wilderness, they call it peace"), and the whole poem explicitly brings to bear upon the local scene a stance, a language, a perspective that is inescapably displaced, uncomfortably detached. In fact it ends with an almost inconsequential, but profoundly expressive image of a travelling witness from elsewhere:

> A Russian freighter bound for home
> Mourns to the city in its gloom.

The poet's unlikely rhyme between the ship's distant "home" and his own homeland in Ulster opens the poem out onto the wider world stage in which the "fog/Of time receives the ideologue". Mahon's strangely neutral, apparently unideological stance represents—and it is part of the drained urbanity and dry-mouthed wit of the poem—a triumph of distancing, and a commentary on its own distance. If this is the work of a "tourist in his own country", it treats the relation of local and global with an admirable lack of political sentimentality. Its 'measurable' metre, like the 'light metre' of 'A Disused Shed in Co Wexford', is a gauge of the inevitable but suspect distance of the poet's art from the politically ravaged city he describes.

The relation between historical violence and artistic concord is explored in two of Mahon's most self-distrusting and important poems, 'The Snow Party' and 'A Disused Shed in Co Wexford', set respectively in seventeenth-century Japan and twentieth-century Ireland. 'The Snow Party' begins with one of his characteristic locations of the artist in place:

> Bashō, coming
> To the city of Nagoya,
> Is asked to a snow party.

The poem is written in the historic or aesthetic present tense, the tense of Keats's 'Ode on a Grecian Urn': "Bashō . . . is asked to a snow party", "There is a tinkling of china", "Snow is falling on Nagoya". The poet's world is a kind of socially exquisite "cold pastoral", and it is captured in the poem's delicate *haiku*-like imagism with its allusions to the immaculate landscape art of Japanese verse. After five self-enclosed three-line stanzas, which are not *haiku* but constantly evoke their ghost, Mahon transforms our view of those viewing the snow by suddenly opening out the whole historical frame—and syntax:

> Elsewhere they are burning
> Witches and heretics
> In the boiling squares,
>
> Thousands have died since dawn
> In the service
> Of barbarous kings;
>
> But there is silence
> In the houses of Nagoya
> And the hills of Ise.

By introducing the unnamed but potent "elsewhere", the poem acknowledges the brutal political history which the exclusive aestheticism of Bashō's Nagoya elides—elides as the snow muffles and hides the details of the land. "There is no document of civilisation which is not at the same time a document of barbarism", as Walter Benjamin has reminded us, and Mahon's poem makes us move beyond the refined civilisation represented by Bashō's *haiku* and the snow party to recognise the barbarity implicit in such an order.[29] The poem's final silence focuses our attention onto what has been *silenced* in this aesthetic world—witchcraft, heresy and war among other things. By the end of the poem what has been thrown into question is the beautiful precisionism of the imagist poetry itself and the chilling aesthetic distance of Bashō's art. According to the film director Akira Kurosawa, the wartime militarist censorship of modern Japan "conducted a two-prong attack on art by mutilating films and encouraging a *haiku* revival to keep people's minds upon chrysanthemums and waterfalls".[30] Mahon's poem simultaneously embodies the social and aesthetic decorum of Bashō's world and recognises the "barbarous" forces which violate it and upon which it turns its back.

The oriental mask Mahon adopts in 'The Snow Party' has a resonance nearer to home, as Dillon Johnson reminds us; its cadences inevitably recall Joyce's description of the snow falling across Ireland at the close of his story 'The Dead' and its vision of "elsewhere" may, in Johnson's words, point "toward the slaughter of Aughrim and the

Boyne, contemporary with Bashō's tour to Nagoya".[31] 'A Disused
Shed in Co Wexford' (Penguin, p. 62) is a more direct reflex of Irish
history. Based on an anecdote about a forgotten shed in the grounds of
a "burnt-out" hotel somewhere in Wexford, it is also, as its dedication
to the author of *Troubles* reminds us, a retrospective meditation on a
time of civil war.[32] Like Yeats in his *Meditations in Time of Civil War*,
but also like Thomas Kinsella in his comparable but more specifically
political and poetically specific poem, 'Tao and Unfitness at Inish-
togue on the River Nore', Mahon uses his poem to tap the hidden
legacy of the "civil war days" when the hotel was burnt and the
"mycologist" expropriated—a legacy embodied in the multiplying
fungi trapped in the dark shed for half a century.

"Even now" the poem begins, "there are places where a thought
might grow", invoking "Peruvian mines" and "Indian compounds"
before moving in on his obscure corner of Co Wicklow. As the poem
develops and its thought grows in its own "abandoned" "worked out"
site, the bizarrely contorted and trapped fungi become not only
symbols of the victims of Anglo-Irish violence, amnesia and repression, but the mycological equivalents of the prisoners' chorus in
Beethoven's *Fidelio*, incongruous personifications of the imprisoned,
the exterminated and disappeared masses across history—"Powdery
prisoners of the old régime", Goyaesque images of the "Lost people
of Treblinka and Pompeii". This is dangerous poetic ground, but if
the poem is about the victims of history, it is also acutely aware of their
exploitation by the present—and even by the poet himself in writing
the poem as he speaks for them:

> 'Save us, save us', they seem to say,
> 'Let the god not abandon us
> Who have come so far in darkness and in pain.
> We too had our lives to live.
> You with your light meter and relaxed itinerary,
> Let not our naive labours have been in vain!'

Like the mushrooms of the poem's central conceit, the lost people
have come alive to us "through the flash-bulb firing squad we wake
them with": the poet with his "light meter" and "relaxed itinerary"
subjects them to his own kind of imaginative violence in making them
subjects and turning them into conceits, even as he tries not to
abandon those whom history has abandoned. By the close the poem
itself has become one of those "places where a thought might grow",

as it makes its starting place into a symbol of the displaced and "lost people" of the world. The pacific scene in Wicklow comes alive in Mahon's art as a theatre of global human violence and becomes a place where art must acknowledge its roots in "darkness and in pain". Thought grows where violence has happened—and among the debris of our ordinary, inhabitable world. Aesthetic concord grows out of inescapable historical discord.

## 5

> We are in one place and one place only
> ('A Garage in Co Cork')

> It might be anywhere,
> That ivory tower
> Approached by a dirt road.
>                                   (Penguin, p. 142)

The "ivory tower" of the opening of 'A Lighthouse in Maine' is of course the lighthouse. It is also described as a "polished Buddha". As "ivory tower" the lighthouse becomes a figure of aestheticism, as Buddha a figure of meditation, and later as "the soul of Adonais" a Shelleyan figure of the poet—a modern "dirt road" equivalent of Baudelaire's *phares*. The motorised but inveterately allegorical poet is struck not only by the emblematic force of the tower's bare architecture but the strange neutrality of the setting:

> It might be anywhere—
> Hokkaido, Mayo, Maine;
> But it is in Maine.

It matters that it is in Maine, but it is expressive for Mahon because it stands for anywhere. Like Wallace Stevens's jar in Tennessee, it takes "dominion everywhere".[33]

Like Wallace Stevens to whom he paid tribute in an uncollected poem called 'The Man who built his city in snow', Derek Mahon is something of a "polished Buddha" himself and in his most achieved meditative lyrics such as 'A Garage in Co Cork' and 'The Globe in North Carolina' he converts place into a figure for our place in the world—or indeed the world itself.[34] At the close of the original version of 'A Garage in Co Cork' and back home in Ireland, Mahon is struck again by what struck him in Maine:

> We might be anywhere—in the Dordogne,
> Iquitos, Bethlehem—wherever the force
> Of gravity secures houses and the sun
> Selects this fan-blade of the universe
> Decelerating while the fates devise
> What outcome for the dawdling galaxies?
>
> But we are in one place and one place only,
> One of the milestones of earth-residence
> Unique in each particular, the thinly–
> Peopled hinterland serenely tense—
> Not in the hope of a resplendent future
> But with a sure sense of its intrinsic nature.[35]

The "intrinsic nature" of the garage's one place, which "Somebody somewhere thinks of . . . as home", represents not a triumph of specificity such as the homely garage in Elizabeth Bishop's 'Filling Station' but a strangely neutral "milestone" of "earth-residence" like the lighthouse, no more than a "fan-blade" of the universe. "We are in one place and one place only" speaks the disappointed language of post-metaphysical pathos which is intrinsic to Mahon's very personal verse music and integral to his curiously impersonal, quasi-anthropological world-view. In Mahon's poems we are almost never "in one place only" and both the "milestones" and the garage itself acknowledge their dependence on travel and travellers. Like the shed in Wicklow, the obscure garage in Cork is the more fascinating to Mahon for being both modern and abandoned—an index, like the cans of 'The Apotheosis of Tins', of the transience of the technological civilisation of which we are all part:

> Left to itself, the functional will cast
> A death-bed glow of picturesque abandon.
> The intact antiquities of the recent past,
> Dropped from the retail catalogues, return
> To the materials that gave rise to them
> And shine with a late sacramental gleam.

Mahon's obsession with leaving and returning home, and with technological and civilisational obsolescence, converts the "quiet corner of Co Cork" into an instance not only of a modern culture based on the "retail catalogue" and automobile but of our "earth-residence" as such. The poem maps its way by reference to more established geographical and mythological co-ordinates—symbols of possible transcendence like Nirvana and Bethlehem, of the classical and Judaic stories of the Flood (Noah and Baucis and Philemon), and of Irish emigration like South Boston and Cricklewood. "Residence" and what he calls in 'Going Home' "a residual poetry" are intimately allied in this poetry of place in which, despite that "late sacramental gleam", "spirit" has deserted place. In this respect the deserted garage is absolutely typical ("it might have nothing behind it but thin air" ). The garage is Mahon's modern equivalent of Goldsmith's Deserted Village—a commentary on Irish emigration, a traveller's view of a lost past—but also a wittily grave 'metaphysical' poem equivalent to Marvell's or Donne's, a poem not about place but our place in the world. At one point the poet ironically greets the desolate garage with the exclamation "Nirvana!" Ironically, but not entirely so; in a review of *Thomas Merton on Zen* he quotes Merton as saying "Nirvana is found in the midst of the world around us; truth is not *somewhere else*".[36] It might even be found in a Garage in Co Cork. With its tight focus on the deserted garage amid its modern rubbish, and its chastened openness to the wider world, I think this is one of the permanent modern Irish poems.

"The earth spins to my finger-tips", 'The Globe in North Carolina' begins, and one of Mahon's most luminous poems of place keeps the idea of the planet earth spinning while it takes another fan-blade of the universe and makes it too a miniature *speculum mundi* under what he calls his "mild theoptic eye". In fact it overtly adopts one of the stock props and tropes of metaphysical poetry, the Globe, and handles it in a form and metre reminiscent of Marvell's 'The Garden':

> From Hatteras to the Blue Ridge
> Night spreads like ink on the unhedged
> Tobacco fields and clucking lakes,
> Bringing the lights on in the rocks
> And swamps, the farms and motor courts,
> Substantial cities, kitsch resorts—
> Until, to the mild theoptic eye,
> America is its own night-sky,
>
> Its own celestial fruit, on which
> Sidereal forms appear, their rich

> Clusters and vague attenuations
> Miming galactic dispositions.
> Hesperus is a lighthouse, Mars
> An air-force base; molecular cars
> Arrowing the turnpikes become
> Lost meteorites in search of home.

Somewhere in the background of this remarkable compounding of the macrocosm and the microcosm, of the topographical and the cosmological, stands Marvell's couplet about poetic coupling from 'The Garden':

> The Mind, that Ocean where each kind
> Does streight its own resemblance find.[37]

Far away from Ireland in North Carolina, the displaced poet, making use of what Christopher Ricks (after Empson) calls the Marvellian "self-inwoven simile", sees America as "its own night-sky/Its own celestial fruit".[38] Through a series of comparable Marvellian conceits or witty Ovidian metamorphoses, an air-force base becomes Mars (both planetary and martial), and cars turn into "lost meteorites in search of home". Like the Garage in Cork, the Carolina landscape represents its own culture, in this case modern America's, while also offering the poet a "resemblance" to his own 'home' across the Atlantic where his lover lies:

> You lie an ocean to the east,
> Your limbs composed, your mind at rest,
> Asleep in a sunrise which will be
> Your mid-day when it reaches me . . .

The paradoxical intimacy of the global and the personal provides a modern equivalent of the intellectual mobility and erotic fidelity of such poems as Donne's 'The Sunne Rising'. But as in Donne, and as in his poem about the garage, Mahon converts the scene into an ironic emblem of the great globe itself. When he addresses the "Great mother", the planet earth ("the dim stone where we were reared"), we recognise a poet consciously modernising the global idioms of English seventeenth-century verse in the light of a post-Christian existentialist worldview—and consciously reappropriating Robert Lowell's adaptation of the Marvellian stanza to modern America in 'Waking

Early Sunday Morning'. In the final stanzas Mahon's usually mistrustful "salt astringency" rises in a mood of rare Wordsworthian or Emersonian trust, to affirm that "true salvation" lies not in action but in:

> the trust
> We place in our peripheral
> Night garden in the glory-hole
> Of space, a home from home, and what
> Devotion we can bring to it!

'The Garden' has become a "night garden", place "space", and the whole planet some kind of "home from home" such as North Carolina presumably was for the poet at the time of writing. Like the meteoric cars of the opening, the whole poem, for all its cosmopolite elegance, is a "search for home", and at its close the poet is left "listening to that lonesome whistle blow". What began as a response to a North Carolina landscape ends as a sort of twentieth-century global love song, a suave metaphysical Blues.

## 6

All places are distant from heaven alike.
(Robert Burton)[39]

*Antarctica*, Mahon's most recent book, takes its title from a continent that represents a kind of degree zero of place—an uninhabitable space—and from a poem about a failed quest for the pole and an explorer who never came back ("He is just going outside and may be some time"). It begins and ends with poems about great twentieth-century writers who have helped define what we mean by modernism and modernity. Both characteristically work by exploring their fraught relationship to places. The first, 'A Kensington Notebook', is a wonderful brief historical critique of early modernism in London, written in the form of a pastiche of Ezra Pound's *Hugh Selwyn Mauberley*, itself a pastiche history of an earlier generation of poets. The last, 'Death and the Sun', is a reflection on the death of Camus. At its centre are two intensely Mahonian soliloquies, one autobiographical, 'Craigvara House', about the writer's uneasy convalescence reading Sartre's *La Nausée* by the sea in his native

North, and the other, 'Tithonus', one of his bleak mythological inventions, a rewriting of the monologue of Tennyson's garrulous eternal depressive in the light of Samuel Beckett's comparable figures. Taken as a whole the book represents a crisis in the writer's engagement with his work, an elegant, icy and despairing achievement.

This crisis comes to a head in a more recently published poem, 'Dawn at St Patricks' in the new *Selected Poems* (VG, pp.104–6). This is a Lowell-like autobiographical life study which describes the poet hospitalised one Christmas, a "make-believe existentialist" on his "protestant bed" in "a Dublin asylum"; the asylum is both a modernised version of "Swift's home/for fools and mad" and another "home from home" for the poet. The poem takes comfort from the Swiftian conceit that if this is the "story of [his] life", it is also "the story of all lives everywhere,/mad fools wherever they are". This is a dubious consolation, one of Mahon's most dangerous universalisations of an "anywhere" into an "everywhere". It is true, however, to his doubly displaced sense of place. In identifying his philosophical displacement with his cultural one, and locating his makeshift existentialism upon that uncomfortable "protestant bed", the poem raises the unresolvable issue of how Mahon's obstinately and elegantly reiterative poetry of place is related to his problematic place in a painfully conflict-ridden Irish culture.

'A Kensington Notebook' (VG pp. 90–95) goes back in time to the conflict-ridden moment of modernism and is a telegrammatic resumé of the life and art of its founding fathers Ford Madox Ford, Ezra Pound, and Wyndham Lewis. It is focused in the first place around their residence in Kensington just before the First War, and then viewed in retrospect in the light of their subsequent careers elsewhere. Mahon uses the clipped ironic mode of the third poem in Pound's *Mauberley* sequence—"The tea-rose, tea-gown, etc./Supplants the mousseline of Cos./The pianola 'replaces'/Sappho's barbitos"—to place Pound himself:[40]

> The operantics of
> Provence and Languedoc
> Shook the Gaudier marbles
> At No. 10 Church Walk
>
> Where 'Ezra Pound, M.A.,
> Author of *Personae*,'
> Twitched his 'nostrils and
> Invisible antennae'.

The Irish poet's antennae here are as beautifully tuned to Pound's caustic cadences and citational mannerisms as Pound's own were to his contemporaries, as in the exactly tuned dissonance of "Langue-doc" and "Church Walk" here, or in the more tragic dissonance between Pound's early ideals, associated with *The Spirit of Romance* and the romance of modernism, and his later political career in Fascist Italy:

> The Spirit of Romance
> Flowered briefly there
> Among jade animals;
> And years later where,
>
> Confucius of the dooryard,
> Prophet of το χαλon,
> He drawls 'treason' into
> A Roman microphone.

The moderno-Greek rhyme of "to kalon" and "microphone" repli-cates the ironic juxtapositions of Pound's "We have the press for wafer,/Franchise for circumcision", while ironically insisting on the uncomfortable juxtapositions of the political and the aesthetic in Pound's career, from Kensington to the Roman microphone and eventually to the "silence of the Alps" and *"le fleuve des morts"*.

The careers of Ford and Lewis are afforded the same treatment, setting their visions of place and the place of their visions against the places they lived in and left. The blue plaque on Ford's South Lodge and his toy soldiers "on the/Razed table of art", for example, are set beside his vision of romantic Tory England as a "great good place" ("Sussex chirped in the sun"). Never such innocence again, however, and with the war the "table of art" and its "toy soldiers" are juxtaposed with later more violent images:

> What price the dewy-eyed
> Pelagianism of home
> To a lost generation
> Dumbfounded on the Somme?
>
> 'The Last of England'
> Crumbles in the rain
> As he embarks for
> Paris and Michigan.

The poignant satiric tones of this count the cost of Ford's visions of England by reference to its consequences abroad—on the battlefields of the war and, via his grandfather's Pre-Raphaelite tableau of emigration 'The Last of England', during Ford's later expatriate life. In some other sense, Mahon infers, this moment itself represents "the last of England". The play between "price" and "Somme", between losing and finding in "lost" and "dumbfounded", combined with the ominous off-rhyme of "Somme" and "home", confound the solidities of Ford's idealisations of the good place; while Ford goes into permanent exile, England "crumbles in the rain". In Mahon's account of Lewis's career too, modernist promise and posturing give way to a more threatening world—"aesthetic bombardiering" and the bohemian "anarchy" of *Blast* yield to the "real thing", the "moonscape" of the shrapnel-pitted landscape of war-torn Europe and his later "Canadian/Exile"; at the time of the artist's eventual death, he is like Ford "a marginal figure still" and captured in one of Mahon's most cruel images of metamorphic displacement as an unsuccessful reincarnation of Milton's Samson, "eyeless in Notting Hill". The *déracinés* gurus of early modernism overshadow Mahon's echoic verse, yet are themselves overshadowed within it by the history which overtakes them and places their art in its brilliant but dubious light. Interestingly the most palpably 'successful' of their number, T.S. Eliot, is left unnamed in this pastiche elegy for modernist London. The title of Mahon's four-part poem, though, is a reminder that Eliot originally intended to name those placeless poems of place *Four Quartets*, the *Kensington Quartets*.

In a sense 'A Kensington Notebook' is Mahon's most bravura poem of place, a caustic elegy for a centre of metropolitan but iconoclastic culture, and a tribute to the confident internationalism of those Lewis called 'The Men of 1914'.[41] Like the earlier 'Beyond Howth Head' the sequence is riddled with titles and place-names from across the world, immaculately mapped onto the poem's Kensington and into the poem's elegant architecture. I am tempted to think of this Kensington as Mahon's equivalent of Yeats's Byzantium.

'Antarctica' on the other hand is its antithesis, an empty place, with no culture:

> The tent recedes beneath its crust of rime
> And frostbite is replaced by vertigo;
> At the heart of the ridiculous, the sublime.
>
> (Penguin, p. 190)

Rhyme here is indeed crusted with the frigidity of "rime", and the poet's sense of wit ("the ridiculous") is embarrassingly implicated in the empty gestures of "the sublime". Somewhere in the background of this you can hear the cadences of William Empson's desolate villanelles, 'Villanelle' and 'Missing Dates', and in reading Mahon's later work I have often been reminded of the close of Empson's 'This Last Pain', with its urge to "build an edifice of form/For house where phantoms may keep warm". Empson's poem ends with a formulation that goes to the heart of Mahon's work:

> Imagine, then, by miracle, with me,
> (Ambiguous gifts, as what gods give must be)
> What could not possibly be there,
> And learn a style from a despair.[42]

Plenitude and poverty, culture and *anomie*, style and despair, are close neighbours in Mahon's search for a sufficient "edifice of form".

In his introduction to his translations of the French poet Philippe Jaccottet, Mahon describes him as follows:

> He is a secular mystic, an explorer of '*le vrai lieu*' (the real place). 'The natural object is always the adequate symbol', says Pound; and Jaccottet's symbols are the elemental, pre-Socratic ones: tree, flower, sun, moon, road, mountain, wind, water, bird, house, lamp. He is fascinated by light, especially what John Le Carré calls 'the religious light between dawn and morning'; and by lamplit twilight, *l'heure bleue*. 'I wonder', mused Geoffrey Grigson in *Notes from an Odd Country*, 'if deity and art don't originate in sparkle, glitter, crystal, refracted light, an abstracted portion of sun'.[43]

This might almost be a description of Mahon's own art, not only because of its search for adequate natural symbols but because of its *bricolage*, the way it seeks to piece together an aesthetic (or a creed?) out of eclectic literary bric-à-brac. Though Mahon shares some of the cultural predicaments of "the charmed circle" of fellow Irish poets such as Michael Longley, John Montague, Seamus Heaney and Thomas Kinsella, he also, like Philippe Jaccottet, forms part of what might be called the defrocked visionary company of modern poets— like Rilke in Germany, Seferis in Greece, Thomas Tranströmer in Sweden, Stevens and Ashbery in the U.S., and Thomas Hardy in England. Mahon confesses to missing in Jaccottet "humour, the demotic, the abrasive surfaces of the modern world". That is a measure of his own divided allegiances as a "make-believe existentialist" from Ireland, acknowledging both his "secular mysticism" and the realities of "the modern world", his sense of a divided Anglo-Irish culture and the fictive "globe" imaginable in the later twentieth-century. His own poetry sets the quest for "*le vrai lieu*" within the abrasive world of those surfaces—and in real places.

NOTES

The quotation in the title comes from 'A Disused Shed in Co Wexford'. SP of DM VG 1991, p.62. All quotations in the text refer to this edition. The epigraphs come from Louis MacNeice, 'Valediction', *Collected Poems*, ed. E. R. Dodds (London: Faber & Faber 1966), p.52; Samuel Beckett, 'Hommage à Jack B. Yeats', *Disjecta* (London: John Calder, 1983), p. 148.

1.  *Time Was Away: the World of Louis MacNeice*, ed. Terence Brown and Alec Reid, (Dublin: Dolmen, 1974), pp. 113–122.
2.  Seamus Heaney, *Place and Displacement: Recent Poetry of Northern Ireland*, Pete Laver Memorial Lecture, delivered at Grasmere 2nd August 1984, published by the Trustees of Dove Cottage, 1984.
3.  *Time Was Away*, p. 117.
4.  *Ecclesiastes*, Phoenix Pamphlet Poets No. 9, 1970.
5.  *Twentieth Century Studies*, No. 4, (November 1970), pp. 89–93.
6.  *ibid.*, p. 91.
7.  *ibid.*, p. 90.
8.  A version of this charge was levelled against Mahon by Stan Smith in *Inviolable Voice: History and 20th Century Poetry* (Dublin: Gill and Macmillan, 1982). Smith aligns him with "the sceptical Protestant tradition of Louis MacNeice", and calls him a "tourist poet" who writes in "accents familiar from The Movement' and "with a tone of shell-shocked Georgianism that could easily be mistaken for indifference before the ugly realities of life and death in Ulster" *(ibid.,* p. 189).
9.  'The Sheep and the Goats', a review of Paul Muldoon's Faber anthology of contemporary Irish poetry, *Irish Times*, 7th June 1986, p. 13.
10. *Twentieth Century Studies*, p. 93.
11. *New Statesman*, 29th March 1974, pp. 451–2.
12. 'The Irish Writer', a paper read to a meeting of the Modern Language Association, New York, December 1966, reprinted in *Davis, Mangan, Ferguson: Tradition and the Irish Writer*, The Tower Series of Anglo-Irish Studies 11, Dublin: Dolmen (1970), p. 66 and Chester Springs: Dufour Editions.
13. *The Penguin Book of Contemporary Irish Poetry*, London: Penguin Books (1990), p. xx.
14. 'Cavafy', *The Snow Party*, 1975, pp. 18–20. Another poem, 'After Cavafy' in *Lives*, 1972, p. 24, was later revised and entitled 'Poem Beginning with a line by Cavafy' in *Poems 1962–78*, (1979) p. 45.
15. Seamus Deane, *Celtic Revivals* (London: Faber & Faber (1985), p. 156.
16. *Poems 1962–78*, p. 44.
17. Its own order is a violation and revision of the earlier version of the poem in *Lives* (1972) which was printed in regular stanza form. It has been excluded from the VG *Selected Poems* altogether.

18. 'In Belfast', *The Night Crossing*, p. 6. Later entitled 'The Spring Vacation' in *Poems 1962–1978*.

19. The poem was first published in the Trinity College Dublin magazine *Icarus* 42, March 1964, p. 31. There it ended very differently:

> Poetry and fluent drivel, know your place
> Take shape in some more glib environment,
> Away from shipyard gantry, bolt and rivet,
> Elsewhere assess existence, ask to what end
> It tends, wherefore and why. In Belfast live it.

Political changes in Ulster between 1964 and 1968 when it was published in book form must have contributed to Mahon's later reshaping of the poem. Interestingly, Paul Muldoon entitled his first pamphlet *Knowing my Place* and in *Station Island* Seamus Heaney protested "I hate how quick I was to know my place".

20. Edna Longley discusses this in 'The Singing Line: Form in Derek Mahon's Poetry' in *Poetry in the Wars* (Newcastle upon Tyne: Bloodaxe, 1986), pp.170–184.

21. It was published in *Icarus* 42, March 1964, pp. 8–10. All quotations from this source.

22. Wallace Stevens, 'Adagia', *Opus Posthumous* (New York: Alfred A. Knopf, 1957), p. 158.

23. *The Penguin Book of Contemporary Irish Poetry P*, p. xxii.

24. 'Going Home', *The Snow Party*, p. 7, *Poems 1962–78*, p. 63.

25. Seamus Heaney, *Wintering Out*, London: Faber and Faber (1972), pp.47–8.

26. John Keats, *The Complete Poems*, ed. John Barnard (Harmondsworth: Penguin Books, 1973), p. 341.

27. In its first published version the poem was significantly different: "Europe thrives, but the English decline", it said, and it ended with a much more distinctively Irish 'spirit of place' associated with the music 'Of bagpipe and *bodhrán*', *The Honest Ulsterman* No. 36, July/October, 1980. The later version, while avoiding the discriminatory 'the English' and the divisively imperial 'British Isles', brackets the English and Irish under the neutral umbrella "off-shore islanders", setting the "sectarian banter" of Belfast against the "faded Georgian bricks" of Brighton without giving either poetic dominion over the other.

28. *The Hunt by Night*, 1982, p. 10. The VG Mahon cuts this last stanza and reverts to the pamphlet form of the poem, *Courtyards in Delft*, 1981, p. 21, which ends with the image of his companions dreaming of war. Even in this shorter version the poem is overshadowed by the implicit threat of those dreams of war and the moment when the "ruined dykes admit the esurient sea".

29. Walter Benjamin, *Illuminations*, ed. Hannah Arendt, translated Harry Zohn (London: Cape, 1970), p. 258.

30. Quoted in Robert Hass, 'Images', *Twentieth Century Pleasures* (New York: 1984), p. 289.

31. Dillon Johnson, *Irish Poetry after Joyce* (Notre Dame: University of Notre Dame Press and Dublin, 1985), p. 229.

32. Mahon wrote an obituary for J.G. Farrell in *The New Statesman*, 25 June, 1976, p. 854, praising him as "a novelist who stood back, who took the long view".

33. Wallace Stevens, 'Anecdote of the Jar', *Collected Poems* (London: Faber & Faber, 1955), p. 76.

34. 'The man who built his city in snow: In memory of Wallace Stevens 1879–1955', Poem of the Month Club, London, 1972.

35. *The Hunt by Night*, p. 56. The end has been altered and shortened in the VG *Selected Poems*, 1991. The phrase that provides the epigraph for this section has been revised by Mahon to "we might be anywhere but are in one place only".

36. *New Statesman*, 25 June, 1976, p.854.

37. Andrew Marvell, 'The Garden', *The Complete Poems*, ed. Elizabeth Story Donno (Harmondsworth: Penguin Books, 1972), p. 100.

38. Christopher Ricks's discussion of Marvell's use of this device, 'Andrew Marvell: 'Its own Resemblance", is reprinted in *The Force of Poetry*, 1984, p. 34 ff. Ricks, though he doesn't quote this example, notes the currency of this trope in Mahon and other contemporary Ulster poets, suggesting it relates to their comparable experience of civil war and self-divisive unity.

39. Robert Burton, *The Anatomy of Melancholy*, 1621, 2.2.4.

40. Ezra Pound, *Hugh Selwyn Mauberley (Life and Contacts)*, *Collected Shorter Poems*, 1949, reprinted (London: Faber & Faber, 1984), p. 189.

41. Wyndham Lewis, *Blasting and Bombardiering* (London: Eyre and Spottiswoode, 1937).

42. William Empson, *Collected Poems* (London: Chatto and Windus, 1953), p. 33.

43. Phillippe Jaccotet, *Selected Poems*, selected and translated with an introduction by Derek Mahon (Harmondsworth: Penguin Books, 1988), pp. 11–12.

**Clair Wills**
The Lie of the Land: Language, Imperialism and
Trade in Paul Muldoon's *Meeting the British*

# The Lie of the Land

Violence always organised itself into a *scene*: the most transitive of behaviour (to eliminate, to kill, to wound, to humble) was also the most theatrical, and it was really this kind of semantic scandal he so resisted (is not meaning by its very nature opposed to action?).[1]

Paul Muldoon's 'Quoof' has become his trademark, signalling above all the desire to create in poetry a private, intransitive word, to experience the world of poetry as a paradise, an Eden, untainted by the corruption of the 'real'. And in response to this perceived desire his poetry has been both championed for a certain reluctance to draw links between poetry and politics in Northern Ireland, and condemned for its irresponsible hermeticism. While these discrepancies may afford important insights into the nature of Muldoon's poetic community, and the poet's ability to 'mean what he says', both readings ignore the ways in which Muldoon himself consciously problematises questions of the private and the political in poetic discourse. Throughout *Meeting the British* he plays with notions of poetic language as an abstraction from or magical transformation of everyday discourse, and explores the ways in which such a 'rarefied' language may refer to or act on public events and the shared language of ordinary communication. The vacillation between the 'everyday' meaning and the transformed 'poetic' meaning of words is imaged in alchemical terms, a hermetic process in which new substance is distilled from old. Yet this alchemical twist is less a departure than a logical progression from Muldoon's earlier experiments in creating meaning through recontextualising old myths, stories and phrases, giving them a new function by placing them in a new context.

Perhaps the most contentious example of this method is the fantastic and violent language of 'The More a Man Has the More a Man Wants'. Muldoon has said of the language in the poem that "I hoped to purge myself of the very public vocabulary it employs, the kennings of the hourly news bulletin".[2] The 'raw material' of the poem is the 'deadening' public language which is used to describe violent events in Northern Ireland. The events come to us already filtered through varieties of public language: governmental, literary, journalistic, cinematographic, all of which necessarily compromise the actual experience of those events since they can only objectify and glamourize the fact of violence.[3] Muldoon chooses to undermine the dead official language of the media by repeating it, thereby emphasising its clichéd nature. This method can reach almost obscene proportions, as in the description of the effects of a booby-trap bomb: "Once they collect his smithereens/He doesn't quite add up./They're shy of a foot, and a calf . . .". It is missing the point simply to criticize this use of language for its tastelessness. Ironically it raises the question of what could be the "decent" language which might successfully signify such violence. In one way, Muldoon is saying, the language of poetry is more central to an accurate description of events than the public language of documentary reportage; by their relegation to 'fiction' such events achieve once again a deadly and unnerving prominence. For the poet it is precisely in the 'private' poetic world that a heightened responsibility to public events may be found. And yet one may question whether the transferral of such language from the journalistic scene of violence to the poetic scene can be sufficient to "purge" it of its abuses. For though Muldoon can place language in a new context, he is not able to control absolutely the way it is read. (Moreover, if the 'staging' of violence is integral to violence itself, if it is always necessarily dramatised, by 'repeating' this staging Muldoon is unable to reinvest the language with its lost transitivity, but only to emphasise its loss). It is this issue of the controlling of readings which proves crucial in analyzing the question of the 'responsibility' of poetic language in *Meeting the British*.

## The Extent of Limits

I think that the writer should be alert to all these possible readings. And alert to the curtailing of possible readings that are not productive. And I don't care what people say, it's the writer who does that. And the points at which he doesn't do it are the points at which there is confusion . . . Because that's what the process of writing is about. It's about opening himself, or herself to the floodgates, what it's about is discovering the extent of limits, the confinement, the controlling of readings, of possible readings.[4]

Muldoon claims that it is possible for poetic discourse to be harnessed to the particular function of expressing the writer's meaning and intention; the writer's task is to 'control' and 'confine' meanings which words may carry in everyday discourse, by constructing a type of discourse which is closed off from the normal communicative functions of language—a hermetic, poetic 'world'. Such a theory attempts to deny both the role of historical context and change, and the activity of the reader in the process of interpretation, and suggests that it is possible for the writer to 'own' completely the keys to interpretation. By taking words out of circulation the poet can ascribe to them a value of his own.[5] And yet the very fact that artistic discourse is to some extent "at a remove" from the normal functions of everyday communication, may ensure that the writer has less rather than more control over his or her intended meaning. As Roland Barthès claims in his discussion of the 'encyclopaedic' word in modern poetry, once the word is abstracted from social reality the poet's intention can never be fully adequate to its meaning, which now comprises all the word's possible meanings in history and society.[6] He argues for the "magical" and "mysterious" quality of poetic language. In modern (post 1848) poetry:

> poets give to their speech the status of a closed Nature, which covers both the function and structure of a language. Poetry is then no longer a Prose either ornamental or shorn of liberties. It is a quality *sui generis* and without antecedents. It is no longer an attribute but a substance, and therefore it can very well renounce signs, since it carries its own nature within itself, and does not need to signal its nature outwardly.[7]

Barthès's assertion is that modern poetry deals with the linguistic rather than social relationships between words. It

> destroys the spontaneously functional nature of language and leaves only its lexical basis. It retains only the outward shape of relationships, their music and not their reality. The Word shines forth above a line of relationships emptied of their content, grammar is bereft of its purpose,

it becomes prosody and is no longer anything but an inflexion which lasts only to present the Word. Connections are not properly speaking abolished, they are merely reserved areas, a parody of themselves, and this void is necessary for the density of the Word to rise out of a magic vacuum, like a sound and a sign devoid of background, like 'fury and mystery'.[8]

Because of the lack of the necessity for connections, the meaning of the word in 'discontinuous speech' is 'encyclopaedic'—it contains all the possible associations and connotations "from which a relational discourse might have required it to choose". Abstracted from the workings of everyday discourse, the syntagmatic relations of the word are suppressed, and it therefore achieves a state possible otherwise only in the dictionary, "where the noun can live without the article— reduced to zero degree—pregnant with all past and future specifications".[9] So for Barthes the loss (or the distancing) of the social function of language in poetry ensures that the poetic word forgoes the "stability of intention"—since it can mean in one moment all the meanings it has ever had. Muldoon's claim to wish to limit readings is all the more strange in that the poetry itself exemplifies to a marked extent Barthes's "degree zero" writing, a poetry characterised by gaps and discontinuities, where connections are made often only on the level of the signifier. Muldoon characteristically fragments narrative continuity; the poems are not held together syntactically (so, for example, he often uses gaps marked by asterisks to encourage the reader to 'leap' from one fragment to the next): instead, different tones and styles are brought together by the 'vertical' relationships between meanings. Reading the poems necessitates shifting between different levels of meaning which act as clues to the narrative 'behind' the paradigmatic structure. Even those poems which seem more obviously syntagmatically constructed, such as 'Immram', 'The More a Man Has' and '7 Middagh Street' tend to hide narrative connections, offering the reader instead sometimes heavily disguised repetitions of single words and images with which to 'build' links.

The difficulty of 'holding on' to the meaning of words once abstracted from syntagmatic relations is examined in 'Chinook':

> I was micro-tagging Chinook salmon
> on the Qu'appelle
> river.

> I surged through the melt-water
> in my crocus
> waders.
>
> I would give each brash,
> cherubic
> face its number.
>
> *Melt*-water? These were sultry
> autumn
> fish hang-gliding downstream.
>
> Chinook. Their very name
> a semantic
> quibble.
>
> The autumn, then, of Solidarity,
> your last in Cracow.
> Your father
>
> rising between borsch
> and carp,
> relinquishing the table to Pompeii.

The speaker stands in the river "that calls" and tries to arrest the movement of the fish, to name them. But he realises that so far from being able to place a limit on the salmon, he has even mistaken the meaning of his own activity. The melt-water and crocus waders of spring are out of place in this narrative—these are "sultry/autumn/ fish hang-gliding downstream". Just as Spring and Autumn are interchangeable in the speaker's memory, so the names are unsuited to the activity of the fish, since when they make their way upstream to spawn it is their "autumn". Thus they are not the angelic children the speaker thinks he sees. Similarly the "sultry autumn fish" are the young, newly hatched. So the meaning changes according to the context of the utterance and the situation of the speaker, just as it changes depending on whether you are a fish or a fisherman. In the same way the very name of the salmon is "a semantic quibble", since it gathers several meanings to itself—the 'enclyclopaedic' nature of words in poetry becomes the very subject of the poem. Apart from the name of a salmon, Chinook is the native name of an Indian tribe on the Columbia river in North America. It is also the name of a creole language which originated in the dealings of the Hudson Bay company's servants with the Native Americans. It was then used by the Indians as a means of communication between the different tribes and with the colonizers. Moreover the Chinook wind is an ocean wind which is warm in winter and cool in summer. (Like the Spring/ Autumn confusion, the temperature of the wind depends on the temperature of the surroundings—it is contextual. And indeed the wind itself *creates* seasonal confusion as the warmth of the winter wind heralds a false spring, encouraging plant life to flower only to be destroyed by the 'real' winter).

But probably the most immediately recognisable reference of the term 'Chinook' for contemporary readers is as a name for a type of military helicopter; the Chinook became famous in news coverage of the Vietnam, and more recently the Falklands war. This usage of the name seems qualitatively different from the others mentioned, since it arises out of a distinctively modern and self-conscious process of naming. And indeed the name for the helicopter does differ in its linguistic relation to the other objects designated by the word Chinook. For although it may be impossible to say which came first, the names for a wind, a salmon and a tribe are the same because of geographical proximity—they share a contextual, or metonymic relation with each other. In the same way the language Chinook is so named because of its use by the Chinook tribe—the process by which names are conferred in society depends on contextual relations. In contrast, the name for the helicopter arises out of a metaphorical relation between the Chinook wind and the wind made by the action of the helicopter's blades. And the poem as a whole records the self-conscious artistic process by which such metaphorical relations are created. For the activity of "micro-tagging" the fish is itself a metaphor for designating objects and events in poetry. So the poem in fact records the *difference* between the social process of naming which depends on metonymic displacement, and the metaphorical relation which arises when such naming becomes self-conscious or 'artistic'.

Within the poem all the meanings of the word Chinook exist simultaneously—as Barthès says the poetic word is magically 'whole':

> it shines with an infinite freedom and prepares to radiate towards innumerable uncertain and possible connections. Fixed connections being abolished, the World is left only with a vertical project, it is like a monolith, or a pillar which plunges into a totality of meanings, reflexes and recollections.[10]

And this totality of meanings is self-consciously harnessed by the poet, so that the "semantic quibble" becomes productive not

disruptive of meaning. At least one of the meanings of 'Chinook'—
that of the trading patois—is significant not only within this poem but
in the poem 'Meeting the British' (where it is made clear that a
language which seems to be a third language, created in order to
communicate and more specifically to trade, in fact works as a means
of domination over the colonized). In contrast to the patois the nouns
in the final two stanzas at first sight suggest stability and untrans-
latability. Borsch, carp and Pompeii are all words which carry a single,
identifiable meaning. However, the reason that they don't need
translation is that they are already borrowings from one language to
another, and in this sense they perform exactly the same function as a
patois, a means of representing one culture to another. Just as
'borsch' and 'carp' are words which suggest a stable meaning as well as
a country of origin, so "Cracow" 'means' Poland. (And here the false
spring born by the Chinook wind may act as a reminder of the Prague
Spring, with all the difficulties of "holding on" to political change
which it connotes). 'Pompeii' similarly has 'one' meaning although it
is not of the same order as Cracow—the word has passed into another
realm because of an event, so that it now 'stands' for stasis in
movement, or the sudden petrification of events. Solidarity, although
translated from the Polish, stands for a political movement rather than
an abstract concept, but the displaced concept 'solidity' works on the
level of metaphor in the poem. The word works with 'Pompeii' as a
symbol of the solidification of events and meanings, due to departure,
which the speaker's failed attempt at micro-tagging could not achieve.
The speaker, unlike his addressee in the poem, has not been able to
place a limit on experience by cutting it off at a certain point, and it is
for this reason that he can't hold down events in his memory.

The only way out of this impasse for the writer is to be aware of all
the possible meanings and readings of his work, but of course this is
impossible to achieve. And as if to point this out (in contradistinction
to Muldoon's stated belief about intention), the nouns in the final
stanza are not as univocal as one might think. For the meanings of
borsch, carp, Pompeii and Solidarity which the poet is attempting to
utilize in the poem (Eastern Europe, petrification of events, solidity)
are metonyms derived from the associations of places and events, in
exactly the same way as the language meaning of Chinook is derived
from its designation of a tribe. (So in Eastern Europe borsch
designates a type of soup rather than a Russian dish). In the same way,
though the word does not change, people understand very different

things by Solidarity depending on their political allegiances and personal understanding, i.e. depending on the context which the word inhabits for them. Moreover, the reader takes 'borsch' and 'carp' to be examples of particular types of food—so particular that they don't need to be translated into English. But of course 'carp' also means discourse, argument and complaint, and thus it shares with 'Chinook' not merely the meanings of a type of discourse and a fish but also a semantic duplicitousness.

In the poem words are undecidable both because of their lexical richness (the entirely different meanings which a word such as 'carp' may denote), and because of the various connotations which the single meaning of a word may carry (just as the fishing scenario depends on contextual interpretation, so the meaning of the final stanzas may alter depending on different understandings of the events in Poland). But the poem reduces the gap between the polysemous word and the word rich in social connotation by showing that both depend on the same processes. For example, the word 'borsch' (which is in some senses representative of an early stage of development of Chinook's poly-semousness) initially begins to carry the different meanings of soup and Russian food because it becomes weighted with a new social connotation (Russianness).

Interestingly my analysis of the poem 'Chinook' which has as its subject the instability and polysemousness of words, has tended to confirm Muldoon's theory of creative writing as the control and limitation of linguistic meaning. Even as the poem emphasises the number and diversity of meanings of words, the poet must be aware of them all in order to include them in his statement about poly-semousness. Such a writing project opens up two methodological difficulties. On the one hand the reader is encouraged to read the poetry in terms of what Barthes has termed the 'fullness' or 'wholeness' of the word in poetry, displaced from its position within a relational discourse. But on the other s/he is constrained by the knowledge that all this has been planned and controlled by the author in order to give the *illusion* of instability. This in turn produces a difficulty for Muldoon: the fragmentation of narrative connections which encourages words to perform to their "zero degree", also opens up the way for interpretations which the writer may not have accounted for. (Significantly, the authority of the reader in deter-mining meaning also includes the ability to discover *political* readings, i.e. linguistic polysemousness need not necessarily increase the 'hermeticism' of the poetry but can equally encourage socially 'responsible' readings.) Of course this is all a matter of degree since words can never be absolutely confined to intended meanings. Nevertheless, Muldoon's continual destruction of the syntagmatic relations which serve to some extent to limit the encyclopaedic reference of poetic words, sits oddly with his prescriptivist insistence on his own control of meaning.

## Roots and Origins

Quinquereme of Nineveh from distant Ophir,
Rowing home to haven in sunny Palestine
With a cargo of ivory,
And apes and peacocks,
Sandalwood, cedarwood, and sweet white wine.

Stately Spanish galleon coming from the Isthmus,
Dipping through the Tropics by the palm-green shores,
With a cargo of diamonds,
Emeralds and amethysts,
Topazes, and cinnamon, and gold moidores.

Dirty British coaster with a salt-caked smoke stack,
Butting through the Channel in the mad March days,
With a cargo of Tyne coal,
Road-rail, pig-lead,
Firewood, ironware, and cheap tin trays.[11]

Chinook, the language of trade, is constructed by means of the trading of words, the replacement of words from one context to another where, like borsch, they take on an altered meaning in order to represent one culture to another. Yet if the role of the trading language is to translate cultures for each other, its end lies not in translation but in substitution, as objects, cargoes are exchanged for one another. My analysis of 'Chinook' has suggested the difficulty which arises for the writer in stopping the process of alchemical translation (a one-way process in which objects are transformed into gold) from sliding into one of infinite substitution (when gold itself becomes a means of barter). Once objects are transformed by the Midas touch of poetry, how can the difference which gives them meaning and value in the world be maintained between them?

The distinction between 'everyday' and 'poetic' symbolic processes
lies at the heart of 'Sushi', a poem which sets up an opposition
between argumentative discourse and a magical, silent, alchemical
matching of essences. While the two people sit having (or not having)
an argument about the lack of productivity in arguing, alongside them
the master and his apprentice transform objects into precious works of
art:

> I saw, when the steam
> cleared, how this apprentice
> had scrimshandered a rose's
> exquisite petals
> not from some precious metal
> or wood or stone
> ('I might as well be eating alone.')
> but the tail-end of a carrot:
> how when he submitted this work of art
> to the master—
> *Is it not the height of arrogance*
> *to propose that God's no more arcane*
> *than the smack of oregano,*
> *orgone,*
> *the inner organs*
> *of beasts and fowls, the mines of Arigna,*
> *the poems of Louis Aragon?—*
> it might have been alabaster
> or jade
> the master so gravely weighed
> from hand to hand
> with the look of a man unlikely to confound
> Duns Scotus, say, with Scotus Eriugena.

The carrot becomes a rose which "might have been alabaster or
jade": any material will serve for this mysterious alchemy since
"God's no more arcane" than the indiscriminate list of things
displaced from their origins. The activity of the 'volatile' (a name for
an alchemical compound) apprentice suggests that arbitrary connections, not systematic analysis, are the fundamentals of creation—
the carrot and rose are both red, but there is nothing more essential in
their connection. What is strange about the poem is that such an
arbitrary, metonymic link between the material of creation and the
finished product should be associated with the alchemical search for

essences, and the philosophy of Duns Scotus.[12] The poem attempts to find some common ground between the arbitrariness of relations between words, and between words and their referents, and the transmutation of ordinary reality into art, a process which seems to depend on extracting the true 'essence' from the raw materials of creation.

But the linguistic capriciousness of the central italicised section sits uneasily with the Master's training in magical and mystical trans-formation. The name Louis Aragon is a reminder of the surrealist project of juxtaposing opposites in language and image so that perception may be renewed, and of the surrealist mentor Rimbaud's faith in the "alchemy of the word". Rimbaud believed that it was possible to transform existing reality with its limited logic, by effecting free substitution, the miracle of the word. But the very arbitrariness of the substitution undercuts any notion of 'essence' so necessary to the process of alchemy, since the slippage between objects and words (oregano, orgone, organs) implies the impossibility of returning to a 'truth' before the objects existed, i.e. it denies the fact that there is an essence in ordinary reality or everyday language to be extracted and transformed. The alchemical magic is a pretence. This philosopher is a hack—the value of the gold/philosopher's stone has degenerated to that of exchange. In fact Muldoon has gone further than the usual capitalist structure of exchange in which some commodities are more valuable than others. Here everything is exchangeable, since everything is comparable to everything else. The mention of Arigna might suggest the mining of precious metals but in effect Muldoon is less of a prospector who digs deep than a pirate who plunders whatever cargo comes his way.

The cargoes of Masefield's poem are scattered throughout the volume, and the colonizing effects of this imperialist trade are evident in poems such as 'Meeting the British' and 'Chinook'. In both poems trade depends on the ability of a language to translate one culture for another, in other words to erase the difference and unknowability of the cultures enough that they may interact (but not so much that the colonized culture may think of itself as the 'same' or the 'equal' of the colonizers). As the poem 'Profumo' points out ("Haven't I told you, time and time again,/that you and she are chalk/and cheese? Away and read Masefield's 'Cargoes' ") difference must be maintained in the interests of hierarchy, a hierarchy which results in the domination of one culture by another. In 'Meeting the British' this asymmetry is imaged in the lack of equality of the objects of exchange—the Native

Americans will cede their land and wealth in return for fish-hooks, blankets and smallpox. It is precisely this difference between objects which Muldoon's plundering method, his association of any word or object with any other, denies. In piracy the trade (exchange) value of the object is lost, it becomes arbitrary as the pure 'value' is exalted. The pirate's cargo brings together all different types of value from different ships and nations, but the notion of value itself must depend on maintaining difference. If everything is equally substitutable the hierarchical value of the commodity is lost. This could be read then as a utopian, anti-colonialist move, in which all the products of imperialism are stolen and stuffed together so that they lose their singularity. But if the capitalist impulse is to substitute a quantitative measure of value for a qualitative, then it is premised upon everything being the same in a certain way—everything can be judged by the same standard of value. In this case piracy is merely an extension of capitalism's mode of substitutability, for pirates don't work for colonized nations, but hoard wealth for themselves.

As Mick Imlah points out, all the end words of the italicised passage in 'Sushi' are variations on the consonantal theme "rgn":

> This fragment (which might convey a complaint against Muldoon's indiscriminate plundering method) is only joined to the rest of the poem by its rhymes with, again, the first and last lines of the poem—'arguing' and 'Scotus Eriugena'—and with 'erogenous' in the middle. When we find further variants ('organza', 'Oregon') dispersed through other poems an enigma presents itself; . . . it does make sense if the origin of this rhyme sequence (which like the theme behind the Enigma Variations doesn't itself appear) is the word 'origin'.[13]

But in the end this alchemical mystery, which seems predicated on words being the 'same', or the same in essence, depends on being able to tell the difference like the master (who knows that things aren't just all versions of the same thing).

As Muldoon has said in an interview, Masefield's poem 'Cargoes' is "essentially about one idea: the distinction between the colour, beauty, possibility of the imagination that we associate with far-off lands and the down-to-earth ordinariness of our day-to-day world of dirty British coasters".[14] So the imagination doesn't 'confound' objects and ideas, the real and the ideal, in the way that the central section of 'Sushi' suggests: the distinction between carrot and rose must be maintained. The sight of the carrot 'through' the rose does not amount to a perception of the 'essence' of the work of art (for the carrot is not its referent) or of the rose. But while the referent is the 'real' rose, and this is gestured towards in the work of art, the carrot (the "root"), the place from which the art has been taken and cut, can nonetheless be *seen*.

The assertion of absolute relativity between all found objects may in certain contexts be read as a utopian project which breaks down hierarchical barriers (the 'essence' of post-modernism), but on the other hand, as the poetry shows, a mere declaration of similarity can't effect the determining grounds on which such hierarchies have been built. As Imlah suggests, throughout the book the rhyme words are often joined by little more than the letters they have in common. Like false etymology this process depends on an idea of common but displaced origin—so in '7 Middagh Street', 'Auden' speaks of his willingness to return to "Eden" (Europe), but also suggests that in going to America the emigrants are searching for their origins as they move away from them:

> For history's a twisted root
> with art its small, translucent fruit
>
> and never the other way round.
> The roots by which we were once bound
>
> are severed here, in any case,
> and we are all now dispossessed;
>
> prince, poet, construction worker,
> salesman, soda fountain jerker—
>
> all equally isolated.
> Each loads flour, sugar and salted
>
> beef into a covered wagon
> and strikes out for his Oregon. . .

Here, in an equation of the loss of hierarchy gained in severing class from its social roots with democracy, Muldoon's Auden asserts that just such a move frees art from its roots in the social world. In other words social levelling leads to a type of 'origin' outside the social and political orientation of human beings. Similarly, in the metonymical displacements which the poems effect all words are weighted equally, and, as Freud explains of the dream-work, they lose the hierarchy of importance accruing to them in the dream thoughts. Auden wishes to leap from the England of the industrial revolution "with its mills, canals and railway bridges/into this great void", wherein words, like the landscape, will be empty and ready to be filled with whatever meaning he wishes to assign them. Words then are bereft of responsibility just as they are bereft of any type of effect on history. However as MacNeice/Yeats points out in 'Louis', "In dreams begin responsibilities"—even the dream (where words are liberated from their order in the social world, where words can stand for anything through displacement and condensation) has a social conscience.

## *White Writing*

As for his crass, rhetorical

posturing, 'Did that play of mine
send out certain men (*certain* men?)

the English shot . . .?'
the answer is 'Certainly not'.

The consideration of the writer's 'responsibility' to his community is of course one of the main themes in circulation through the volume; repeatedly the question of poetry's agency in the social world is couched less in terms of the role self-consciously taken up by the writer than of a debate between linguistic arbitrariness and stability. Continually in tension with the infinite meaningfulness or meaninglessness of "zero degree" writing (a writing whose social agency is absolutely divorced from any intention on the writer's part) is Muldoon's own insistence on the writer's role as one of determining and controlling readings. This optimistic, declarative mode in which words mean what the author means them to mean is characteristic not only of Muldoon's 'Wystan' but also of his Robert Frost, and yet the alchemical translation in the American polity which Frost celebrated is undercut by the actual and verbal mutability in the poem 'Gold'.

The difficulty isolated in the poem 'Chinook' of fixing the magical alchemical moment, the moment of metaphorical translation, recurs in 'Gold'. The sorcerer-like quality of the child's teacher (his soutane like a wizard's cloak) is analogous to the optimism accompanying

Kennedy's presidency—a golden age of magical political transformation which, according to Frost, was to be heralded by and to herald a transformation in the status of poetry ("A golden age of poetry and power"). But the poem charts a movement away from such enchanted transmutation and towards a social reality characterized above all by impermanence. In the poem the personal history of Gerard Quinn (though unknown to the general reader) meshes with the more 'public' histories of Kennedy and Monroe. No longer a Brother, and having suffered a near-fatal car accident, Quinn 'cancels' faith in eternal transmutations:

> Twenty years on you reach
> into the breast
> of a wind-cheater
>
> for your blue pencil:
> 'All cancelled;
> *Nothing gold can stay*'.

The blue pencil is a corrective—blue is the colour used for writer's corrections—to the optimism of the early 1960s. But like the ink in 'Something Else' the blue is a 'fugitive' colour, an ink that disappears. It is used specifically so that the correction won't show up in printing. So a self-destructing statement, written in an ink that fades, is used to undermine the definitive statements characteristic of Frost and the teacher's red pen. The only way Muldoon will offer a critique of the belief that statements can assert identity, that they have any identity, is by offering a vanishing, ironic, momentary gloss and then disappearing, "by the back door of Muldoon's". The critique also encompasses the connection Frost made between poetry and power, democracy and the arts:

> Our venture in revolution and outlawry
> Has justified itself in Freedom's story
> Right down to now in glory upon glory—
> It makes the prophet in us all presage
> The glory of a next Augustan age
> Of a power leading from its strength and pride,
> Of young ambition eager to be tried,
> Firm in our free beliefs without dismay,
> In any game the nations want to play
> A golden age of poetry and power
> Of which this noonday's the beginning hour.[15]

Frost's declarative statement links the democratic freedoms America offers with the possibility for art to play a role in the workings of the state, to intervene in the moulding of society (as in the popular conception of the role of art in the Augustan age). Unlike the later Auden then, who similarly celebrates the democratic levelling of society in America, Frost believes that within such a society the hierarchy whereby the poet takes on the role of spokesperson and laureate of the community, may be maintained. But the ability of art to make enduring statements for society is undercut by events; the poem shows how the change and transformation heralded by Frost's poem cannot be stopped, like ink which isn't fast: "Nothing gold can stay". But of course the impermanence of the poetic statement, the alteration of its meaning according to historical context, is a condition which also affects Quinn's correction, as it does all of Muldoon's poetry. As I discussed in relation to 'Chinook', the poetry seems to send out contradictory messages which on the one hand insist on the writer's control over the statements he makes and on the other undercut that very possibility.

Blue inks appear again in 'Something Else', this time more openly connected with the inability to 'freeze' a moment, even in writing. The opening stanza describes the changing colour of a cooking lobster, in terms of disappearing inks—"madders" are a type of "fugitive" colour, a colour which fades very quickly. Muldoon describes the poem as about "the inability to capture a moment except in the archaeological sense—well that's even a metaphor for the capturing of a moment, you know, seeing the dog curled with its litter under the table at Pompeii".[16] Language, metaphor, always intercede so that the 'moment' is dead or gone by the time it is expressed. The 'freezing' of a moment by making a tableau out of history (the metaphorical 'Pompeii' of 'Chinook') involves, even requires the death of its referent. Unwilling to choose the archaeological method of disinterring a moment or event which has remained intact, Muldoon goes so far as to assert the impossibility of such an enterprise, because of the inevitable slippage from 'something else', to 'something else again'.

The "gossamer thread" which causes this slippage and connects these associations runs throughout the book as various inflections of blues and dyes appear in the poetry. But this isn't simply a theme or code which can be traced through the different "frequencies" and plays on the notion of writing-ink. For the various configurations of the trope frustrate an easy analysis of the 'meaning' behind

Muldoon's project as the images slip into one another. Like the characteristic use of paradigmatic relationships to build a structure within each poem, similar 'vertical' connections are used to make links not only within but across poems in the volume. Tracing through the thread of images connected with blue ink and white fibre which link many of the poems necessarily feeds off a contradiction in the poetry itself. For the complex of images which play on the impermanence of inscriptions in ink tends to parody the notion of a secret lurking behind the writing, waiting to be uncovered. The play on the colours blue and white in the volume is above all self-referential; through it poems qualify and comment on each other, rather than on anything external to the book. And yet it is only by uncovering the 'secret' or hidden links between the references to the green furrow, flax, indigo, asbestos and gold that this irony may be 'read'.

The blue dye of 'Gold' and 'Something Else' reappears in 'Meeting the British', a poem which like 'Chinook' plays on the connections between trade and language; here the poet who has taken on the role of spokesperson for his tribe in fact fulfils the role of go-between and betrayer of his people:[17]

> We met the British in the dead of winter.
> The sky was lavender
>
> and the snow lavender-blue.
> I could hear, far below,
>
> the sound of two streams coming together
> (both were frozen over)
>
> and, no less strange,
> myself calling out in French
>
> across that forest-
> clearing.

Nature is in stasis even while it moves, just as the two sides are in process, "coming together" while they are "frozen over" linguist-ically. The speaker uses his command over language to command our view of nature as he describes the snow as "lavender-blue". This phrase seems almost to be ironizing the stasis of nature, which can be altered merely by a word, so that the "difficulty of holding on to a moment" is compounded by the use of poetic language, cut off from the 'real', to describe it. The lavender is also a bridge of course, between sky and snow, and between the two sides, as the colonel displays his handkerchief of 'peace' (which as in 'Bechbretha' will actually be used to effect conquest). But the lavender is party to a betrayal as the smell masks the disease infecting the gifts brought by the colonizers. The fish-hooks are a reminder of the attempt to tag fish in 'Chinook', and suggest that this is a moment which can be securely 'caught', a moment with real historical effects. In this light the smallpox embroidered into the blankets is an inscription of 'alien' signs very different from the fading inks of 'Something Else' and 'Gold' in that it cannot be washed out. So the words are 'hooked' into a social meaning like the word 'Solidarity' in 'Chinook'. Lavender and smelling salts are used to revive consciousness, to dispel the language of dreams—these actions are signs with a real social meaning, just as the signs are real actions (so the word "dead" can be read less as a metaphor for the height of winter than an actual description of the surroundings, populated by the dead of battle). This is gestured towards in the phrase "forest-clearing", which connotes not merely a description of a place but an activity—the activity of the colonizers in deforestation (a practice ubiquitous to colonizers from sixteenth-century Ireland to twentieth-century Vietnam). Significantly, it is this practice which 'Wystan' forgets or misreads in his lyrical celebration of American democracy, and the activities of the "huge blond-haired lumberjack", the mythical Paul Bunyan. Auden and Benjamin Britten collaborated on an operetta about the legendary American hero (Auden would have been writing the libretto at the time Muldoon imagines him speaking his monologue). Humphrey Carpenter mentions the interpretation Auden placed on the traditional stories: "Bunyan in fact becomes in Auden's hands the spirit or presiding genius of pioneer America, and the Bunyan legends are reconstructed, as Auden put it, into a parable of "the development of the continent from a virgin forest—to settlement and cultivation".[18] At the end of the operetta Paul describes the new challenge of industrialised America:

> The pattern is already clear
> That machinery imposes
> On you as the frontier closes,
> Gone the natural disciplines
> And the choice of life begins—

America's destroyed and recreated, America is what you do,
America is you and I, America is what you choose to make it.

The lumberjack's destruction of the virgin forest is seen from the other side in 'Meeting the British' where the forest-clearing also involves the destruction, or attempt to destroy, those who previously inhabited it. Thus the "Oregon" Auden seeks is only an origin if it refuses to recognise the settlement already there.[19]

The idea of the betrayal and destruction of a nation through language is also one of the themes of the celebrated poem 'Quoof'. The poem tends to be read as primarily concerned with the barriers to communication between individuals. The speaker carries his private, or rather familial, word for a hot-water bottle, like a private world. The word becomes a sword, which may be used to pierce or break barriers but here is used to create one. The lack of communication in the first stanza leaves language inert in the second, which contains no main verb:

> An hotel room in New York City
> with a girl who spoke hardly any English,
> my hand on her breast
> like the smouldering one-off spoor of the yeti
> or some other shy beast
> that has yet to enter the language.

The spoor, like the hand, is the signal of the presence of an alien being, possibly savage, but unseen and unknown. The spoor of the yeti on the snow (like the pony's "glib cairn", and the horse's dung in 'Gathering Mushrooms') is dark on white, but his hand on her breast reverses this scheme, since the implication is perhaps that the woman is not white (although her race is defined only in terms of her non-Englishness). Both snow and breast are defiled by a sign of something which cannot be known or named. Language here becomes almost synonymous with the social world as the entrance of the beast into the realm of language signals a step forward in communication. The implication is both that there exists outside the closed linguistic world something which threatens it, and also that such beasts cannot exist in our minds (and therefore in actuality, since the yeti has not been seen) before words exist for them—the yeti is named as it is conceptualised. But beyond this rather abstract argument about the nature of linguistic reference lie suggestions of the power of an imposed language. For what is the significance of the girl "who spoke hardly any English"? Even if she had perfect command of the English language the word "quoof" would be unintelligible to her since it is a 'familial' rather than a 'national' word. The poem hints at the way language is used to colonise and, conversely, to empower. There are dangers as well as gains in allowing the beast/the hand to enter the language (in this case the language of the girl which is other than English). Like the Indians in the poem 'Meeting the British', the danger in opening up to new forms of communication is colonization, a loss of 'self-containment'. And of course this is the situation for Muldoon, who has perfect command of the English language though he was born in Ireland, where English is in one sense an 'alien' language. Like 'Aisling' the poem can on one level be read as another version of the traditional trope in which the female represents the land to be colonised by the male. Here however the woman resists—the poem ends still lacking a verb, the 'entering' unaccomplished.[20]

The suggestion in 'Meeting the British' that the language of poetry is necessarily "hooked into" or implicated in destructive events, that it can work equally to "speak for" or to "betray" a people, is in turn qualified by further allusions which put into question the very possibility of statement-making in poetry. And yet the very process of tracing through these allusions places the reader at Muldoon's mercy, with the suspicion that he is merely playing on our credulity. As well as being linked to 'Chinook' and 'Wystan', the poem also alludes to a passage in the 'Louis' section of '7 Middagh Street'. Again this connection is made through the motif of colour: "C'est la lavande,/ une fleur mauve comme le ciel" is echoed in the linnet's contemptuous comparison of the "grey skies of an Irish Republic" to the "blue-dome" of the Northern flax-growing area (the comparison of the blueness of the sky to flax is common). This passage in turn, through the transformations of the motif of the girl in the bin-liner dress, refers the reader back to the first poem of the book, 'Ontario', and to 'Christo's' in the middle (repeating the structural balance of *Quoof*). The figure which provokes fears of declining sexual potency in 'Ontario' is again specifically associated with fertility and the desire to have children in 'The Toe-Tag'. The woman/body bag seems to work as a sort of nodal point to which associations of personal and racial identity accrue.

In 'Christo's', which like 'Aisling' can be read as a counter-vision of maiden Ireland, she becomes the focal point for a recollection of Ireland during the hunger strikes, with the suggestion that the men died in order to preserve the already diseased body of the nation. The "green furrow" of the woman's back in 'Ontario' is transformed from fertility to the deadly asbestos, of which the landscape is now constituted:

> Two workmen were carrying a sheet of asbestos
> down the Main Street of Dingle;
> it must have been nailed, at a slight angle,
> to the same sized gap between Brandon
>
> and whichever's the next mountain.
> Nine o'clock. We watched the village dogs
> take turns to spritz the hotel's refuse-sacks.
> I remembered Tralee's unbiodegradable flags
>
> from the time of the hunger-strikes.

As the speaker and his companion drive from Dingle, in the South West of Ireland, to Belfast, Ireland hides as in a body-bag from the wind blowing from the North-East. 'Asbestos' can be read as a Barthesian 'full' or 'encyclopaedic' word: the *Oxford English Dictionary* 'yields' a (false) connection to flax. The fibrous material was thought to be a "kind of incombustible flax", as well as an "unquenchable stone". It was thought of as a magic stone since although it seemed to burn it didn't burn away—it was always alight and white (like bleached flax). This then may be Muldoon's ironic, alchemical philosopher's stone, the white page on which he is to inscribe his deadly secrets. The green furrow of 'Ontario' is transformed into a white fibre, which appears again in 'Louis' as the productivity of Northern Ireland's linen industry is compared to a "great winding sheet of linen".[21] Productivity takes over from fertility—the green furrow becomes white; the natural gives way to the post-industrial world, which is based not on the mining of wealth but on its production. MacNeice quotes from a *Belfast Newsletter* of 1937:

> *Imagine a great white highway*
> *a quarter of a mile broad*
> *extending the length of Ireland*
> *from the Giant's Causeway*
> *to Mizen Head*
> *and you can grasp the magnitude*
> *of our annual output of linen.*

The drive from Dingle to Belfast has been transformed into a bleaching-ground for the North's linen industry. The green furrow is whitened by its use as a 'bleach-green' (linen was bleached by sun and air, pegged out on the ground). The process of linen production involves a transformation of the blue of the flowers of the flax plant into a white cloth (a cloth which in 'Bechbretha', 'Crossing the Line' and 'Meeting the British' is used as an instrument of betrayal). In 'Louis' the whole of the Irish landscape is transformed into a white fibre, which through its connection with asbestos in 'Christo's' again carries the taint of death. In 'Meeting the British' the process of writing, of gaining power over language, and becoming a spokesperson, seems to be implicated in a betrayal which results in the destruction of the tribe. However, writing could equally be construed as the very opposite of the process of transformation which bleaches out the blue flax to produce white fibre, since it involves the reinscription of blue ink onto a white page.

The *Encyclopedia Americana* describes indigo as a pigment used in paints, lacquers, printing inks and rubber (it both imprints and erases). And the process of indigo dyeing is described as one of oxidization (i.e. it is the same 'airing' process by which the blue/grey flax is bleached). Indigo flowers are mainly orange in America; through a process of oxidization the blue dye is made. But indigo is insoluble in water, so it is mixed with an alkaline solution to make a liquid known as indigo white. The fabric to be dyed is immersed in this white liquid. When the fabric is exposed to air the indigo white on the fibres is oxidized back into blue indigo. The dyeing process is then the exact opposite of the bleaching process by which the fabric is made in the first place. Muldoon seems to want to claim that he is writing in disappearing ink, making 'fugitive' statements that are the opposite of a Frostian (or Audenesque) declarative public mode. But the process of publication could be read as analogous to the 'oxidization' or 'airing' of the dyed inscription in the public realm. Once published, the ink remains fast, although interpretations of the poetry may differ.

This ambivalence is brought out by the reaction of the linnet in 'Louis' to the "figure of speech" which compared linen productivity to the length of Ireland:

> Among the blue flowers of the flax a linnet
> sang out 'Lundy'
>
> at the implications of that bleach-
> green. 'It was merely a figure of speech'.

> 'Call it what you like.
> The grey skies of an Irish Republic
>
> are as nothing compared to this blue dome'.
> He tailed off over the flax-dam
>
> to return with a charm of goldfinches
> who assailed me with their 'Not an inch'
>
> and their 'No', and yet again, 'No'.
> As they asperged me with kerosene
>
> I recognised the voice of Sir Edward Carson;
> 'Bid me strike a match and blow'.

The linnet takes the comparison literally; although it was *intended* as a figure of speech, MacNeice has lost control over its reception. The incantation the birds set up in response to his arbitrary "figure" is one loaded with political meaning, an easily recognizable complaint to the tune of 'No Surrender' and the more recent 'Ulster Says No' to the Anglo-Irish Agreement. The ambivalent status of a writing which attempts to undercut its own statements is brought out also by the fact that the very naming of the linnet depends on context. The bird is known, we gather from the dictionary, as an 'indigo bird' in America—but flax and indigo are opposites, one turning from blue to white, and the other from white to blue.

As my elucidation of the linked allusions concealed in these passages suggests, there is a contradiction between dreams and arbitrary slippage, the notion of writing as a vanishing act, and the demands made on the reader. The poetry is on the one hand anti-declarative, and on the other expects a great deal of work from the reader whose task is to uncover something, even if that something is the fact that there is no secret, that what seem to be themes pointing towards a message, are in fact syntactical tropes revealing that there is nothing underneath. So the play on disappearing ink suggests a kind of invisible writing, whose secret may be unlocked by means of a code, or at least a very good dictionary. Muldoon seems to be aware of the contradictory messages the poetry sends out as it both attempts to undercut the authority of the writer and expects the reader to trace through the writer's whims. This is evidenced not only by his insistence that the writer's intention controls the meaning of the work (writing as concerned with "the controlling of readings") in spite of his own understanding that the connotations of words are beyond the writer's control, but also by his exaggerated prescriptiveness, as in 'Away and read Masefield's Cargoes" (for the poem is a necessary 'key' to many of the connections in the volume).[22] In one way the references to bleaching could be read as a metaphor for the poetry's extreme distantiation from the world of actual experience—its hermeticism. The tropological links between flax, indigo and asbestos can be made without hint of an external object. The poem/book becomes sustained by the purely internal relation of its component parts, impervious to external pressures. What I have termed the characteristic 'hermeticism' of Muldoon's poetry is partly based on its polysemousness, the instability of meaning and reference encouraged by the loose structures of the poems, and the 'enclyclopaedic' nature of words divorced from the single and particular meanings they are required to carry in 'relational' discourse. But, as I have argued, it is precisely through such linguistic polysemousness that the poetry is opened onto the public domain, by revealing the struggle over the meanings and differences between words in everyday discourse. Thus the social 'responsibility' of such poetry derives not only from the fact that the reader can invest the poems with a public and political meaning once they are dissociated from authorial control, but also because the 'unstable' language of the poetry itself reveals the struggle over context.

The debate between arbitrariness and stability is played out between Wystan and Louis, the two corner-stones of the last poem. Arbitrariness is connected to the belief that, since there is no stable meaning in the word, the author can start afresh with a 'new' meaning—and this is Auden's idea of the democracy of the word. But the creation of such a new beginning necessitates clearing away old meanings (in 'Meeting the British' this process is imaged through the activity of "forest-clearing"). As Bakhtin points out of the structure of forms of the poetic:

> the trajectory of the poetic word towards its own object and towards the unity of language is a path along which the poetic word is continually encountering someone else's word, and each takes new bearings from the other; the records of the passage remain in the slag of the creative process, which is then cleared away (as scaffolding is cleared away once construction is finished), so that the finished work may rise as unitary speech, one co-extensive with its object, as it were speech about an 'Edenic' world.[23]

It is precisely this scaffolding which reappears in the final lines of the poem as MacNeice draws attention to the politicization of words in Northern Ireland:

> The one-eyed foreman had strayed out of Homer;
> 'MacNeice? That's a Fenian name'.
> As if to say, 'None of your sort, none of you
> will as much as go for a rubber hammer
> never mind chalk a rivet, never mind caulk a seam
> on the quinquereme of Nineveh'.

The foreman's hold over the name (which is false, since 'MacNeice' goes back to the pre-Fenian King Conor MacNessa) helps to uphold a system of social injustice, the effects of which are felt not least in the area of employment. Here Muldoon admits the social rootedness of the language he uses:

> the name as just the word on its own doesn't exist, as a signifier . . . but in fact it has connotations that it cannot itself allow for. It exists in other realms. [MacNeice] is strictly speaking a name that is more than likely an Irish name, a name that was in Ireland before the Plantation, let's put it like that, or before the arrival of the Normans . . . So MacNeice is a much older name than that shipyardman would perhaps allow for.[24]

The foreman echoes not only the goldfinches' cry of 'No Surrender' but the dictat of the mother in 'Profumo': "chalk" reminds us that "you and she are chalk and cheese". Chalk and cheese, symbols for irreducible difference, however similar in sound, are such because of social (and parental) pressure. The words, as alike as the esker and whisker of 'Brock', will not, like them, simply dissolve into one another, transform into dreams of supra-rational reality.

NOTES

1. Roland Barthes, *Roland Barthes*, trans. Richard Howard (1975, London: Macmillan, 1977), p. 160.
2. 'Paul Muldoon Writes . . .', *Poetry Book Society Bulletin* 118 (Autumn 1982): p. 2.
3. Michael Herr notes the impossibility of dissociating the glamorous 'filmic' version of war from the actual thing in his account of the coverage of the Vietnam war. See *Dispatches* (London: Picador, 1979), p. 169, 173.
4. Paul Muldoon, personal interview, June, 1987.

5.  For a discussion of the way in which the "poetic" word works actively to negate the history of the word and the object in the world see Mikhail Bakhtin, 'Discourse and the Novel', in Michael Holquist ed., *The Dialogic Imagination* (Austin and London, University of Texas Press, 1981), pp. 259–422.

6.  Roland Barthes, *Writing Degree Zero*, trans. Annette Lavers and Colin Smith, ed. Susan Sontag (1953, New York: Hill and Wang, 1968). See also Jean-Paul Sartre, *What is Literature?*, trans. Bernard Frechtman (1950, London: Methuen, 1967), pp. 4–11.

7.  Barthes, *Writing Degree Zero*, pp. 42–3.

8.  Barthes, *ibid., pp. 46.*

9.  Barthes, *ibid., pp. 48.*

10. Barthes, *ibid., pp. 47.*

11. John Masefield, 'Cargoes', *Poems* (London: Heinemann, 1966), p. 906.

12. Eriugena, or 'John the Irishman', called into question the transcendence of God with respect to the natural world in a sophisticated version of pantheism, whereas Scotists believed that man's intellect has a direct, intuitive knowledge of the singular material object, and not merely an indirect knowledge of it gained by reflecting on the material image. Duns Scotus's theory of "haecceitas", or the "thisness" of a thing, recurs in altered form in Michael Heffernan's "quidditas" in 'The Soap Pig'.

13. Mick Imlah, 'Abandoned Origins', rev. of *Meeting the British, Times Literary Supplement*, September 4th 1987, p. 946.

14. Muldoon, personal interview, June 1987.

15. Robert Frost, "For John F. Kennedy His Inauguration", *Selected Poems*, ed. Ian Hamilton (Harmondsworth: Penguin, 1973), p. 224–5.

16. Muldoon, personal interview, June 1987.

17. See also the poem 'Yggdrassil' (*Quoof*, pp. 26–7) for Muldoon's parodic use of the notion of the poet as a spokesperson for his 'tribe'.

18. Humphrey Carpenter, *W.H. Auden: A Biography* (London: George Allen  Unwin, 1981), p. 68.

19. Hence his monologue really is 'monologic' in Bakhtin's sense since it insists on self-generation. In this respect it is interesting that the end of Muldoon's poem (mis)quotes Auden himself quoting Shakespeare. Here he states that Chester is his ("historical") origin, his "onlie begetter", and gives him his own initials. But this is in fact a version of the title of a poem he wrote while an undergraduate, 'To the onlie begetter Mr. W.L.' (McElwie). Auden sees himself as the origin and controller of his own words but as Derrida points out, even original performatives ("America is what you do") depend on citation. 'Signature, Event, Context', *Margins of Philosophy*, trans. Alan Bass (Brighton: Harvester, 1982), pp. 321–327.

20. As in 'Aisling' however, it is debatable whether Muldoon successfully avoids the charge of misogynism. In the context of the literature on maiden and mother Ireland, 'Aisling' can be read less as a distasteful confession than as a way of representing the poet's orientation towards history. Because of her diseased state the figure of the woman does not function as a productive national symbol. Rather than an image which can be used to legitimate a particular version of Irish history, in which the men of the nation continue to fight their alien oppressor, the female figure introduces discontinuity (in the form of death and disease) into the historical process. In this way the figure could be read as one which resists colonization by the poet/myth-maker's narrative (in the same way that the girl in 'Quoof' could be read as resisting linguistic colonization). However, this reading necessitates two methodological inconsistencies for the critic. For it is not enough that Muldoon's *intention* should be that the figure of

the woman resists co-option by the nationalist historical narrative, since on one very obvious level the female figure is entirely subordinated to the poet's 'use' of her. In other words she does not resist the poet's alternative parodic narrative which may easily be read as a misogynist indictment of woman's supposed 'productivity' rather than as an ironic comment on nationalist historical and political rhetoric. This difficulty in reading Muldoon's narcissistic feminine tropes is a general one, and it is related to the second methodological problem which concerns the 'hidden' or coded nature of Muldoon's comments on historical and political ('public') narratives. For since it is in tracing the associations of his private 'hermetic' symbols, such as the various 'meanings' of mushrooms, twins or indigo, that it becomes clear that Muldoon is ironising the notion that poetic language cannot or should not encompass public narratives, a reading of the poems which is unaware of these hidden meanings will tend to read poems such as 'Aisling' in terms of their surface misogynism.

21.  Muldoon, personal interview, June 1987.
22.  Muldoon's parody of the use of myth and the manipulation of a declarative tone is part of his rejection of the notion of an homogenous Irish culture and reading community. Yet his allusive technique reveals the importance of the growth of an institutional audience based on an 'ideal' academic literate reader, cultivated by university and Arts Council readings.
23.  Bakhtin, *Imagination*, p. 331.
24.  Muldoon, personal interview, June 1987.

**Richard Brown**
Bog poems and book poems: doubleness, self-translation and pun in Seamus Heaney and Paul Muldoon

# Bog Poems and Book Poems

"So you drive on to the frontier of writing
where it happens again."

In a note written for the Poetry Book Society some years ago, Seamus Heaney offers a familiar way in to the 'Bog Poems' of *Wintering Out* and *North* by discussing the word 'bog'. He writes that 'bog', the Gaelic word for 'soft', is one of the few English borrowings from the Irish language, and that in his family idiom he might as likely use the Norse word 'moss'.[1] Etymology and the "past of invasion, colonization and language shift" that may be inferred from its discoveries are among the concerns that have become familiar to readers of Heaney and recent Northern Irish poetry and we are here firmly pointed to the "*bog* meaning soft" in section two of 'Kinship' and to the etymological lessons of 'Belderg', where conflicting English and Irish elements in the place-name Mossbawn reveal a common Viking root.[2]

Origins are the stuff of Heaney's curiosity in *North* as we have learned to read it. He sniffs at them "like a dog turning/its memories of wilderness/on the kitchen mat". They are exhumed in the Viking ghosts that are the "old fathers" of the city of Dublin, in memories of the sagas, in the longship builders who speak to him again in the title poem and they are remembered in the Norse etymologies ('althing', 'graiping', 'holmgang', 'felloe' and 'floe') that are scattered among the rich vocabularies of these poems.

But words may contain modern as well as ancient mysteries within the complex structure of their meanings. There may be hosts of other connotations and undersenses to be explored, even in such a word as 'bog'. In following the entrails of ancient Nordicisms may we not be in danger of overlooking, for instance, the polylingual coincidence whereby *bog*, in modern Danish, is the word for book? "Some day I

will go to Aarhus", the poet dreams in 'The Tollund Man', slipping
into a semi-mythologised past of "man-killing parishes", which
almost entirely conceals what might be suggested to a modern Danish
speaker: that it may be more in the close relationship between bog and
book than in any closeness to linguistic origins, symbolic Irish
landscape or atavistic rituals that Heaney's poetic energy resides.

Heaney's poems themselves rarely conceal this relationship. It
provides a structural ambiguity on which they build. Naturalness and
literariness jostle for ascendancy in every reading of his verse. Should
we find in him the contemporary Ulster Green, fledged on simple
rural memories and associations, a Wordsworthian whose own
marriage to nature is stormily commemorated in 'The Betrothal of
Cavehill'? Or should we rather see the Harvard and now Oxford
Professor, skilled in the postmodern rhetoric of Deconstruction: a
self-consciously intertextual poet who does not so much innocently
resemble as cunningly name Wordsworth for us, exploring and
adverting to a pantheon of "exemplary figures" in his work, as if to
admit that there is no nature outside the language that describes it, no
poetry that is not poetry about poetry itself?

Bog poems; book poems. We might at first think that the pun, at
least so baldly stated, could hardly be made without offending the
serious and sensuous decorum we have come to expect of Heaney's
poetry. But expectations may deceive. 'The Digging Skeleton' draws
on just this ambiguity, playing on the resemblance between the
archaeologist who digs into the subterranean past and the literary
browser who may find "anatomical plates/Buried along these dusty
quays/Among books yellowed like mummies". The "book people" of
these anatomical plates are themselves Heaneyan diggers and bodies
to be exhumed no less than bog-browned corpses. They provide
another key to the elaborate configurations of analogy and association
in the poems.

'The Digging Skeleton', with its overt acknowledgement 'After
Baudelaire', points to the books that are buried in *North*, or the extent
to which we might say that Heaney's poems are buried in books.
Besides Wordsworth and Hopkins, the writing of *North* unearths
shards of Yeats, Kavanagh, Owen, Hopkins, Mansfield, Lowell,
Shelley and Keats. Its picturing names Breughel and Goya. Its
history sifts through layers of Patrick Pearse and *Hamlet* and Walter
Raleigh, to Tacitus and Diodorus. We should by no means allow the
force of archaeological metaphor to make us overlook, or to leave at
some unstated level, the crux of Heaney's sensuousness. He does not

simply describe the unearthing of bodies from the bog. He re-enacts the mysterious unearthing of the sensuous body from the language of the book: that is the mystery of writing itself.

This pun is only one of the pattern of shifting or punning identities that reveal the profound doublenesses implicit in the metaphorical textures of Heaney's poems. Digging (the paternal prototypic activity that defined Heaney's writing from his first volume[3]) provides a mysterious analogy not only with reading and writing but with the act of unblanketing ("he stripped off blanket bog"), erotic undressing ("the dark-bowered queen,/Whom I unpin") and with an anatomising ("I unwrap skins") that recalls Donne. The "bone house" can be a field, a cemetery, the body, a skeleton, a skull, a room, or a pot. Each skeleton may be a landscape according to that deep congruence of natural forms that also inspired the sculpture of Henry Moore. In the eye of the mind, each object of knowledge becomes an object of necrophiliac desire.

In the ancient past we may see the immediate present. In the alternation of vowel and consonant we find an analogy for that deep alternative: "the shock of gender". In 'Act of Union' the geographical shapes of Britain, Ireland and Ulster reveal the troubled romance and ominous birthing that may be said to make up their complex fate. In Heaney's poetic language there is no escape from resemblances. Visiting the Prado in 'Summer 1969' as if to escape on a Summer Holiday of art, Heaney's persona only finds the Goya picture, "that holmgang/Where two berserks club each other to death", that most reminds him of home.[4]

There are two kinds of 'kinship' in these poems. One (the kinship of Levi-Strauss) speaks of those deep familial and community loyalties, those forces of "our tribe's complicity" whose violence Heaney never condones but whose obligations he can never disown. "I grew out of all this/ like a weeping willow/ inclined to/ the appetites of gravity," he writes in 'Kinship'. But there are also those kinships (the family resemblances of Wittgenstein) of metaphor and imagination, elective affinities that make of Heaney a "Freedman" in poetry.

His use of visual puns made Heaney the most important example for the younger generation of English poets at the start of the 1980s and put his work at the heart of *The Penguin Book of Contemporary British Poetry*, from which (despite his verse protest) no-one has thought to remove it.[5] Puns are the acts of union that make possible a poem like 'Act of Union'. (Its title, for the sake of the pun, elides the 1801 Act of Union with the Government of Ireland Act of 1922 or

Northern Ireland Act of 1949, which are arguably its more precise
historical referents). They imply a postmodern world where identities
may be neither historical nor even stable but may continually be
created and re-created out of ever more precise conceptions of
difference. In terms of national politics this may offer a glimpse of a
multi- or even post-national situation where cultural differences are so
nearly in danger of absorption on a global scale that they become
instantly sought as the stuff of cultural commodity rather than
conflict.[6]

Modern readers of poetry retain strong Arnoldian assumptions that
the highest excellences are those of seriousness (and Victorian 'high'
seriousness at that) and equally strong prejudices (inherited from
Enlightenment Rationalism) against the pun as a trivial and irrelevant
literary device. But such assumptions can easily be seen as a paradox
of our modernity or postmodernity itself. Freed from the immediate
dangers of political struggle by contemporary affluence and liberalism,
English and American readers of poetry are curiously attracted to the
gravity of a Northern Irish 'situation'. Readers of Heaney in
particular have hungered for a justifying seriousness that may now be
characteristically political rather than moral but is still unmistakeably
Victorian in its assumptions. Not even Heaney's most fashionably
politicised of critics can avoid the recognition that, as Seamus Deane
has put it, "Artists can often be more troubled by the idea that they
should be troubled by a crisis than they are by the crisis itself."[7]

Puns in Heaney may hardly dare speak their name for fear of an
apparent levity that transgresses the assumptions by which his poetry
has become so popular: finding, as he has done, a delicate balance
between the unpalatable historical and political weight of John
Montague and the "unbearable lightness" of Paul Muldoon. Yet
recent work in literary theory finds in the pun a new kind of
intellectual significance. Indeed, according to the critic Gregory
Ulmer, the apparently foppish fondness for puns in the most
celebrated of poststructuralist critics may herald a new intellectual
climate or, to use the favoured term, a new 'episteme'. Having
outgrown the Enlightenment epistemological reliance on difference,
we may now be entering a moment where the perception of pun or
'brisure' becomes itself the condition of a new knowledge: the
'homonymic episteme' of Deconstruction.[8]

Such may be the seriousness of the punning that underpins and is
inevitably secreted within the title of a poem like 'Punishment',
which, with its structural play on the resemblance between ancient

and modern ritual condemnations of adultery, has become the *locus classicus* of a certain kind of debate about Heaney. According to Blake Morrison the poem, with its final confession of an ability to "understand" "revenge", should be understood like Auden's 'Spain', in Orwell's famous stricture, as a dangerous defence of, almost an incitement to violence.[9] But unlike Auden's poem, which searches for a doomed unity in a dramatic gesture of political certainty, Heaney's poem enacts a contrary motion of critical self-questioning and doubt. Typically the tell-tale resemblance the poet is forced to discern calls up a series of guilty questions. Would he have punished the girl's adultery? Still worse, he asks, would he have "cast the stones of silence" that might have condemned her in some more cowardly and treacherous way? Indeed can he be sure that in his meditation on her plight he is any more than an "artful voyeur", whose crime is further compounded by more than a trace of necrophilia? Heaney's enquiry into culpability always comes up with the answer that no-one is more culpable than he.

Who does the pun punish? As commonly used in the eighteenth century the pun, small point or *punctilio* might be thought to have inflicted a wound on the credibility of an intellectual opponent. However we now more familiarly talk as if the pun, with its associations of loudness or vulgarity, is something which 'punishes' the feelings of someone with better literary 'taste'. Literary theorists may argue that the pun constitutes an attack on the semantic order, on its assumptions of traditional unitary significance. The pun attacks the authority of the word and of The Word and the propriety of the name. Representatives of linguistic nominalism and referentiality may tremble at its appearance, though paradoxically the pun (as for Stephen Dedalus) may reinforce an identity between name and fate. Early authorities, following the pun's own logic of association, linked it with the Carthaginians and their brave and long though ultimately self-destructive war of attrition against Rome: the Punic wars.[10]

At first sight the main casualty of Heaney's puns is the poet or his persona himself. This is nowhere more apparent than in 'Casualty' from *Field Work*, the poem that, as several critics have pointed out, may be at once Heaney's 'Fisherman', his 'In Memory of W.B. Yeats' and his 'Easter 1916' and which, by means of a well-noted pun on the connotations of the word 'rhythm', becomes a poem about poetry itself.[11] Morrison commented on how Heaney's changes from earlier drafts of the poem confirmed his susceptibility to the pull of tribal loyalty. However we might go further and explore the extent to which the poem's changing emphases during composition re-inforce its determination to focus on the plight of the poet as much as that of the unfortunate O'Neill.

In each version the poem plays with the paradox that O'Neill's back is turned toward the poet but that it is a "turned observant back". Heaney's descriptive art might apparently enjoy the privilege of being invisible but, despite the tricks by which he tries to conceal it, O'Neill's "turned back watches too". Morrison pointed to the social embrace of symbolic circles in the elegy but, beyond the circle, its most characteristic and repeated figure is that of twisting or inverting. He remembers O'Neill "as he turned", the boat's screw is at once itself "turning" and "turning/Indolent fathoms white". This image of turning and turning back in upon oneself is evident in the impossible logic of the poem's tenses (the back "watches" yet "was blown to bits"), in the reflexive action of its pun and in its revision. As well as placing the question at the end, perhaps Heaney's most striking change from the early versions was his introduction of other voices into the poem. In the final version the Bogside walls speak their obscene message and, in a magical act of reversal, the dead man becomes revenant and answers back:

> 'Now you're supposed to be
> An educated man,'
> I hear him say. 'Puzzle me
> The right answer to that one.'[12]

* * *

It may be a coincidence that the odd polylingualism of 'bog' first started to puzzle me in Copenhagen at an academic conference devoted to the study of James Joyce. But what is coincidence? It is Joyce through whose life of exile Heaney's confessional persona "sweated" in 'Summer 1969' and Joyce whose presence vies with that of Yeats as primary exemplar for a reading of the work.

Joyce developed as an exemplary figure in Heaney's work from before *North*. Hints of a linguistic nationalism in some of Stephen's remarks in *A Portrait* serve as epigraph to 'The Wool Trade' and Joyce's Dublin-centredness is used as an instance in 'Gravities'. Even a self-willed exile like Joyce may have been subject to "gravities" but equally Heaney could by no means have avoided gravitating toward Joyce. Such is the implication of the final poem in *Station Island*, which (after a series of encounters with old teachers, ghosts of victims of violence, etc.) pays its ultimate act of literary homage to Joyce.[13] Here again Joyce is enlisted as the representative of the language politics which became visible at the start of the 1980s in Paulin and Friel and in the criticism of Seamus Deane as well as in that of Colin MacCabe. Heaney enthuses on the odd coincidence that his birthday, April 13th (a birthday which by an even odder coincidence he shared with Samuel Beckett) is the date on which Stephen Dedalus's diary triumphantly notes down the vindication of his Irish English use of the "good old blunt English" word "tundish".

However, especially in an earlier published version written for a Joyce centenary conference in 1982 and published in the *James Joyce Broadsheet*, he also stresses the dissenting, lonely, apostate Joyce ("When I refused to take the sacrament"; "What I did on my own/ was done for others but not with them").[14] This Joyce is a liberating example of (and a binding obligation to) imaginative freedom:

> And don't be so earnest,
>
> Let others wear the sackcloth and the ashes.
> Let go, let fly, forget.
> You've listened long enough. Now strike your note.

'Leaving the Island' is an extraordinary poem not least in that in its punning relevance it mingles Heaney with Joyce and in that it seems to effect a link between the almost irreconcilable traditions of the Joycean writer-as-exile and the more contemporary national tradition of writers like Sean O'Faolain. More importantly it confirms and enthuses in a literary ambition which is neither narrowly provincial nor atavistically anti-modernist but seeks to "swim out on your own" to find those frontiers at which writing is genuinely difficult and genuinely new.

★   ★   ★

It may in some ways seem a surprise that Heaney's next writing should have been the series of lyrics entitled 'Sweeney Redivivus' written in connection with his translation of the middle Irish *Buile Suibhne* under the teasingly Eliotic title *Sweeney Astray*.[15] Heaney's Sweeney poems have been among the slowest to have been absorbed into critical discussion of his work, perhaps because it is often hard for the critic to know how best to discuss translation, but no doubt also because the self-translating myth that they provide is a highly self-oriented one and one which it is hard to reconcile with a version of Heaney as a poet who is in any straightforward way 'engaged'.

The lyrics capture a series of moments neither in nor out of the original narrative so much as in what the epigraphic 'First Gloss' calls "the margin". Written, like free translations of the interpolated lyrics in the romance, in the first person, they dramatise various moments of poetic exile and questing as an analogy for poetry itself, from Sweeney's half-surprised recognition of his new status "incredible to myself/ among people far too eager to believe me/ and my story, even if it happened to be true", to taking up residence in the "hidebound boundary tree. My tree of knowledge", to his encounter with the cleric and to his representation of himself as a yuppy version (in the Dordogne) of the rich man ordered by Christ to give half his possessions to the poor.

Though it inverts the usual order of precedence, we might want to see an influence of, or at least a congruence with Paul Muldoon in these lyrics. There is an attempt to capture some of the lightness of tone and opacity that Heaney had admired in his 1978 RTE review of *Mules* and an obvious relationship with the lyrics and narratives of mysterious flight in *Why Brownlee Left* and *Quoof* (where Heaney's 'Broagh' is itself parodied).[16] Interestingly, another Joyce appears in the *Station Island* volume in 'A Bat on the Road': the sensitive, fugitive, self-conscious spirit implied in Stephen's reference to the "batlike soul" of his race in *A Portrait*.[17] Writing itself is defined here and in the 'Sweeney Redivivus' lyrics as flitting, fugitive, verging on the pathological (as in the critical work of one of Heaney's earliest supporters, Karl Miller[18]), as a kind of mental fugue or flight.

In *Sweeney Astray*, rather than being a heroic Joycean exile Sweeney is a shy Celtic soul, a defeated combatant with the ascendant Christian forces of moral authority. Like many of Yeats's early Celticist writings, the romance lends itself to be read as a drama-tisation of the historical and ideological conflict between Christianity and whatever opposed, opposes or evades it in Irish history. Heaney stresses that the figure of Sweeney is not mythic in the sense of that of Finn or Cuchulain but is "historically situated" and represents "a tension between the newly dominant Christian ethos and the older, recalcitrant Celtic temperament."[19] As in 'The Wanderings of Oisin', the story is told with a sympathetic perspective on the wandering, the defeated, the pre- or non-Christian, the "shy and wounded temperament" of Ernest Renan and Matthew Arnold's Celtic idea that becomes a melancholic Faustian metaphor for modern art.[20]

Such a plunge into myth may in itself be seen as something of a regressive gesture, an attempt to return to the pre-Oedipal world of Yeats's earliest poetry that, at least under the Leavisite programme of modern literary values, critics had been happy to repress or to ignore.[21] Flann O'Brien, as Heaney's note points out, was the last writer to give currency to the myth and in his *At Swim-Two-Birds* was profoundly double about the myth.[22] At one level he used it as a parody of the Celtic twilight and displays a kind of irreverent student resentment at its imposition on the Irish education system. At another level it provides a curiously valid myth for a novel whose commitment to literary artificiality and experiment properly demand a deliberately anti-mythological attitude. The story of the recusant monarch and his flight into madness becomes an emblem of modern madness and the Absurd. The whole book, by its very title, is, as modern culture seemed to be in 1939, at Swim-Two-Birds and places the artist in the postmodern tragi-comic situtation in which O'Brien found James Joyce:

> Sitting fully dressed, innerly locked in the toilet of a locked coach where he has no right to be, resentfully drinking someone else's whiskey, being whisked hither and thither by anonymous shunters, keeping fastidiously the while on the outer face of his door the simple word, ENGAGED.[23]

Heaney's embrace of the myth represents an ability to be reconciled to self and to community far more than O'Brien with his "transgressor's resentment of the nongressor" ever could have been but is in some ways more similar than might at first appear. At any rate to erect too hasty a contrast between the inspired and inebriated prophet of postmodern chaos and some regressive neo-Arnoldian moralist would serve as no valid representation of either author.

Heaney stresses the tragedy of Sweeney's defeat. The cleric asks if he be contented and he replies:

> I am so terrified,
> so panicky, so haunted
> I dare not bat an eyelid.

> The flight of a small wren
> scares me as much, bell-man,
> as a great expedition
> out to hunt me down.

In his version, as in O'Brien's, the myth becomes an occasion to re-open the debate that is now most familiarly glossed as a debate about artistic autonomy: whether its necessary freedoms outweigh its undoubted costs.[24] It retranslates Heaney's other self-translating translation, the Ugolino story from Cantos XXII and XXIII of Dante's *Inferno*, where, in that circle of Hell set aside for those guilty of treachery, Dante is far quicker to condemn the savagery of the punishers than the "traitor".[25] Though there may be differences of emphasis, both Heaney and O'Brien might be using a myth to demonstrate the inevitable conundrum by which we realise that a pure artistic autonomy can be as mad as even a limitedly constrained art can be dull.

Heaney's introductory note asserts that his main reason for translating the Sweeney poem is his immersion in its topography, its sense of place. That is once again to leave unsaid on grounds of taste the obvious self-punishing of the pun on Heaney's own name. In this, of course, it forms a companion to Muldoon's 'Immram' with its equally unstated punning dependence on the "Immram Mael Duin".[26] Both poets engage in the practice not so much of par-onomasia as of autonomasia: an authorial self-naming that might suggestively be placed in the context of Michel Foucault's idea (which Salman Rushdie has recently had cause to quote) that the very concept of authorial identification came into existence when discourses became transgressive and "to the extent that authors became subject to punishment".[27]

Of the two poets, Muldoon's mixture of postmodernism and myth is more apparently O'Brienesque. Mixture is the artistic quality that Muldoon celebrates throughout his work: in, for instance, the mules of the poem 'Mules' that might "have the best of both worlds" and the surrealistically mixed images that are the "centaurs" in the poem of that name.[28] He offers (as in the line in 'The More a Man has the More a Man Wants') "a shamrock after the school/ of Pollock, Jackson Pollock", leaving us to wonder whether that is a representational possibility or a joke at his own expense.[29] He uses myth and puns on names in the McEwan-esque surreal sexual nightmare 'Whim' where a whimsical *CuChulain* (who appears as a modern urban Don Juan) suffers an obscene, canine fate that the punning potential of his name (which means the hound of Chulain) might be said to foreshadow. Muldoon can translate himself into an Oisin of whose ageing return to the land of time he says "I know something of how he felt" and a post-Leopold Bloom Odysseus for whom sexual uncertainty might suggest that he should have taken his bow with him, not left it at home with Penelope.[30]

Most of all though, he is the hero of 'Immram': a quest poem done in a Chandleresque mode that is the mirror image of Heaney's. One poem may be read as a search for; the other as an escape from. In Heaney's poem the defeated fugitive tries to escape but finds that the only sanctuary is with the opponent from whom he flees. In Muldoon the son's search for a father turns out to be a disappointment: a revolving door rather than a "door into the dark" where the father may not be an original but may rather be more 'modern' than the son. It is a confrontation with the fact that originals are always lost, never recoverable, that the goals of an insatiable post-Freudian desire may be nothing more than self-delusion and that the act of searching may only reveal the traces of the searching that has been done before.

The extent to which, and the level at which Muldoon's poetry also takes on the question of artistic autonomy can be seen in 'Lunch with Pancho Villa' where the politician's rebuke of the poet's lack of relevance turns into a self-destructive, self-inverting quest that is a parodic exaggeration of the movement seen in Heaney. He also treats the relationship between naming and the submission to authority in 'Anseo': a poem that is one of the most telling of all recent poems from the North of Ireland in its contribution to the politics-of-language debate. Here the poet recounts how in his school, when register was taken and names read out, he replied with "Anseo": "the first word of Irish I spoke". That reply, it would seem, defines him as a political subject in relation to language within the society of the classroom and, still further, serves to define the class scapegoat Joseph Mary Plunkett Ward who becomes the commander of a hideaway paramilitary group where he can exact the same subjection in the same response.[31] Not least among the postmodern features of Muldoon's poetry is the extent to which we may be tempted to read it as a mocking translation or parody of Heaneyan modes. Rather than displacing the original as different, as an old Icarian father to a new Dedalian son, this may, of course, serve rather to bring out the postmodernism latent in the original itself.

Self-translation, the possibility of artistic autonomy and indeed punning on names are all renegotiated in '7, Middagh Street', the extraordinary long poem that concludes Muldoon's *Meeting the British*.[32] Perhaps itself a translation of 'Station Island', the poem is an overtly postmodern literary pilgrimage, written as a series of parodic monologues that combine the voices of the cultural ghosts that inhabit the New York apartment building of the title: Auden, Gypsy Rose Lee, Benjamin Britten, Salvador Dali, Carson McCullers and Louis MacNeice. From Auden's point of view Yeats's worries about the political impact of his art are nonsense:

> If Yeats had saved his pencil-lead
> would certain men have stayed in bed?

The unpeeling layers of significance in Yeats's symbolic rose have, courtesy of David Lodge's Morris Zapp,[33] become the deft unpeeling of the art of striptease:

> It's knowing exactly when to stop
> that matters,
> what to hold back, some sweet disorder . . .
> The same goes for the world of letters.

The last word, though, ties up the twisting circle of the roller coaster by reminding us in the quoted voice of Lorca through MacNeice that (in MacNeice's case at least) assumptions about names may be deceptive and that:

> poetry *can* make things happen—
> not only can, but *must*—

Though to call this or anything the last word in a poem like '7, Middagh Street' would be to miss its parodic, punning, postmodern and MacNeicean point that:

> World is crazier and more of it than we think,
> Incorrigeably plural.[34]

To arrive at these readings is, in part, to offer a retrospect on important aspects of the cultural scene of the 1980s. Some significant relation clearly exists between the watershed moments of English political neo-Victorianism, the collapse of literary criticism into the literary theories of Marxism, Feminism and Deconstruction, the identification of Joyce in the massive Joyce Centenary Year Celebration as *the* exemplary modern writer, the identification of contemporary poetry as the poetry of Northern Ireland, the 'Martian' ethos of the *Penguin Book of Contemporary British Poetry*. The establishment of Heaney as the essential poetic voice of the decade and of his concerns of artistic autonomy as the essential writerly concerns form an important part of this pattern. It is a pattern which may seem local in its significance but rapidly comes to seem global at the end of the decade as the political power of artists and the traditional belief in national identities is confirmed in the revolutions in Eastern Europe and as the madness or impossibility of artistic autonomy is tested out again in the affair of *The Satanic Verses*.

To impose any simple set of relations or to offer any simplistic interpretation of them would clearly be in error, but connections of this scale, rather than ones which only refer to locality or to province, may need to be drawn to understand the politics of a poet in the postmodern world. To see Heaney as implicated in this larger pattern would not be to depoliticise but to repoliticise his poetry at what he has called in *The Haw Lantern* the "frontier of writing":[35] a frontier that may subtly overlap with the literary frontiers created by the last writings of Joyce and Yeats, the departure for America by Auden, the going underground of Samuel Beckett or into a dark tunnel by Flann O'Brien in 1939.

We may remember the invitation made by Orson Welles, as he grumbled into the camera in *The Third Man*, to consider the warring nations of the world and their rich artistic harvest on the one hand, whilst on the other hand he asks of neutral Switzerland: "What has it produced? The cuckoo clock." It is, of course, an old wartime joke and, moreover, one that denies the real artistic contributions made by Switzerland not least to the pacific ocean of Joyce's art. In the criticism of Heaney's poetry it has become familiar to talk of war: a talk to which the poetry itself responds in the subtle and moving elegy on Ireland's Wilfred Owen, the First World War poet Francis Ledwidge.

Heaney celebrates Ledwidge's belonging to Irish place and his nostalgic Georgian "twilit note". He is himself nostalgic for it, though careful also to see Ledwidge as a "dead enigma" in whom "all the strains/Criss-cross in useless equilibrium". For what we should never forget is that 'war poetry' itself may be a kind of Georgianism and that nostalgia for Georgian simplicities may at its worst topple over into a dangerous nostalgia for the simplicity of a Georgian kind of war. We should, of course, as readers of poetry, be able to be wary of our metaphors. But equally we must find some formula which does full justice to the telling 'motto' of one of the most powerful (according to Harold Bloom, most "perfect"[36]) of lyrics, 'The Harvest Bow':

> '*The end of art is peace.*'

This is a profoundly simple, profoundly Keatsian and yet also, like Keats's in the 'Ode on a Grecian Urn', a profoundly ambiguous conclusion. It is with its pun on the end (since an end may either be a goal or an extinction) that I conclude. But to stress the importance to Heaney's and Muldoon's art of such ambiguities as this need not be to argue, as Edna Longley has seemed to do in her *Poetry in the Wars*, for a purely autonomous, depoliticised place of art.[37] It is rather to suggest that another "chosen ground" (or to use the title of his recent Richard Ellmann lecture, another "place of writing") that Heaney has made his own, is one that is arguably some way from the Ulster of "Armoured cars and tanks and guns", and is the self-generating, self-consuming postmodern Switzerland of the pun.

## NOTES

1. Reprinted in Jonathan Barker (ed.), *Thirty Years of the Poetry Book Society* (London: Hutchinson, 1986), pp. 126–7.
2. Seamus Heaney, *North* (London: Faber & Faber, 1975), pp. 41 and 14.
3. Seamus Heaney, *Death of a Naturalist* (London: Faber and Faber, 1966), pp. 13–14.
4. Goya, 'Fight with Cudgels' (1820–23), Prado (Madrid).
5. Blake Morrison and Andrew Motion (eds.), *The Penguin Book of Contemporary British Poetry* (Harmondsworth: Penguin, 1982) and Heaney's *An Open Letter* (Derry: Field Day, 1982).
6. See, for instance, Fredric Jameson, 'Postmodernism: The Cultural Logic of Late Capitalism', *New Left Review* 146 (July/August 1984).
7. Seamus Deane, 'The Artist and the Troubles' in Tim Pat Coogan (ed.), *Ireland and the Arts* (London: Quartet Books, 1988), pp. 42–50.
8. Gregory Ulmer, 'The Puncept in Grammatology' in Jonathan Culler (ed.), *On Puns* (Oxford: Blackwell, 1988).
9. Blake Morrison, *Seamus Heaney* (London: Methuen, 1982), p.64.
10. See, for instance, Thomas Sheridan, *The Art of Punning* (Dublin and London, 1719), attributed to Jonathan Swift, or Swift's own 'A Modest Defence of Punning'.
11. Morrison, p. 79 and Neil Corcoran, *Seamus Heaney* (London: Faber & Faber, 1986), p. 137.
12. Seamus Heaney, *Field Work* (London: Faber & Faber, 1979), p. 23.
13. Seamus Heaney, *Station Island* (London: Faber & Faber, 1984), pp. 92–4. [It is worth

noting that the version of 'Station Island' printed in Heaney's *New Selected Poe. 1966–1987* (London: Faber & Faber, 1990) omits this Joycean reference. Ed.]

14. Seamus Heaney, "Leaving the Island", *James Joyce Broadsheet*, No. 8 (June 1982), p.5.
15. Seamus Heaney, *Sweeney Astray* (London: Faber & Faber, 1984).
16. Seamus Heaney, 'The Mixed Marriage', review of Paul Muldoon's *Mules* (London: Faber & Faber, 1977), in *Preoccupations* (London: Faber & Faber, 1980), pp. 211–3; Paul Muldoon *Why Brownlee Left* (London: Faber and Faber, 1980) and *Quoof* (London: Faber & Faber, 1983).
17. *Station Island*, pp. 40–1.
18. Karl Miller, *Doubles* (Oxford: Oxford University Press, 1984).
19. *Sweeney Astray*, Introduction, n.pag.
20. Matthew Arnold, *On the Study of Celtic Literature* (London: Everyman, 1976), p.80.
21. F.R. Leavis, *New Bearings in English Poetry* (Harmondsworth: Penguin, 1963), p.34, where Leavis praises the "public and practical aim" of Yeats's poetry.
22. Flann O'Brien (Brian O'Nolan), *At Swim-Two-Birds* (London: Longmans, Green, 1939).
23. Flann O'Brien (Brian O'Nolan), 'A Bash in the Tunnel', reprinted in *Stories and Plays* (London: Hart-Davis MacGibbon, 1973), p.17.
24. See Terry Eagleton, *The Ideology of the Aesthetic* (Oxford: Blackwell, 1990).
25. *Field Work*, pp. 61–4.
26. Paul Muldoon, 'Immram' in *Why Brownlee Left*, pp. 38–47. Muldoon's note (p. 48) reads "I am indebted to Whitley Stokes's translation of 'Immram Mael Duin' (*Revue Celtique* IX-X)." This, the author has told me in conversation, is a joke.
27. Michel Foucault's essay 'What is an Author?', recently discussed by Salman Rushdie in his Herbert Read Memorial Lecture 'Is Nothing Sacred?', *Granta* 31 (Spring 1990), pp. 106–7.
28. *Mules*, p. 14.
29. Paul Muldoon, *Selected Poems* (London: Faber, 1983), p. 105.
30. *Why Brownlee Left*, p. 7; 'Armageddon, Armageddon' in *Mules*, p. 54; *Making the Move* in *Why Brownlee Left*, p. 32.
31. *Why Brownlee Left*, pp. 20–21.
32. *Meeting the British* (London: Faber & Faber, 1987).
33. David Lodge, *Small World* (Harmondsworth: Penguin, 1985), pp. 25–7. The fictional character Morris Zapp is sometimes said to have been based on the reader-response critic Stanley Fish.
34. Louis MacNeice, 'Snow', in *Collected Poems* ed. E.R. Dodds (London: Faber & Faber, 1966), p.30.
35. Seamus Heaney, "The Frontier of Writing" in *The Haw lantern* (London: Faber and Faber, 1989).
36. Harold Bloom, review of *Field Work*, *TLS*, 8 February 1980.
37. Edna Longley, *Poetry in The Wars* (Newcastle: Bloodaxe, 1986), p.210.

**Bernard O'Donoghue**
Involved Imaginings: Tom Paulin

# Involved Imaginings

The criticisms most commonly made of the poetry of Tom Paulin are, firstly, that it is over-cryptic, and, secondly, that it is more directly concerned with politics than it is proper for poetry to be. In this essay I want to argue that the crypticism is precisely a product of the reluctance to be political in a campaigning way, though Paulin's language and terms of reference are unflinchingly drawn from the public domain. There is no doubt that, in the Western European literary tradition, it is decidely *against* a poet's interests to descend to the political, in our era at least; I want to suggest that Paulin is particularly disinterested in this respect in that his concern with politics runs counter to all his aesthetic and literary instincts. But that a writer of his generation and geographical origins should be concerned with political realities is inevitable, as the following outline of his background establishes.

Paulin was born in Leeds in 1949.[1] His mother is a doctor from Northern Ireland and his father a teacher from Tyneside in the North East of England. When he was four, the family moved to Belfast where his father became a headmaster. Paulin lived and went to school there until 1967 when he went to Hull to do an English degree. In 1970 he went on to Lincoln College, Oxford where he did a B.Litt. on the poetry of Hardy (the basis of his *Thomas Hardy: The Poetry of Perception*, published by Macmillan in 1975). Since 1972 he has lectured in English at the University of Nottingham, where he was appointed Reader in poetry in 1989. To date he has published four main volumes of poetry, all with Faber: *A State of Justice* (1977), *The Strange Museum* (1980), *Liberty Tree* (1983), and *Fivemiletown* (1987). In addition, an important section of *Liberty Tree* was published by Bloodaxe in 1981 under the title *The Book of Juniper*, with drawings by Noel Connor. He has also published a volume of essays and journalism, *Ireland and the English Crisis* (Bloodaxe 1984), and he is the editor of the controversial *Faber Book of Political Verse* (1986). His *Faber Book of Vernacular Verse* was published in 1990.

He is a director of the Field Day Theatre Company in Derry; his fellow-directors are the poets Seamus Deane and Seamus Heaney, singer and broadcaster David Hammond, novelist and playwright Tom Kilroy, and the two founders of the company, playwright Brian Friel and actor Stephen Rea. He has had three plays published by Faber: in 1985 a version of Sophocles's *Antigone* called *The Riot Act* (first staged by Field Day in 1984); in 1987 *The Hillsborough Convention*; and *Seize the Fire*, a dramatic version of *Prometheus Bound*, in spring 1990. Field Day also publishes a continuing pamphlet-series on literary and historical matters, principally concerned with Northern Irish politics, and attempting to represent all Ulster viewpoints (though traditional Unionist opinion, perhaps with some justice, feels itself under-represented, here as in other forums). The first series in 1983 included Paulin's 'A New Look at the Language Question', arguing the desirability of *A Dictionary Of Irish English*, corresponding to Webster's American Dictionary or the acclaimed *Concise Scots Dictionary*.[2] The objective of such a dictionary would be to recognize the separateness of English usage in Ireland from Standard English whose locus Paulin defines as centring on the House of Commons with a patriotic tendency, when pressed, to "speak for England". This essay[3] is still a good introduction to the complex of Paulin's Ulster and Irish loyalties, as sympathetic to Ian Adamson's 'The Language of Ulster'[4] as to traditional discussions of English in Ireland generally.[5] If anything, since 1983 his Ulster affiliations have become more marked and his declared distaste for the politics of the southern Irish Republic more pronounced.

Paulin first came prominently to notice in the second half of the 1970s, as one of the principal figures (a recognition shared with his contemporaries Paul Muldoon and Medbh McGuckian) in the second wave of the post-1969 Ulster poets (though of course clear differentiation of such waves is always problematical). 1969 was the year of the first prominent Civil Rights marches from which the current series of 'Troubles' is traditionally dated. Paulin supported the Civil Rights movement strongly, in common with most poets on all sides of the Ulster poetry-politics community, including some who now diverge from his views with vehemence, such as James Simmons and Michael Longley. Even before 1969, divided politics and the feeling that "that kind of thing could start again"[6] had remained a grumbling undercurrent in Ulster poetry, not only in Heaney and Montague on the Catholic side but also in a less focused way in Protestant poets like MacNeice and 'mannerly' John Hewitt, a socialist poet of a much earlier generation whose standing has risen dramatically in the past twenty years, earning him in 1988 the ultimate Irish literary recognition, a summer school.[7]

It is worth noting in passing that, with the major exception of Richard Murphy, southern Irish poetry of that pre-1969 era was strikingly different, in ways that English criticism still largely ignores. Concern there was predominantly with country life and/or constitutional politics (usually satirically represented): the tradition from Austin Clarke to Thomas McCarthy.[8] A recent exponent of this tradition, Paul Durcan, *has* been taken up, partly perhaps because of the modishly revisionist interpretation that has been taken of his poetry. Patrick Kavanagh belongs here, championed by the *Honest Ulsterman* in the early 1970s as a martyr to the perfidy of Flann O'Brien and the southern capital Dublin, "the meanest little city since Carthage" according to a 1972 issue of the *Ulsterman* (reflecting a rather partial reading of ancient history, it might seem).

But, if the explicitly political was not entirely avoided in Ulster or any Irish poetry between 1940 and 1969, it became impossible to ignore political realities in Ulster after that date. Heaney's experience provides the classic case, a minatory headline for later poets such as Paulin and Muldoon. Heaney moved to the south of Ireland in 1972, pursued by the catcalls of the Paisleyite *Protestant Telegraph* as it bade farewell to "the well- known Papist propagandist". Literary relations too reflected, in more moderate terms, the strains imposed by the 'Troubles': Michael Longley's fine *Selected Poems* in 1984 was a melancholy reminder of days of common purpose, containing exchange poems between himself, Heaney, James Simmons and Derek Mahon—a grouping now broken up in a series of complicated fissures.

This is the context, then, in which the emergence of Paulin's poetry has to be seen, and it should be borne in mind when evaluating the charges against him of an excessively overt 'politicism'. Within that context *A State of Justice* (1977) was a very resonant title, adapted from 'A Just State', one of a series of bleak, violently-expressed political poems in the middle of the volume which ends

> The shadows of watchtowers on public squares,
> A hemp noose over a grease trap.

Reviewers interpreted such poems—neither surprisingly nor in-accurately—as having express reference to Northern Ireland. But their reference is also much wider, bearing more generally on the politics of this momentous last quarter of the twentieth century. The more political poems in this volume (and in fact there are not many in which the politics is overt—which is not, of course, to say that politics are irrelevant to the others) had been published separately in an *Ulsterman* pamphlet under a title which uses a line from one of these poems, 'Theoretical Locations' (from 'The Hyperboreans': a title which evokes Heaney's *North*). 'A Just State' suggests comparison with Eastern European writers like Mandelstam, and clearly applies to any state. The first poem of *A State of Justice* bears the significantly plural title 'States':

> That stretch of water, it's always
> There for you to cross over
> To the other shore, observing
> The lights of cities on blackness.

Certainly this applies well to England-Ireland, but it is an Auden-esque *paysage moralisé*, concerned with general problems of affiliation and political restlessness: the universal dilemma of creating a perfect state to identify with, which is a major set theme in Irish poetry after Yeats. Paulin is already a political idealist, in the tradition of eighteenth-century European republicanism (which he would insist has nothing to do with twentieth-century Irish republicanism).

A *State of Justice* was an acclaimed first volume, nominated as the Choice of the Poetry Book Society in London: a coveted accolade. It is a diverse volume, ranging in theme and subject more widely than its single-minded title and first poem suggest. The poems were written in part while Paulin was working on Hardy, and we might remember in reading poems like 'Under a Roof' that Paulin was a student at Hull during Larkin's librarianship:

> It'll piss all evening now. From next door
> The usual man and woman stuff rants on, then fades.

The second line here sounds like Larkin rounded off by Yeats; indeed some of the most assured poems in the book are in the romantic traditions of which Paulin has always declared a very jaundiced view. But we soon learn, going through Paulin's work, not to expect his affiliations and oppositions to be single-minded or univocal; infamous cases in point are his views of Conor Cruise O'Brien, Ian Paisley and Marxist criticism. It is as if, like Yeats, the poet has a radical distrust of middle-of-the-road, liberal views; this unpredictability is an important element in the effectiveness and vitality of his later poetry. Throughout his work, concern for social responsibility and answerability occurs side by side with assertions of the artistic freedom of the individual against the constraints of consensus. The competing polarities are memorably expressed at the admired, romantic conclusion of 'Inishkeel Parish Church':

> O Absalom, Absalom, my son,
> An hour is too long, there are too many people,
> Too many heads and eyes and thoughts that clutter . . .
>
> Then, before the recognitions and the talk,
> There was an enormous sight of the sea,
> A silent water beyond society.

There are other accomplished romantic moments, such as 'From' with its lyrical ending, "A soft grass covers them and light falls," or the aphoristic "Hard wood is worn by the stone,/So is stone by the softness of feet." Side by side with such romanticism we already find the harshness of diction that has come to be seen as Paulin's most characteristic quality: "the crossroads loony smashed to bits"; "wooden huts on the permafrost"; "something made a fuck of things"; "my loathsome uncle chews his rasher"; "a rain of turds".

The impression given is of an inventive poet under various influences, experimenting for a stable voice; as a parallel his friend Douglas Dunn's uneasy mixture of Scottish, declaredly socialist politics with a romantic declaration of the hegemony of the imagination, comes to mind. But, even if there was unevenness of diction and subject, Paulin was unmistakably a writer of considerable originality and confident forcefulness. What is distinctive in him is a readiness to bring avowedly political reference into his poetry, free of the cosmetic reworking that traditionally precedes its introduction into Western European poetry. To take one example of this quotidian politics, 'Thinking of Iceland' uses the Auden-MacNeice *Letters from Iceland* as a frame for a sociological description of urban Northern Ireland, using Auden's anthropologist's eye. In the course of it though, there is a passing stab at Richard Crossman to whom Auden and MacNeice wrote one of the letters 'unfortunately': the fact is unfortunate simply because Paulin was outraged that Crossman as editor of the *New Statesman* in 1971 argued for Irish unification.

It is a slight instance, but it offers a good discussion point for Paulin: both to see how he proceeds and how he has been partly mis-understood, even by his most distinguished critics such as Edna Longley. Longley has tended to assume two things about him which I think are false: first, that he is a radical critical theorist like his friend and Field Day colleague Seamus Deane.[9] She accordingly opposes him to the writers, from Edward Thomas to Mandelstam to Derek Mahon, who argue for the authority of the poetic imagination over political reality and opinion. Yet this is just the kind of ground on which Paulin swipes Crossman's opinion aside here, and he has argued consistently on this side throughout his career. The second wrong assumption of Longley (and others) about Paulin is that he is well-disposed to the Irish Republic or to the possibility of its subsuming Ulster as a political unity centred on the Dáil; this assumption is implicit when Paulin is described in the misleading phrase "zealous convert".[10] Paulin certainly writes and speaks with zeal, but he is not a convert to anything; as Longley argues elsewhere in that same chapter, his critical spirit is at its most forceful when it is most negative.

If there was no single major influence on *A State of Justice*, there is an important poetic relationship with John Hewitt. Like Paulin, Hewitt had a teacher-father and was an outsider sympathetic to the Northern Irish working class, similarly so across any sectarian divide (though here Hewitt, unlike Paulin, has the occasional lapse). Like Paulin's, part of Hewitt's working life was spent in England (fifteen years in Coventry); they are similarly drawn to the pastoral 'civility' of the English countryside, as a comparison of Paulin's uncollected poem 'The Argument at Great Tew'[11] with Hewitt's Cotswold poems bears out. So it is relevant to note Hewitt's manifesto from the *Irish Times* (4 July 1974), quoted by Alan Warner in his introduction to the *Selected John Hewitt*:

> I'm an Ulsterman, of planter stock. I was born in the island of Ireland, so secondarily I'm an Irishman. I was born in the British archipelago and English is my native tongue, so I am British. The British archipelago consists of offshore islands to the continent of Europe, so I'm European. This is my hierarchy of values and as far as I am concerned anyone who omits one step of that sequence is falsifying the situation.[12]

These are not Paulin's terms; he would not use the apriorist phrase 'British archipelago', and he would be less keen to press for the appellation British. But there is the same dilemma of loyalties, combined with a generosity of spirit expressed in the socialist embrace of all orders, racial or religious. John Montague described Hewitt as "the first (and probably the last) deliberately Ulster, Protestant poet"; again, if this doesn't exactly evoke Paulin's self-definition, it surely describes his subject, inspiration and tradition. What is more, it has become increasingly true throughout his career.

If Edna Longley is right to see Paulin's critical gift as negative, the same is not true of his poetic imagination with its tendency towards the burgeoningly romantic. What Alan Robinson (in one of the best discussions of Paulin to date) calls his "recent recourse to stylistic hermeticism"[13] is already incipient in Paulin's next book *The Strange Museum* (1980) which is more difficult from its first page. It was published in 1980, and it is instructive to bear in mind something Paulin wrote in 1983, in the Introduction to *Ireland and the English Crisis*:

> Until about 1980 I took a different view and believed what most Ulster Protestants still believe—that Northern Ireland was, and ought to remain, permanently wedded to Great Britain. Although I had always hated Ulster Unionism very bitterly and supported the Civil Rights movement from the beginning, I believed that Civil Rights and greater social justice in Northern Ireland could be achieved within the context of the United Kingdom. I rejoiced, therefore, at the fall of Stormont and the same week attacked a Provo supporter who was selling nationalist newspapers . . . But there was something different in the air as the decade ended. I started reading Irish history again and found myself drawn to John Hume's eloquence, his humane and constitutional politics. (p.16)

While the most recurrent image in *A State of Justice* was a state or states, here the focal notion, which has remained central in Paulin's work since, is *history* and its complex relations with contemporary reality.[14] The first poem in *The Strange Museum* is called 'Before History'; it eloquently summarises, in a more assured form, the abstract state, the theoretical location, of the political poems in the earlier volume (as well, incidentally, as anticipating impressively the cold political austerities of 1980s Britain):

> This is the long lulled pause
> Before history happens,

> When the spirit hungers for form,
> Knowing that love is as distant
> As the guarded capital, knowing
> That the tyranny of memories
> And factual establishments
> Has stretched to its breaking.

The volume contains a good deal of lonely hunger for the provincial familiarity of Belfast. But in general the same diversity of theme and form as in *A State of Justice* is in evidence: there is still some uncertainty of tone in a tendency towards pastiche ("hell is very like those Sunday streets" from 'In the Egyptian Gardens') and a rather dry banality ("And academic fellows/ File limericks by the score" from 'Song for February').

There is also a very different personal, lyrical element in some of the poems which should be seen in a biographical context: Paulin and his wife had a car crash in which his wife was badly injured, and she was kept in hospital in Belfast while he lived alone in Nottingham for six months. So some poems here represent an interruption of his thematic development, in the same way that Douglas Dunn's *Elegies* (written on the premature death of his wife) do. The last poem in the book, 'A Lyric Afterwards', represents Paulin's generosity of vision at its most eloquent:

> In your absence I climbed to a square room
> where there were dried flowers, folders of sonnets
> and crossword puzzles . . .
>                 Their bitter
> constraints and formal pleasures were a style
> of being perfect in despair . . .
>
> But that is changed now, and when I see you
> walking by the river, a step from me,
> there is this great kindness everywhere:
> now in the grace of the world and always.

As for the central political strand of the poetry, *The Strange Museum* is a gloomy, even despairing volume, perhaps because of the hardening of hostilities in Northern Ireland into a grim normality. The positive figure of John Hewitt has receded, and the prevailing spirit in many of the poems is a listlessness, unrelieved by much excitement, positive or negative. The term 'mitteleuropa' (Paulin's concentration on which reads prophetically in 1990 as the Russian Empire crumbles) echoes as an evocation of a kind of Sartrian *anomie* from the first poem through several of the others—'Second-Rate Republics', for instance. Similarly, the words 'neap' and 'neapish' appear first here, to recur as expressions of this anomic state of mind in Paulin's poetry and criticism. But an important development is that the theoretical locations are becoming *less* theoretical and more inescapably real; the grey state, with its suggestions of menace, is more explicitly identified with circumstances in Northern Ireland. 'Surveillances' moves from the gulag of its first stanza, the overlooked state (which is 'theoretical' as an image for us), to the Northern Irish image of the surveying helicopter in the second stanza with its brilliant real/unreal closing image: "All this might be happening/ Underwater." The most successful, and most anthologized, poem in the book, 'Anastasia McLaughlin', explicitly marries the Russian and Irish experiences, making one historical event the matrix of another (like a medieval typologist), in the same way that 'Thinking of Iceland' did:

> Her father is sick. He dozes most afternoons.
> The nurse makes tea then and scans *The Newsletter* . . .
>
> He sees his son below the bruised Atlantic,
> And on a summer's morning in Great Victoria Street
> He talks with Thomas Ferguson outside the Iceworks.
> He sees the north stretched out upon the mountains,
> Its dream of fair weather rubbing a bloom on rinsed slates;
> He watches the mills prosper and grow derelict,
> As he starts his journey to the Finland Station.

At this stage of his career Paulin was prominent as polemicist as well as poet, particularly in the heated debates on critical theory. His twin concerns are reflected in the title of his book of essays *Ireland and the English Crisis*; indeed it is commonly felt that the two concerns do not gel very naturally. As late as June 1983, Paulin was still mounting a vigorous attack in an interview with *Oxford Poetry*[15] on what he saw as the negative, destructive element in post-structuralism, accusing Marxist criticism of putting Joyce on "the same level as an advertisement for haemorrhoid cures or the novels of David Lodge". Raymond Williams gets a tick for "some good work done years ago" but is accused now of writing awful prose and having "no love of

poetry", by contrast with the "passion and courage" of Christopher
Ricks and the "noble and inspiring polemic" at the end of Helen
Gardner's *In Defence of the Imagination.*

The fact that Paulin has now modified these views (in some cases,
indeed, reversed them as he brings his radical politics to bear on
literature) should not be allowed to detract from the fundamental
consistency here. He has always emphasized the hegemony of the
creative imagination, as preached by the European Romantics and
their successors in twentieth-century Russia: Mandelstam is the
principal copytext for modern writers. In that same trenchant
interview, he declared his admiration for Derek Mahon and Paul
Muldoon as "pure artists, exemplary figures", defending them
against the charge of turning their backs on political realities in
Northern Ireland. Though Paulin himself has always employed
public matter in his poems, he would stand absolutely by what he says
about Mahon and Muldoon.

The same apparent shift in attitude towards critical theory was
clearly documented in 1982–3. Paulin made a fierce attack in the
*London Review of Books* on Peter Widdowson's *Re-Reading English*
(Methuen *New Accents* 1982) as destructive of this notion of
free artistic expression. But he was even more dismayed by two
rejoinders to the *New Accents* series: *Reconstructing Literature* by
Lawrence Lerner and *Counter-Modernism in Current Critical Theory*
by Geoffrey Thurley (both 1983). In a footnote in *Ireland and the
English Crisis* (p.14) he writes "Both works are remarkable for their
espousal of an aggressive, bullish nationalism, and for their dedication
to an unexamined concept called the 'Anglo-Saxon' mind."

A split between Paulin's *literary* commitment to Gardner-Ricks
and his socialist political convictions was bound to come: it is as if
something had to give, and it is tempting to say that it was his critical
posture that yielded, in conflict with the passionately held subjects of
his poetry. But it is not as simple as that; the poetry has always (and
increasingly) been a complex amalgam of the two sets of convictions,
combining a rather puritan notion of perfectibility with a sense of the
urgent need for greater justice in the body politic. This is a tradition
long pre-dating Romanticism in the English tradition, founded in
Paulin's view of Milton, as his controversial introduction to the *Faber
Book of Political Verse* spells out. It might be seen as the conflict
between two radical traditions: Mandelstam's hunger for freedom for
the literary imagination, as against the English radical tradition
which, paradoxically, perhaps finds its most powerful expression in

the French Revolution as seen by the younger Wordsworth and Tom Paine, and its most potent counter-image in Burke (who accordingly features prominently in Paulin's poetical ethics).[16] Put crudely, the direction of Paulin's development is partially explained by the fact that in present-day Britain freedom of expression is less under threat than the living standards of the unemployed working classes, or the lack of peace for the people of Northern Ireland.

It is increasingly felt though that these issues too are interrelated. Certainly, the relation between them does recall the two concerns of the title of his essays, Ireland (politics) and the English crisis (literary/ artistic freedom). This tension was partly released by finding expression in what I think was Paulin's finest large achievement before *Fivemiletown's* 'The Caravans on Lüneburg Heath', *The Book of Juniper*, published separately by Bloodaxe in 1981 and incorporated in his third full volume, *Liberty Tree*, in 1983. The conclusion of the long and difficult title poem of *The Book of Juniper* has often been quoted, with admiration for the inspirational bringing together of images of the ill-fated, limited extension of the French Revolution to the west of Ireland in 1798 (Killala), and of the trees emblematic of Ireland, North and South, and—unforgettably—of England at the end:

> and I imagine
> that a swelling army is marching
> from Memory Harbour and Killala
> carrying branches
> of green juniper . . .
>
> now dream
> of that sweet
> equal republic
> where the juniper
> talks to the oak,
> the thistle,
> the bandaged elm,
> and the jolly jolly chestnut.

This poem was the flagship and the finest achievement in a book whose coherence and compulsion marked a major advance in Paulin's poetry. All the earlier effects are put to effective common purpose here; the asperities of tone draw on a Northern Irish dialect as a linguistic correlative to Ulster's social and political mix. Like Muldoon, Paulin uses terms coined by John Hewitt from local usage, and extends the practice. A wry poem of Hewitt's, 'The Lass of Richmond Hill; or the Royal Garden Party' (1969) is evoked by Paulin's mythology. Listening to a Belfast band in Jubilee Year playing 'The Lass of Richmond Hill' sets Hewitt's narrator on a Paulinesque train of historical association:

> when the United Irishmen marched in
> to Antrim town that other June day,
> the young men in green jackets, the leaders,
> tried to sing 'The Marseillaise',
> the proper anthem for revolutions,
> and none of the pikemen-peasants knew it . . .
> But Jemmy Hope, that reliable man
> who never postured, rallied all
> by striking-up 'The Lass of Richmond Hill',
> which most knew anyway.
> So, in step together, they swung
> down the long street to meet the enemy.

As well as the allusion to Jemmy Hope the weaver, well-attested in Paulin, there is the same admiration for the complex motivation of the Protestant revolutionaries of 1798 as in *Liberty Tree*. The 'liberty tree' was the icon of French Revolutionary radicalism as it was represented in Ireland (and Britain) in the 1790s, so it provides an inspired symbol for the complex division of loyalties in Paulin. Historically it allies him with Paine and Wolfe Tone against Burke and Grattan: that is, with the radicals against the constitutionalist-royalists. They too, like the Anglo-Irish political leaders of Yeats's 'The Tower', gave though free to refuse, and at greater personal cost.

This division corresponds to and expresses perfectly Paulin's literary-critical position as expounded in the introduction to his *Faber Book of Political Verse*. There Paulin argued the existence of "a strain of religious pessimism which links Arnold to Burke and Eliot and the later Wordsworth", a tradition that Paulin would associate with an imaginative constriction corresponding to its conformist politics. In a poem of seventy-four short lines 'And Where Do You Stand on the National Question?', Paulin gives a remarkably full statement of his priorities, as Hewitt was wont to do. Paulin's heroes are there: Joyce in the epigraph (Stephen Dedalus saying "Told him the shortest way to Tara was via Holyhead"); Paisley with his cult of Bunyan (Paisley is technically an anti-hero, but one better understood by Paulin than by anyone else who has written a serious evaluation, rather than caricature, of him, as in Paulin's astute essay 'Paisley's Progress'[17]); Hewitt; Heaney. His villains are there too: the new British Minister of State, 'Sir Peregrine Falkland', who is "not a high-flyer" (this characterization again might be thought to suggest more fellow-feeling with the people of Ulster as a distinct group than is usually attributed to Paulin); the Unionists in the imaginary fiction called *Molyneaux's Last Hope*; and, in striking alliance, 'Burke and the Cruiser'—Conor Cruise O'Brien whom Paulin sees as the last remnant of traditional Unionism in the south of Ireland.

*Liberty Tree* has a new assurance, confidence and integrity as well as one of Paulin's most brilliant single poems, and it manages to embrace the political-topical (the Falklands, the IRA hunger-strikers) and the international (Polish Solidarity and the OAS in Algeria) within a framework that is largely constructed from 1790s Ulster Protestant Republicanism. It now seems curious that most reactions to the volume at the time saw it as composed of the icons of Irish republicanism. Apart from Tone (who, despite his Dublin origins, is primarily associated with Ulster Protestant leaders such as Monroe and McCracken), there is none of the southern Irish legendary here (except 'Dev' and the hunger-striker Michael Devine in a sardonic fiction). But the pages are full of northern 'high-flyers': Paisley, Brookeborough, Molyneaux, Craig, Biggar, McCracken. Equally important is Mandelstam, "the leavening priest of the Word . . . exiled in Voronezh", representing the "Word" as the artistic imagination.

Paulin's most recent complete book, *Fivemiletown* (1987), was said by some commentators to be concerned with the unionist experience as distinct from the Protestant repubiicanism of *Liberty Tree*: a movement implicit, it was suggested, in the title of one of the poems, 'Now for the Orange Card'. In fact though, this distinction hardly even makes sense in Paulin's corpus. On closer scrutiny the book can be seen to be concerned with the same twin subjects—artistic imagination and political/historical reality—if it does lack the graphic colour and zestful wit of *Liberty Tree*. The continuity is easily illustrated: Bowden Beggs as the parodic northern name takes over from memorable 'Professor "Deeko" Kerr' of 'Local Histories' in *Liberty Tree*. The provincialism of which ultimately the poet is accusing himself is a major theme, as it was in the comedy of the earlier poem, with 'Samuel Twaddell: a Co. Down man at the Cape'.

The ways in which *Fivemiletown* is less positive than *Liberty Tree*, and the reasons for it, are clear enough. The book is dominated by the imagery of Protestant experience: defenestration (of Thirty-Years-War Prague, as well as Masaryk), masonic symbolism (Catholics are not allowed to become masons: and the drift here is to connect masonic symbolism itself with the French), Calvin, Luther, Hus. Paulin is here dramatizing what he sees as a rather desperate attempt to supply the lack of a local historical mythology (of which Irish republicanism is full—perhaps to a fault) by drawing on the whole history of Protestantism in Europe. The reason why this mythology is depressed in the current Northern Irish context is patent: the suspension of Stormont, Northern Ireland's parliament (in 'Sure I'm a Cheat Aren't We All?', and 'An Ulster Unionist Walks the Streets of London'), and the signing of the Anglo-Irish Agreement. The choice for the Northern Unionists is put starkly at the end of 'The Defenestration of Hillsborough' (the leaders of the Democratic Unionist Party have more than once complained that they have been pushed out on to the window-ledge):

> This means we have a choice:
>
> either to jump or get pushed.

This disenfranchisement is associated with various images of frustration: loveless sex, skinheads, permafrost, inexpressive words. Its most depressing (and maybe wittiest) statement is 'Waftage: An Irregular Ode', where the propositioning lover who is rejected because his "breath stinks" and his "taste is simply foul" makes a ludicrous, Bogartian bid for dignity at the end:

> So, real cool, I growled
> 'Lady, no way you'll walk
> right over *me*.'
> Dead on. I chucked her then.

There is no doubt that part of the reference of the *post-factum* "chucked" lover here is to Margaret Thatcher. But the weight of sympathy in these poems is decidedly with the frustrated protagonists who feel themselves betrayed. That is not to say that they are propagandist clarion-calls for the Protestant cause; but they are powerful dramatisations of the emotion and dilemma of its interests, by evoking with creative imagination what that desolate, unloved situation is like.

Where the book is *more* declaratory than its predecessors is in the second area I have been tracing, the social function of literature. Tsvetayeva, Mayakovsky and Akhmatova are all here to represent the literary imagination under duress, and there is a joke on deconstruction: "some grand universal/called Paul de Man or Poor Tom" while "the weight of the social moment/is just breaking me up". But the major text on the matter, in Paulin's *oeuvre* to date, is the long closing poem on Heidegger, 'The Caravans on Lüneburg Heath'. The significance of this poem is that it weds the two major themes better than any previous work of Paulin's. The addressee is Simon Dach, a German poet of the time of the Thirty Years War which Paulin sees as the most crucial period in Protestantism as it fought for survival in Europe during the heyday of the Counter-Reformation: a condition comparable with that of Ulster Protestant Unionists of the present era. Into the address to Dach is woven the poetic commentary of 'Simplex', a character taken from another Thirty-Years-War text, the *Simplicius Simplicissimus* (1669) of Grimmelshausen.[18] This is a picaresque novel describing the horrific experiences of the narrator, a virtuous naif, and his fellow peasants during the Thirty Years War, as the shifting fortunes of the conflicting armies and religions affect them as the real victims. (Simplicius changes from Protestant to Catholic in the course of events, but not with any great significance.)

The politics of Paulin's poem, and by extension of the volume, clearly relate to this. Seamus Heaney quoted as expressive of the desperation of Ulster writers in the whole post-1969 period these desolate lines from early in Paulin's poem:[19]

> what I have to say's dead obvious
> we've had x years of blood and shit
> and some of us have written poems
> or issued too many credos through the press.

The whole poem is a challenge to the straightforward views of 'Simplex' on either side, and it is Paulin's most intricate use of the device noted above, the running together of two (or more) historical periods and places.

The story that brings together politics and literary matters here ('Ireland and the English crisis' again) is the relationship of the philosophers Husserl and Heidegger. Paulin's Heidegger pleads the arts-politics divide to justify himself against the charge of capitalizing on the persecution of Husserl, his Jewish predecessor in the chair of Philosophy at Freiburg:

> *but some felt guilt*
> *guilt is not my subject.*

It is clear that Paulin is not persuaded by this defence, both from his footnote in *Fivemiletown* ("certain evasive, and probably mendacious public statements which Heidegger issued in order to justify his conduct under the Nazi regime": p.67), and from the comment of a *kleine Judenbube* in the poem:

> 'Go chew acorns
> Mr Heidegger
> You went with the Nazis'

(The phrase *ein kleine Judenbube* comes from Arno Mayer, a member of the Princeton History Department, who describes having been at the age of nineteen the 'morale officer' whose task it was to make life pleasant at the end of the war for captured Nazi scientists including Wernher von Braun whom the Americans wished to make use of. They could use the contemptuous phrase, 'little Jew-boy', of him, their captor, with impunity because they were useful.)[20]

Paulin could hardly have found a better set of parables for the dilemma of reconciling politics and the academic. It is this involved complexity of judgement that leads to Paulin's crypticism—a point made with sophistication by Alan Robinson: "obliquity is interpreted not as escapist or pragmatic, but instead as a subversive form of engagement".[21] Also relevant to this dilemma in Paulin is Tzvetan Todorov's brilliant essay 'Jakobson's Poetics' where he discusses realism and art-for-art's-sake by distinguishing between "the 'reality' that literature designates" and "the means whereby the text gives us the impression of doing this—the plausibility of literature rather than its truth".[22] This seems to describe precisely the case of writers like Paulin and Muldoon who use the material of contemporary events without imposing a judgmental shape on them. It is obvious that the classic case is Paulin's principal literary hero Joyce who draws all his material from the Dublin that has survived with supreme circumstantiality in his head. It is an art that strives for realism-for-realism's sake.

Finally, this places Paulin in a late Romantic tradition (Todorov discusses Jakobson in terms of the motivated symbolism he traces in Mallarmé; Paulin is also concerned to 'purify the language of the tribe' by adding to its stretch). He belongs there with Joyce and Mahon and Muldoon—his "exemplary artists". Throughout his career the mutual reinforcement of the artistic imagination and political reality has stayed consistent, remaining through changes of subject and theme true to the central European traditions of Romantic realism.

## NOTES

1. For much of the earlier section of this essay I am drawing on my article 'Tom Paulin: Theoretical Locations and Public Positions', in *Verse* 3, no.3 (1987), pp.29–39. I am grateful to the editors of *Verse* for permission to do so.

2. *The Scots Language in One Volume from the First Records to the Present Day*, editor-in-chief Mairi Robinson (Aberdeen: Aberdeen University Press, 1985).

3. *Field Day Pamphlets*-1 (Derry 1983). Reprinted in *Ireland and the English Crisis* (Newcastle upon Tyne: Bloodaxe, 1984), pp. 178–93.

4. 'The Language of Ulster' in *The Identity of Ulster* (Belfast: 1982).

5. For example P.W.Joyce, *English as we Speak it in Ireland* (Dublin: M.H. Gill, 1910); A.J. Bliss, *Spoken English in Ireland: 1600–1740* (Dublin: Dolmen, 1979).

6. Seamus Heaney, 'Docker' in *Death of a Naturalist* (London: Faber & Faber, 1966), p. 41.

7. The last of Hewitt's ten volumes of poems was *Freehold and other poems* (Belfast: Blackstaff, 1986). *The Selected John Hewitt* was edited by Alan Warner (also Belfast: Blackstaff, 1981).

8. McCarthy's book about the deaths of his parents *The Sorrow Garden* won the London Poetry Society's Bartlett Award in 1981. It is significant that his much more ambitious and imaginative *The Non-Aligned Storyteller* (London: Anvil 1984), with its witty mock-international view of Irish politics, was less noticed because its terms of reference were less familiar.

9. *Poetry in the Wars* (Newcastle-upon-Tyne: Bloodaxe, 1986), p. 197. It is very foreign to Paulin's whole view of art to ally him with "structuralist . . .'discourse' ", against the imagination.

10. *ibid.*, p. 206.

11. Published in *London Review of Books*, vol. 4, no.20 (4–17 Nov. 1982), p. 19; and in *Irish University Review* (with a brief introduction by Paulin) Vol. 13, No. 1 (Spring 1983), pp. 83–5.

12. *The Selected John Hewitt*, ed. Alan Warner (Belfast: Blackstaff, 1981), p. 6.

13. Alan Robinson, *Instabilities in Contemporary British Poetry* (London: Macmillan, 1988), p. 115. Robinson too takes Mandelstam in Paulin as the prototype of faith in the transubstantiating power of art.

14. There is a vigorous attack on this notion of 'history' as manifest in Field Day ideology

in Longley's *Poetry in the Wars*, p. 190 ff., with particular reference to Brian Friel's play *Translations*.

15. *Oxford Poetry* 1, no. 1 (June 1983), pp. 20–3.

16. In the introduction to *Ireland and the English Crisis* Paulin attacks T.S. Eliot's penchant for English monarchism. His discussion of Eliot's "problem of disaffiliation" (p. 19) is interesting for my argument generally.

17. *London Review of Books*, Vol. 4, No. 6, (1–14 April 1982), pp. 18–21. Reprinted in *Ireland and the English Crisis*, pp. 155–73.

18. English translation by S. Goodrich (Sawtry, Cambs.: Dedalus, 1989), of *Die Abentheuer des Simplicissimus, Ein Roman aus der Zeit des dreissigjahrigen Krieges* (ed. E. von Bulow, Leipzig 1836).

19. Seamus Heaney, 'Anglo-Irish Occasions', *London Review of Books*, vol. 10, no. 9 (5 May 1988), p. 9.

20. The story is told in Studs Terkel, '*The Good War*' (London: Hamish Hamilton, 1985), p. 467.

21. *Instabilities*, p. 118.

22. T. Todorov, *Theories of the Symbol* (1977), translated by Catherine Porter (Oxford: Blackwell, 1982), p. 275.

**Thomas Docherty**
Initiations, Tempers, Seductions:
Postmodern McGuckian

# Postmodern McGuckian

## Introduction

McGuckian's poetry is pointless, in a sense akin to the way in which Molly Bloom's soliloquy is without point, unpunctuated or unpunctual. A typical sentence meanders around a point, apostrophically veering from it whenever it seems to be about to touch ground, so to speak:

> You call me aspen, tree of the woman's
> Tongue, but if my longer and longer sentences
> Prove me wholly female, I'd be persimmon,
> And good kindling, to us both.[1]

It has become fashionable to read McGuckian as a poet whose language, grammar and syntax all serve to question masculinism, and to see her as a poet in a literary lineage deriving from Joyce's Molly. There may be some truth in this, but at the outset it might be worth suggesting that the lines from 'Aviary' just quoted provide strong circumstantial evidence for a hunch one has while reading McGuckian. Like another predecessor aligned with a feminist poetic, Emily Dickinson (and also like McDiarmid), McGuckian seems to be a keen reader of the dictionary. The OED, for instance, under 'aspen', gives an etymology linking the word to 'asp' and offers, as an example of a particular usage of the word, 'aspen tongue', meaning 'the tongue of a woman'. It looks more than likely that these lines were dictated not by any specifically feminist intention preceding the poem, but rather by a reading of the dictionary.

The verse often reads as if the language itself, a language devoid of a consciousness, were directing it:

> Asleep on the coast I dream of the city.
> A poem dreams of being written
> Without the pronoun 'I'.[2]

Often it is difficult to locate any single position from which the poem can be spoken. In philosophical terms, we have a kind of 'blank phenomenology': the relation between the speaking Subject or 'I' and the Object of its intention is mobile or fluid. It reads as if the space afforded the 'I' is vacant: instead of a stable 'persona', all we have is a potential of personality, a voice which cannot yet be identified. The poetry becomes a poetry of 'villainy':

> This house is the shell of a perfect marriage
> Someone has dug out completely; so its mind
> Is somewhere above its body, and its body
> Stumbles after its voice like a man who needs
> A woman for every book.[3]

A recurring feature of McGuckian is an 'untimeliness', the sense of a gap between what is said and the voice which says it. There is a fractured 'unpunctual' consciousness here. That 'untimeliness' is consonant with a current in contemporary philosophies of the postmodern. Deleuze, for instance, often relates his philosophy to the notion that 'the time is out of joint', and he considers a Nietzschean untimeliness to be inherent in anything which can be genuinely called 'thinking'. Similarly, Lyotard indicates that the postmodern art-work exists in a 'future anterior' tense and is always contaminated by the artist's own unreadiness for it. If the ripeness or readiness is all, then the artist and philosopher is she or he who is never 'ripe':

> work and text . . . arrive always too late for their author, or, what amounts to the same thing, their being put into work always begins too soon.[4]

In the present essay, I argue for a postmodern McGuckian. She offers the availability of a poetry which is not defined by its relation to a tradition or place; rather, her writing offers a way of breaking away from the 'place- logic' which is central to the formulation of a national culture, tradition or lineage.[5]

The three major collections construct a specific trajectory. *The Flower Master* (1982) is an initiatory collection. Many of its poems are concerned with different kinds of initiation rites and with the transgressions of borders or boundaries. These borders, however, are not the expected geographical border (though that one is here too), but are more symbolic borders, such as the boundary between infancy and adulthood; the border between an Edenic garden and a secular world, and so on. A concern for our secular ('fallen') condition is apparent from the earliest poems such as 'Problem Girl' with its Eve-like girl, eating her apple; or 'Lychees' delineating a degeneracy from religious life into secularity. From these and other poems, it becomes clear that McGuckian's real 'Flower Master' is none other than the nineteenth-century poet of diabolism, Baudelaire, whose *Fleurs du mal* ghost this text.

*Venus and the Rain* (1984) has as its dominant trait a concern for space, both inner and outer. The 'inner space' is that of the vacuous Subject of the blank phenomenology; the outer space that suggested by the planetary turn of the title poem. Here, one finds traces of another French thinker, the mathematician, philosopher and Catholic Pascal, whose *pensées* were both thoughts and flowers (pansies), and whose writings interlace in the same fragmentary fashion as McGuckian's poetry, with overlaps from one text into the next. Pascal, of course, was a man terrified by "Le silence éternel de ces espaces infinis".[6]

One might immediately be tempted to think of *On Ballycastle Beach* (1988) as McGuckian's *North*, for its title refers to a geographical location at one of the northernmost points of Ireland, in County Antrim. But once again, if the reader searches here for the kind of explicit or mythic politics found in other contemporary Irish poets, she or he will be disappointed. These poems are organised around a 'French-born' idea, *le temps perdu*. *Temps*, meaning both time and weather, allows McGuckian a trope which organises poems obsessed with seasonal change. Here, it is as if the rituals which interest her are the pagan rites which have been latent in all her writing. There is also here a governing figure of 'seduction' or *temptation*, as if the texts were written by a Lilith figure, and as if the texts were an attempt, or essay, at constructing a literary lineage deriving from Eve and her apples.

The present argument falls into three sections. Firstly, I chart some 'initiations', to demonstrate McGuckian's concern for ritual and artifice and to probe the resulting idealism in the writing. Secondly, I 'take the temperature' or temper of the verse, exploring the ethos of

McGuckian's blank phenomenology, her vacuous 'idealist' Subjectivity. Thirdly, I link her writing to surrealism and superrealist movements, and through this describe a politics of her postmodern questioning of the real.

## *1 Initiations*

A prevalent conception of art is that it occupies a different order from the secular world. Many, following an Arnoldian argument, subscribe to the notion that art is a substitute for religion and that it therefore sets up an opposition between the secular and the sacred. In its crudest forms, this is pure idealism; yet, as Eliade and Girard argue, with some sophistication, there is a sense in which the ritualisation of everyday life is crucial: societies require rituals as markers of time's passage. A simple unmarked flow of time would be difficult to understand as time at all. Time and history have to be narrativised; and narratives organise themselves around temporal markers such as birthdays, funerals, anniversaries, solstices and so on. Kermode argues that the endings of narratives cast sense retrospectively upon them; but these endings are moveable feasts.[7]

McGuckian is concerned with two such deictic moments. The first is that we call puberty, a shift from infancy into adulthood, from 'non-speaking' (*infans*) into a voice. Hence the first initiation rite is one concerned with sexuality and with language, the acquisition of a voice, the possibility of 'being listened to'. The second such instant, often located within the first, is a mythic moment of a beginning or birthing of sorts. She often writes of maternity or pregnancy; but these are related to another beginning, the mythic biblical beginning in the fall from grace. This second initiation moment, then, is the moment of the entry into history as such. Both moments of initiation are tantalisingly implicated with each other in the opening poems of *The Flower Master*.

'That Year' opens with a description of a young woman's discovery of some aspects of her body:

> That year it was something to do with your hands:
> To play about with rings, to harness rhythm
> In staging bleach or henna on the hair,
> Or shackling, unshackling the breasts.

A memory, linking "that year" with another, earlier one, follows, introducing the two colours which are important here:

> I remembered as a child the red kite
> Lost forever over our heads, the white ball
> A pin-prick on the tide, and studied
> The leaf-patterned linoleum, the elaborate
>
> Stitches on my pleated bodice.
> It was like a bee's sting or a bullet
> Left in me, this mark, this sticking pins in dolls,
> Listening for the red and white
>
> Particles of time to trickle slow . . .

The memory, linking a moment of childhood play with "that year", hinges on a red kite and a white ball like a pin-prick. The girl looks at her own body with its elaborate—or laboured—stitches. Then there is the wait for "red and white/Particles". Given the suggestion in 'Slips'[8] that poetry operates partly by metaphor and partly by euphemism, it becomes impossible—if we 'listen'—to miss the allusion here to red and white corpuscles, and hence the suggestion that what is being awaited is a menarche. The ritual nature of this moment, "that year", is hinted at in the linking of the menarche with magic, the voodoo of "sticking pins in dolls". Yet there is, of course, also that other year being hinted at: the later year of a birthing, as suggested in those laboured stitches on the bodice, themselves 'slips' for a Caesarian birth. The poem closes with the image of a curtained, cushioned woman, brought to bed.

This pubescent initiation is reiterated in 'Tulips'. Here is the first tacit appearance of a 'master', who is not, as might be expected in this poem, the Wordsworth whose daffodils are tacitly alluded to by the poem's description of flowers dancing "ballets of revenge". Rather, the second stanza offers an elaborate intertextual weaving into Henry James's novella, *The Turn of the Screw*, itself a thoroughly ambiguous tale of frustrated sexuality and of a young woman's relations with a 'Master'. The governess in James was 'raped' or 'carried away' in London at the Master's house; but this sexual overtone, apparent in the tale as in the poem, is also linked to a linguistic issue. The word 'metaphor' means 'carrying across' or 'carrying away': the sexual initiation is also a linguistic initiation, as here in 'Tulips', another poem in which the reader must listen for the slips.

The poem constantly displaces its reader, and is difficult to read due to the elongation of its sentences and the resulting complexity of syntax. The first part of the first sentence (lines 1 to 6) tempts the reader to come to syntactic and semantic rest some seven times, as she or he searches more desperately for the ending of the sentence (its "that year") which will enable the retrospective making of sense. The tulips have the presence of mind to defend themselves against the unwanted intrusion of rain which falls into the daffodil. If McGuckian is a reader of the dictionary, she might be aware that the OED offers a definition of 'tulip' alongside its meaning as flower with phallic stem: a 'tulip' is "a showy person; one greatly admired"—a kind of flower-master, in short. The poem, with this allusion to James's novella, enables the reader to hear the difficult phrase "grocery of soul" as an echo of Mrs Grose, whose own "grossery of soul" is that she is illiterate: the one character in the James text who cannot read and yet also the one who knows what's going on. Letters—mislaid, stolen, intercepted or unread—form the focus of *The Turn of the Screw*, a text whose *raison d'être* is the paralysis of interpretation, the stymying of understanding, as has been argued by Felman and Brooke-Rose.[9] The same difficulty arises here, and one suddenly has to read the letters which constitute the poem differently.

Its opening phrase, "Touching the tulips was a shyness", is an odd phrase as it stands; yet, if one listens to the flower, one can also make a different sense: touching the *two-lips* was a shyness. Heard in this 'American' inflection (*à la* James), one has the image of a speaker demonstrating her shyness by actually touching her finger to her lips. But, at this point, and given the "absence of mirrors", one can also begin to hear the feminist input into this dense, complex poem.

Irigaray, especially in *Speculum* and in *This sex which is not one*, has proposed that the entire history of Western thinking has been inescapably masculinist for the primary reason of its prioritisation of the specular gaze and of the sense of vision. If we replace this with tactility, she suggests, we might be able to counter the inevitability of masculinist thinking, which is complicit with a denial of subjectivity and a denial of the voice to woman. Irigaray argues that while men require some external effect to articulate their sexuality (woman, hand, object of sorts), women are always in touch with themselves, for their genitals are formed by two lips in continual tactile arrangement. It is the intrusion of the male tulip-like stalk of the phallus which arrests auto-erotic pleasure and self-presence (or present-mind-edness). Given the absence of mirrors in 'Tulips', one might realise that the tactile overcomes the visual here. But now, "touching the tulips/two-lips" is thoroughly ambiguous. On the one hand, touching the tulips might suggest an obvious touching of the phallus; but on the other, it also suggests the woman touching her own lips, both mouth and vagina. The poem thus becomes one of covert masturbation, a "womanliness of tulips".

The feminist problematic is that of "not being listened to"[10]. Hence the necessity for circumlocution or 'slips', most obviously in the euphemistic language of flowers deployed by other unheard women such as Ophelia or Perdita. In 'Tulips', the touching of the fingers to the oral lips describes the woman as silenced. But, listening to the slips here, the availability of a "womanliness of tulips", a womanly voice, can be discovered. To hear this voice is the critical task. This poem simply describes the moment of a ritual transgression in which the poet loses infancy in the articulation of sexuality (literally: for sexuality is articulacy, literacy, here).

Initiation, and with it linguistic and gendered authority, implies a rite of passage or transgression of a boundary. This symbolic boundary in McGuckian replaces the geo-political border in other poets' work. She thinks the boundary symbolically, which is conventional enough, deploying a christian mythology of the expulsion from a paradise into history, the theme which dominates *On Ballycastle Beach* where the sands of time replace the gardens implied by *The Flower Master*, after the journey through space in *Venus and the Rain*. But the symbolic geography opens another issue which haunts the poetry: the construction of an 'economy' or law of the household.

This begins in the first collection, where it is as if 'Admiring the Furs' gets too close to the political situation for comfort. The passage across the checkpoints in this poem brings to the speaker's mind her "measurements at nine", a memory of a pre-pubertal state. But this is related to the furs in the window and the violence which brings them there for human warmth and comfort. The animal skin—our own covering—is produced through an act of violence; and in this poem, it is as if the 'preoccupation', as Heaney would think it, causes a pain, the pain which "tells you what to wear".[11] The Irish state, bifurcated on a boundary, *is* an agonising death, a wounded skin which has to be sloughed off. The checkpoint is, like the window-pane, a boundary which serves to cover the presence of pain, that pain which is the wounding of Ireland, the killing of Ireland through the act of partition.

The transgression of this very political boundary is rare in McGuckian. More frequently the boundary to be transgressed takes on a more ritualised and sacral aspect, and operates under a symbolism of domesticity. One example is 'Mr McGregor's Garden', which alludes—as do all gardens in this poetry—to a primal garden, an Edenic state once lost and always remembered with nostalgia.[12] The more immediate allusion—to Beatrix Potter—gives a more ambivalent character to the garden here, and appropriately so, as I will show. The poem starts darkly, with "Some women save their sanity with needles". On one hand, this might be an item from a domestic lexicon, suggesting knitting-needles used with the pin as in the "pin-prick" of 'That Year'. But there is a darker side to this, with the hint of a witch-like injection, and hence the idea of saving sanity through drugs. Attention immediately turns to the mode of saving sanity proposed by the speaker:

> I complicate my life with studies
> Of my favourite rabbit's head, his vulgar volatility.

This "Bunny" becomes her furry comforter later in the poem. But the "vulgar volatility" is the essential issue here. The rabbit's head, of course, is classically used in theories of visual perception to demonstrate a particular boundary in the way we see. The drawing of a rabbit's head is also a drawing of a duck, depending on how we choose to view it. It is impossible to see both at once, yet it is also impossible to see the volatility, the shift as the rabbit crosses the threshold of perception to become a duck.

Perception, sight itself, involves us in a transgression of the very same kind of boundary which caused the pain in 'Admiring the Furs'. Here is an articulation of those Irigarayan theories which acknowledge the pain caused to women by perception as we think it, by the prioritisation of the visual as the determining element of modern western culture. McGuckian answers this directly in 'Painter and Poet' where she seems to favour not the replacement of vision with tactility as in Irigaray, but rather the replacement of vision with words, language, poetry.

This perceptual transgression operates in much of her domestic imagery, where doors and windows are forever being opened and closed, indicating a threshold boundary which invites danger. Similarly, letters frequently go unread, whether the envelope remains whole or is violently torn open. It is as if the act of reading her letters were itself an act of violence or transgression, an act of the same kind of initiatory violence which causes the personal pain described in

'That Year'. Such windows and doors appear, for fine examples, in 'The Sofa' or 'The Sitting'.

But the window, as Bachelard might say, produces the house.[13] The threshold which is a doorway immediately implies not just a threatening outside, but also a domestic interior, of the kind described in 'The Flitting' (which also "has cost me" much discomfort) or throughout the poetry in incidental references to domestic scenes, furniture, the architecture of rooms, beds and so on. This becomes of some importance in 'The Sun-Trap'. In the greenhouse whose hygroscope says "orchid", the flower associated with testicles (from the Greek *orkhis* = testicle), the speaker is:

> touched by even the strange gesture
> Of rain stopping, your penetration
> Of my mask of 'bon viveur', my crested notepaper,
> My lined envelopes. From your last letter
> I construed at least the word
> For kisses, if not quite a kindred spirit.

Reading this last letter, then, there is the suggestion firstly of the "penetration" of the envelope, a transgression of a lining, together with the idea of a sexual relation in those kisses. However, something is not quite right in that the letter cannot easily be deciphered: it is misread, and the reader is searching for a "kindred spirit" while finding only the "word/For kisses". The letter clearly brings disturbing news, of "the magically fertile German girl/Who sleeps in the bunk above you", and who

> seems
> To me quite flirtatious
>
> Though you say she's the sort of girl
> You'd rather have as a daughter.

This reminds the speaker of some previous "near-tragedy" of a weekend spent with a "cousin once-removed". And at this moment, three things coalesce. Firstly, the trapping of the sun, its capturing within the space of the house, and hence its transgression of a boundary, produces the warmth of an interior set against the sickly rain and threatening weather of the outside: the house, thus, as a site of a mutation or transformation. Secondly, this relates to the search for a 'kindred spirit', with its hint of some familial or domestic relation. Thirdly, the near-explicit references to incest, in the idea of the German girl as the flirtatious daughter sleeping in the same room (actually, technically the same bed) as the correspondent, and the unspoken event between speaker and cousin once-removed. Transgression, then, involves the building of a house as a ritual or sacral space called the family which exists as an apotropaic warder-off of death and history. But the production of the house and its interiorised space, together with the necessity of sexual relations as the mode of initiation which makes the house possible in the first place, produces what Freud well knew about, the taboo of incest.

The domestic poems of McGuckian are contaminated thus by the dark and guilty question of endogamy; and it is the guilt associated with this tribal sectarianism which brings *The Flower Master* more clearly into line with Baudelaire's *Fleurs du mal*, a collection also dotted with domestic imagery, but a book which was gothically obsessed with the revelation of an evil which lay behind—and indeed founded—the decorous nature of a bourgeois existence. In McGuckian's case, there is a link between the necessity of transgression (sexual initiation and entry into secular history) and the inevitability of an evil introspection, an 'endogamous' looking inwards towards a guilt perceived in the space 'within', the interior produced by the transgression and its theshold. "Look within" urged the modernist Woolf, famously; and when McGuckian does, she sees guilt. The much-vaunted erotics of her writing are all tinged with the sense of a maleficence, a diabolism, and with the need to find a pure genealogy, but one which in its purity would be uncontaminated by this taboo of interiority, this incestuous thinking and introspection.

A postmodern sublime lies available here. We have the necessity of a transgression, the idea of a breakthrough across some threshold of perception, together with the recalcitrance which that transgression provokes: this is the pleasurable pain of interpretation in McGuckian. It is like the seduction of a letter unread, a letter which remains tantalisingly visible beneath or within its envelope; but the tearing open of the envelope reveals that the letter is not there after all: what we thought was a meaningful missive turns out to be a pattern on the envelope. Throughout the verse, it is precisely at the moment of taking root, or of finding a single place from which to understand a poem, that it melts away again into ambivalence and ambiguity. "A newly-understood poem will melt/And be hard again".[14] And even the point of transgression, the threshold, cannot be properly or adequately identified: "The point when I sleep is not known/By me, and words cannot carry me/Over it".[15]

The reader of McGuckian is in the position of the person who moves from the state of being awake to that of being asleep; either she is awake or asleep, and it is impossible to locate her at the precise moment of the change between the two. The 'checkpoint', in this way, magically is made to disappear, in something of the same sophisticated way in which death is made disappear in Augustine or Wittgenstein or Camus.[16] Yet, of course, the checkpoint undeniably exists: this hovering uncertainly between existence and non-existence is its 'sublimity'. It is both there and not there, like Venus herself who is described like a Malevich painting: "White on white, I can never be viewed/Against a heavy sky"[17] precisely the heavy sky which dominates the "sickly Irish weather".[18]

The letter in McGuckian, the text or poem as well as its very constituent letters, is the site of this refusal of representation. Each poem is, as it were, a threshold inviting the initiation of its reader into some meaning; yet it also denies that meaning at the very instant of its perception. This is McGuckian as Malvolio, a McGuckian who does not play ducks and drakes so much as ducks and rabbits. Initiation promises change; and it is the precise moment of initiation which McGuckian wants to locate. Yet, because of its very characterisation as the site of mobility and mutability, as a point of transgression or change, the locus of initiation cannot properly be identified, represented or described. It is, as it were, immaterial, invisible as Venus in the rain. The point of initiation, the 'checkpoint', is itself pointless.

## 2. Tempers

One neat mutation central to McGuckian is the linguistic slippage between 'tempt' and 'temporal'. In Christian mythology, Eve, eater of the apples that figure so widely in McGuckian, tempted or tried or tested the apple and Adam's resistance to it. This temptation by and of the woman provokes the fall into temporality, the condition in which McGuckian must now write what Stevens would have called 'The Poems of our Climate': that is, poems in which she takes a secular 'temper' or temperature, measuring the flow and sequence of the seasons which coordinate or order secular life. But, due to the 'blank phenomenology' of her writing, she is condemned to live in a kind of temporal absence. She is always—temporally and temperamentally—

at odds with herself: the poems chart a dislocation in their speaker, who always occupies some different temporal moment from the moment actually being described in the poem. There is a gap, a *différance*, between the moment of the enunication and the moment of the enunciated. As in Heidegger, the poet is always living alongside herself. She is like the character who lives in a cold climate in 'Minus 18 Street':

> I never loved you more
> Than when I let you sleep another hour,
> As if you intended to make such a gate of time
> Your home.[19]

As a being-in-time, and one living that time as a gate or threshold of transgression, the poet is never present-to-herself. Caught in a late- or neo- romantic predicament, her voice is always temporally out-of-step with what it says. Her time, like that of Hamlet, is "out of joint".[20]

*On Ballycastle Beach*, despite its parochial title, is among the more exotic of McGuckian's collections, delighting in words derived from Eastern Europe, Africa and Asia as well as the more domestic kinds of detail expected after her earlier work. But it is worth starting closer to home, in the poem 'Not Pleasing Mama', whose only 'foreign' phrase is the French "à la belle étoile", meaning "under the open sky". This poem opens with the odd suggestion that the weather is unsure:

> If rain begins as snow, then the weather
> Has slipped down as between walls, is not
> To be trusted any more
> Than any other magic.[21]

This weather is out of its proper place.[22] The French speaker who interjects might hear an interlingual pun here: *temps* as both weather and time. This text, thus, is not to be trusted for it is the site of another 'slipping' between meanings, between languages and countries, between cultures. If the weather is misplaced, it is also—to the French voice of the text—a *temps perdu*; and this opens the text to its interrelation with Proust, whose text begins not only with not pleasing Mama but also with not being pleased by the Mama who withholds the goodnight kiss. Proust, if he is about anything, is about the loss or waste of time, about a time out of joint.

'Not Pleasing Mama', with its tempting apple, is a key poem: it casts retrospective light on the opening poems of the collection, 'What

Does "Early" Mean?', 'Staying in a Better Hotel', 'Apple Flesh' and 'Grainne's Sleep Song', all texts which share the Proustian and Wordsworthian seduction by time and weather.

'What Does "Early" Mean?' It means "before the proper or appointed time". The poem describes a temporal displacement in which a house is out of step with the season: "Yet I think winter has ended/Privately in you".[23] This is related to McGuckian's own writing, which is equally "untimely":

> None of my doors has slammed
> Like that, every sentence is the same
> Old workshop sentence, ending
> Rightly or wrongly in the ruins
> Of an evening spent in puzzling
> Over the meaning of six o'clock or seven . . .

"Early" is a deictic term, depending for its meaning upon a situation: "six o'clock" is not by definition early. Hence the meaning of the term is itself untimely, as if the meaning of the word resided elsewhere or in a different time from that of the word's actual articulation. It also demands a relation between at least two times: to be "early" implies an appointment; yet it also demands a disappointment, a failure of correspondence between the two or more elements destined to coincide at the proper moment. To be early is to be out of place as well as out of time: it is to be 'flitting', to be on the nomadic move, between situations. No echoes of Hardy ghost this verse.[24]

Moreover, "early", in its implication of (dis)appointment, also demands narrative, for it demands a link to be forged in the plotting of two disparate moments. The narrative of "early" is produced in 'Grainne's Sleep Song',[25] in which untimeliness is directly related to "a novel rough to the touch", presumably the narrative referred to later, that "Uncompleted story, something sterile/I contracted fourteen years ago on the beach,/Entitled 'Wild Without Love' ". The speaker steps out of this narrative, a past moment, to enter a present relation; but the temporal relation between the fourteen-years-old narrative and the situation of "The day that I got up to" is fused and confused. The narrative is incomplete, as the meaning of the poem is also incomplete, falling back to "initials" or beginnings. The sleep-song, then, is once more about the temporal relation between beginning and end; the sleep is a mediation or meditation between the two states or two times, and mutability or uncertainty becomes the order of the day.

It is this which makes McGuckian's poetry a 'critical poetry', in the same senses as Kant's philosophy was a 'critical philosophy' or Frankfurt School political theory is a 'critical theory'. All are formulated in a mode of proleptic difference. Deleuze offers the most succinct description of what is at stake here in Kantian and post-Kantian (for which read postmodern) thinking:

> Time is out of joint, time is unhinged . . . As long as time remains on its hinges, it is subordinate to movement: it is the measure of movement, interval or number. This was the view of ancient philosophy. But time out of joint signifies the reversal of the movement-time relationship. It is now movement which is subordinate to time. Everything changes, including movement.[26]

Movement, the movement of transgression across the 'door' hinged by time, is what McGuckian was after in earlier poems. Here, she has discovered the reversal which makes movement itself subordinate to time, secularism. An allegorisation of this in terms of the political scenario—if one is needed—might run like this: there will be no movement over the border so long as time remains on its hinges—so long, that is, as a particular relation to secularity is maintained whereby the secular is but a pale shadow of the eternal or sacred. Movement will not come so long as Ireland remains 'pre-critical' or 'pre-historic'. A critical reversal of priorities is needed which acknowledges that movement over the border will only be possible if such movement becomes subordinate to time—that is, if the being of people on both sides of the border becomes a being-in-time, a being determined by historicity and not by fixed, eternal or transcendental claims upon a true identity, a 'chosen ground' for a chosen people. The poetry is a call to a critical historicism: not just an awareness of time past, but an awareness that one must 'disappoint' the history or narrative seemingly determined by that time past: time past must be misplaced, *perdu*.

## 3. *The Force of Seduction and the Play of Surrealism*

The crudity of that allegory of politics in McGuckian does not do justice to the force of her poetry, which finds more indirect—but, I shall argue, more powerful—ways of intervening in the political culture in which she writes. As might be expected in any literature which might be called a literature of decolonisation, there is in much contemporary Irish poetry a concern with power: the ambivalent desire for an autonomous national power even in the very instant when the culture is striving to escape the legacy of a suffering caused by such a power. Mastery, in *The Flower Master*, is the shape this takes in early McGuckian; but this quickly comes under speculative pressure in the writing.

Power, like temporality, depends upon relation and narrative: power is, as it were, shaped deictically. Specifically, it depends upon 'under-standing'; yet it is precisely understanding that McGuckian mistrusts. She replaces understanding, with its inherent notion of the availability of stable positions of 'mastery' (she who speaks enigmatically) and 'subjection' (she who would understand and subscribe to the master), with a notion of mere interrelation. The form this takes is one of seduction. Seduction here is taken in a sense close to that proposed by Baudrillard: it is not simply a sexual event; rather, it describes a state of relation between powers or forces, and one which explicitly excludes production. Production would here mean the end of seduction. Seduction is, for instance, the play of forces which keeps the planets in mutual interrelation: one subject of *Venus and the Rain*.

'Venus and the Sun'[27] describes the pull which the Sun exerts on Venus, and an opposing pull, in the opposite direction, exerted by Mars. Seduction is the play of forces, attraction and repulsion, which enables such relation. The resulting tension *produces* the entity we call 'Venus', or that we call 'Mars' and so on. In other words, to identify something as 'Venus' is artificially to arrest the play of forces: to make a fiction from a "mécanique des fluides".[28] The important thing is that the forces come first; there is no essence of 'Mars', 'Venus' or the 'Sun' which generates a specific force: those names are but the effect of a configuration of forces. To stabilise them with such a name or identification is a fictive arresting of time itself; McGuckian reverses the priorities of 'modern' thinking.

To put things this way, of course, is to add the corollary to the Kantian revolution described by Deleuze. In conventional thought, there already exists a mass called the Sun which exerts a force on other stable and identifiable masses called the various planets. This enables a belief in the stability and identity of 'Venus', 'Mars' and so on; and by extension, a belief in some essential 'meaning' for all the elements of the universe, some intrinsic nature. But McGuckian, whose writing is properly aligned with the postmodern thinking of Deleuze, Baudrillard and others, reverses this set of priorities. There is no

Venus without Mars; there is no Sun without these and the play of forces by which they are constituted. Rather than subscribing to some desire to identify what is produced, McGuckian prefers to work at the level of the seduction itself. This way, she questions the modern belief in the availability of identity. The arrangement of matter we call 'Venus' is, as it were, the taking root or forming an earth of a play of forces which McGuckian wishes to keep in play and in place; the arrangement of matter may appear stable, but it is invisible ("white on white'); by extension, of course, 'North' would also have no intrinsic meaning, nor would 'Ireland', nor would 'McGuckian' and so on. "*Le monde n'est qu'une branloire perenne.*"[29]

'Venus', then, is held together, instant by instant, only through a kind of *stasis*, internal dissent and tension or civil war. This kind of seductive attraction depends upon gravity, or *mass*. Much of McGuckian's imagery is drawn from the pull she feels towards a christian iconography and lexicon. But it is a corollary of her post-Kantian poetry that her aesthetic world must be guided not by a christian onto-theology, but rather by a pagan consciousness. Paganism, of course, is not atheist, but prefers a heterotheology, a multiplicity of forces called 'gods' which activate the world.

A number of poems reveal this paganism and relate it to a hieroglyphic questioning of the letter. 'Vanessa's Bower'[30] is a poem with a misunderstood letter, specifically the letter "E":

> . . . Dear owner, you write,
> Don't put me into your pocket: I am not
> A willow in your folly-studded garden
> Which you hope will weep the right way:
> And there are three trains leaving, none
> Of which connects me to your E-shaped
> Cottage. Alas, I have still the feeling,
> Half fatherly, half different, we are
> Travelling together in the train with this letter,
> Though my strange hand will never be your sin.

This E-shaped cottage is like a railway station, from which there run three parallel lines of flight. Seduction here is the gravitational pull away from the cottage and its folly-studded Edenic garden with its weeping tree. That journey is taken with "this letter", meaning both a missive (the poem, perhaps) and also the letter "E". Interestingly, the Hebrew letter    , which looks like an E on its side, is pronounced 'sin'. This letter in Hebrew, the language of the Bible, provokes the weeping. But another intertext appears here. Erasmus, in *In Praise of Folly*, describes this Hebrew letter and its pronunciation in a passage demonstrating the folly of a belief in an original or God-given language (the Word, the logos).[31] We are always in flight—or in multiple lines of flight—from such a language, always out of step with it in time and space. It is not the case that the apple-laden language of woman is folly or madness; rather, what is folly is the garden itself and the belief that there ever was one pure or original language of sanity, one Word which was there in the beginning and which was God.

Frequently in her poems, McGuckian makes a turn towards nomadism, towards a chosen ground which is, strictly speaking, nowhere in particular. The nomad simply moves around, with no specific home except a 'Querencia',[32] the idea of a home, occupying whatever space is needed and available at any given moment. This attitude clearly marks McGuckian off from other Irish poets, like Deane, Montague or Heaney, who have questioned the geography of Ireland as a specific and historically-determined plot of earth or rough field. McGuckian is more interested in symbolic space and in the occupation of a language or a voice. Always in flight, her poems—like her own voice and identity—are never fixed in historical time or geographical space: their meaning is always untimely, never present-to-themselves, and hence never 'available'. In this way, her text is always 'temperable', marked by a promiscuous mingling of different meanings held together in a play of internal forces which allows her never to lose her 'temper'.

Given this difference from her contemporaries, it becomes apparent that if one were to look for predecessors for McGuckian, it would be an error to search among the Irish poets of the twentieth century. In terms of linguistic styles, she has more in common with both nineteenth-century decadence and with twentieth-century sur-realism, both internationalist movements. Much of her imagery could be derived from Neruda or Aragon rather than from Clarke or Kavanagh. Yet there is one way in which she overlaps with a thematics of flight which dominates much Irish writing this century. Yeats, for instance, starts by looking west, then makes successive leaps east-wards to Greece and Byzantium for the sources of his poetry; Joyce and Beckett, famously, exile themselves; Heaney begins from an archaeology of Irish soil, and then, like Yeats, makes a symbolic geographic move eastwards in his alignment of himself with the dissident poets of Eastern Europe. Heaney also leaves the soil in another sense, becoming 'Mad Sweeney', the bird among the trees which Yeats had also dreamt of becoming.[33] It is this 'line of flight' which McGuckian adopts, and in her it becomes a structural determinant of the language and syntax of her writing.

There is an exoticism in McGuckian, very apparent in the vocabulary of *On Ballycastle Beach* for instance, which literally "unsettles" the text and its readers. The predominantly Latinate and Anglo-Saxon vocabulary of the first two collections is interrupted here by words like "Ylang-Ylang" (Malaysian), "vetiver" (from African languages), "Mazurka" (Polish), "Querencia" (Spanish), "balakhana" (Persian) and so on. McGuckian here reiterates some of the symbolic geographical manoeuvres of Yeats, Heaney and others; but its effects are different.

'Querencia', for instance, suggests a kind of 'land of heart's desire', or desired homeland; but it is odd that an Irish poet should use a Spanish word to describe this. The word is actually used in Spanish to describe the terrain of the bull in a bull-fight: it is the 'stamping-ground' of the threatening and dangerous animal. The term thus provides her with an ambivalent word describing her relation to 'home', a home which is 'elsewhere', a home riven by stasis or dissent, a home which is desired but which also threatens. "Balakhana" is the word describing the upper storey of a Persian house, the room in which nomadic travellers would be put to pass the night. This balakhana (a near homonym for Ballycastle, of course) is not a stable home either, but a nomadic place of encampment, a temporary abode.

This kind of language works to suggest an alienation in McGuckian's own relation to her language. Like her, the reader has to become a reader of dictionaries in the endless search for meaning, and the language is thus always at odds with the mouth speaking it, always untimely, always a blank phenomenology. There is no single governing Logos, no monotheology of Truth here, no originary language: McGuckian, like the 'character' in Christine Brooke-Rose's 'novel', *Thru*, lives increasingly in the space between languages. She does not live between English and Gaelic, but between English and the languages of Europe, Asia, Africa. This linguistic internationalism contributes to the instabilities which enable her work to be characterised as late surrealist.

In the present century, surrealism has had a chequered history. Initially an art dedicated to revolution, it became more and more explicitly reactionary. Yet it has always served one critical purpose well: it always questions the nature of the real. In its later development into superrealism, it is not so much the nature of reality so much as the very principle of ontological reality which is questioned. A superrealist painting, say, proposes the question: 'which is more real—object or image?' The postmodern simulacrum, as Baudrillard points out, can question the very principle of reality itself by its parodic duplication; and this is its potentially most radical function. McGuckian is close to this, though her means of achieving it are not through the 'more perfect than perfect' mimesis of superrealism, but rather through the contortions of surrealism. Reality in her writing constantly slips away, leaving a reader to puzzle where she or he stands. Her sentences meander from *étrangeté* to *bizarrerie*, dislocating metaphor and being 'easily carried away' in this language which is dictated by no consciousness, and leaving a reader stranded in flight from multivalent realities. The early writing is concerned with a fall into temporality or secularity; the later with finding a means to cope with that 'fall' not by fleeing history but rather by fleeing the principle of a monotheological Reality, which is seen to be imprisoning. All here is image: there is no presence, only representations. It is worth remembering that, in Ireland, there are two Ballycastles.

NOTES

1. Medbh McGuckian, 'Aviary', *Venus and the Rain*. OUP, 1984, p. 21.
2. McGuckian, 'Harem Trousers', On Ballycastle Beach, OUP, 1988, p. 43.
3. McGuckian, 'The Villain', *Venus and the Rain*, p. 19. It is as if a Cartesian 'cognito' here has been replaced by a 'loquor' as the subject of the voice. For a fuller argument documenting this as a trait in contemporary writing, see my *Reading (Absent) Character* (Oxford University Press, 1983), pp. 34–6, 87–123 and *passim*.
4. Jean-François Lyotard, *The Postmodern Condition* (Manchester: Manchester University Press, 1984), p. 81. Cf. for instances, Gilles Deleuze, *Kant's Critical Philosophy* (Minneapolis: University of Minnesota Press, 1984) (hereafter KCP), and *Nietzsche and Philosophy* (Athlone Press, 1983).
5. On 'place-logic' in the thinking of Rudolph Agricola, see Walter J. Ong., *Ramus: Method and the Decay of Dialogue* (Cambridge, Mass.: Harvard University Press, 1958), p. 121. The present essay characterises such place-logic as 'modernist'. For an argument describing the modifications of space and time in postmodernity, see David Harvey, *The Condition of Postmodernity* (Oxford: Blackwell, 1989).
6. Blaise Pascal, *Pensées Oeuvres complètes* (Paris: Editions du Seuil, 1963), p. 528, no.201.
7. See, for examples, Mircea Eliade, *Le mythe de l'éternel retour* (Paris: nrf, 1949); René Girard, *passim*; Erving Goffman, *The Presentation of Self in Everyday Life* (Edinburgh: University of Edinburgh, 1956); Frank Kermode, *The Sense of an Ending* (New York: Oxford University Press, 1967).

8.  McGuckian, 'Slips', *The Flower Master*, OUP, 1982, p. 21.
9.  Shoshana Felman, 'Turning the Screw of Interpretation', in Felman, ed., *Literature and Psychoanalysis* (Baltimore: Johns Hopkins University Press, 1982), pp. 94–207; Christine Brooke-Rose, *A Rhetoric of the Unreal* (Cambridge: Cambridge University Press, 1981), pp. 128–187
10. McGuckian, *On Ballycastle Beach*, p. 51.
11. McGuckian, *Venus and the Rain*, p. 40.
12. This poem works in the tradition of the 'garden-poem' which dates at least from the Renaissance.
13. See Gaston Bachelard, *La Poétique de l'Espace* (Paris: Presses universitaires de France, 1957).
14. McGuckian, 'Mazurka', *On Ballycastle Beach*, p. 22.
15. McGuckian, 'A Dream in Three Colours', *ibid.*, p. 44.
16. See Augustine, *City of God* (Harmondsworth: Penguin, 1972), pp. 519–20; Ludwig Wittgenstein, *Tractatus Logico-Philosophicus*, 6, 4311; Albert Camus, *Le mythe de Sisyphe* (Gallimard, Paris: nrf, 1942), pp. 29–30.
17. McGuckian, 'Venus and the Rain', *Venus and the Rain*, p. 31.
18. McGuckian, 'The Sun Trap', *The Flower Master*, p. 24.
19. McGuckian, *On Ballycastle Beach*, p. 19.
20. In Romanticism itself, of course, this predicament was that of idealism. The poet typically desires an ontological empathy with the world of the natural which—it is claimed—was enjoyed by the rustic; but the poet, blessed or cursed (or both) with consciousness can enjoy, at best, an epistemological empathy with nature, an empathy gained, however, precisely at the cost of her or his ontological alientation from that world. The autobiographical impetus is thus produced from a project in which the subject aims temporally to coincide with itself, a project doomed, as Sterne had clearly prefigured, to a sublime failure. For an argument characterising this as also a 'modernist' predicament, see my 'Anti-Mimesis', in *Forum for Modern Language Studies* vol. 26, no. 3 (1990) pp. 272–281.
21. McGuckian, *On Ballycastle Beach*, p. 20.
22. The French voice which interjects in this text might hear the Rabelaisian joke, "Between walls" is between 'mur' and 'mur'. Rabelais: "ou mur y a et devant et derrière, y a force murmur, envie et conspiration mutue"; see François Rabelais, *Gargantua in Oeuvres complètes,* tome 1, ed. P. Jourda (Paris: Garnier Frères, 1962), p. 189.
23. McGuckian, *On Ballycastle Beach*, p. 11.
24. Hardy's poetry, especially in the famous instance of 'The Convergence of the Twain', is about keeping an appointment with fate; cf. Beckett, whose characters in *Waiting for Godot* pride themselves on keeping their appointment, but an appointment which is, by the play's formal definition, necessarily a disappointment.
25. McGuckian, *On Ballycastle Beach*, p. 16.
26. Gilles Deleuze, op. cit. (note 4), vii.
27. McGuckian, *Venus and the Rain*, p. 9.
28. Luce Irigaray, *This sex which is not one* (New York: Cornell University Press, 1985), pp. 106–118.
29. Michel de Montaigne, *Essais* in 3 vols (Paris: Garnier-Flammarion, 1969), vol 3, 20.
30. McGuckian, *Venus and the Rain*, p. 10.
31. Desiderius Erasmus, *In Praise of Folly*, in John P. Dolan, ed., *The Essential Erasmus* (New York: Mentor Books, 1964), pp. 151–2.
32. McGuckian, *On Ballycastle Beach*, p. 25.
33. For a more detailed argument making this point, see my *After Theory* (Routledge, 1990), pp. 173–190.

**Neil Corcoran**
One Step Forward, Two Steps Back:
Ciaran Carson's *The Irish for No*

# One Step Forward, Two Steps Back

## *1*

When Seamus Heaney published *North* in 1975, Ciaran Carson reviewed it in the Belfast *Honest Ulsterman*. The review has been frequently cited in discussions of *North*, since it makes the opposition's case with memorably caustic incisiveness. Carson castigates Heaney as "the laureate of violence—a mythmaker, an anthropologist of ritual killing, an apologist for 'the situation', in the last resort, a mystifier". Taking his title from one of Heaney's phrases for himself in the volume's final poem 'Exposure', Carson ironises it with a query: 'Escaped from the Massacre?'; and answers his own question: "No one really escapes from the massacre, of course—the only way you can do that is by falsifying issues, by applying wrong notions of history, instead of seeing what's before your eyes."[1] I do not intend here to take up this debate again: I have tried to define elsewhere some of the ways in which I think *North* may be defended against such charges.[2] It should be said, however, that the criticism is one that has also been pursued relentlessly by Edna Longley, and implied by Paul Muldoon when, in his *Faber Book of Contemporary Irish Poetry*, he (outrageously) publishes only the dedicatory poems from *North*.[3] It is also possible to read aspects of Heaney's career since *North* as an implicit criticism of the procedures he adopts there. Yet those procedures were also, manifestly, an attempt to break through the crust of the 'well-made poem' which the first generation of Northern poets inherited from their origins in the English Movement and the Belfast Group: as Heaney observed at the time, he wanted "to take the English lyric and make it eat stuff that it has never eaten before . . . and make it still an English lyric".[4] The publication in 1987 of Ciaran

Carson's second full volume of poems, *The Irish for No*, which seems to me (as it seemed to an exceptionally well-harmonised chorus of its first reviewers) one of the very finest books to have come out of Northern Ireland since 1968, puts the criticism into a newly illuminated perspective, making it clear that in rejecting the Heaney procedures Carson was equally certain that the lyric tradition needed to be disrupted if the Northern matter was to be adequately expressed.[5]

The book's title poem itself contains a veiled reference to Heaney. 'The Irish for No' weaves apparently haphazardly in and out of several intermittent narratives before it climaxes with an evocation of a blackly almost surreal suicide:

> What's all this to the Belfast business-man who drilled
> Thirteen holes in his head with a Black & Decker? It was just
>     a normal morning
> When they came. The tennis-court shone with dew or frost, a
>     little before dawn.
> The border, it seemed, was not yet crossed: the Milky Way
>     trailed snowy brambles,
> The stars clustered thick as blackberries. They opened the door
>     into the dark:
> *The murmurous haunt of flies on summer eves.* Empty jam-jars.
> Mish-mash. Hotch-potch.

Given that this is a poem which, throughout, almost uninterpretably plays Keats's 'Ode to a Nightingale' across its own wayward surface, it would be too heavy-handed to describe this *briocolage* of reference as straightforwardly satirical at Heaney's expense, and in any case the Heaney allusions are not sufficiently sustained to gauge a tone adequately from them. However, if they register something of the wryly good-humoured acknowledgement of Heaney also to be found in poems by Paul Muldoon and Tom Paulin,[6] they nevertheless appear to imply a sense of unease and limitation. The grotesquerie of the Belfast suicide and the unspecific minatory narrative in which 'they' are coming with, presumably, some underhand purpose in mind (murder, kidnapping, extortion?) consort oddly with, and must intend some judgement on the sensorial opulence of Heaney's early work. The allusions focus on his second volume, *Door into the Dark*, published in 1969, the second year of the 'Troubles'. The word 'dark' resounds through the book; but it would appear that Carson's poem finds behind the door of Heaney's earlier work not contemporary terror but literature, not the dark of Northern Ireland's nightmare but the luxuriance of Keats's ode; and those jam-jars which are full of frogspawn and blackberries in Heaney's 'Death of a Naturalist' and 'Blackberry-Picking' are, in Carson, ominously empty, the sufferers of an imaginative reduction. We may infer from the sly allegorising of 'The Irish for No' that, in the dark of contemporary social and political attrition, Carson finds Heaney's poetic of late Romantic expansiveness wanting.

Carson's review of *North* is continuous with this subversive interlude, suggesting a deep suspicion of the yearning for imaginative plenitude which may be read out of Heaney's mythical and anthropological structures, structures in which the poetic imagination appears to respond to present depredation by inviting it into the potential assuagement of a form of transcendence. If these are "wrong ideas of history" since, in Carson's view, they translate all sense of political consequence into the "realm of inevitability", they are also, presumably, wrong ideas of literature, deriving too calculatedly from the traditions of Romanticism and High Modernism. The structures of *North*, however they may be thought to ironise themselves in the book's self-diversion, may be read as deeply continuous with what Eliot, reading *Ulysses*, famously christened the "mythical method".[7] Recent philosophy and literary theory have proposed to us the concept of a culture and a consciousness of the 'postmodern' (whether the term is understood to imply a temporal sequence or a kind of opposition-from-within of modernism to its own deepest structures, forms and presumptions). The will to such mythical, trans-historical coherence is castigated in this writing as an ideologically fraught 'master narrative' or 'metanarrative', a tale of suspect plenary interpretation. An "incredulity toward metanarratives" is, for Fredric Jameson, the simplest definition of the postmodern;[8] and, in the book Jameson is introducing when he makes this remark, Jean-François Lyotard actually goes further, declaring that the signal of the postmodern is not merely the lack of credibility of the grand narrative but the end of the "period of mourning" for it.[9]

In the challenge to the earlier phase of Heaney's work represented by Carson's review it is surely possible to see the ground of a Northern Irish poetry of the postmodern beginning to prepare itself; and it is tempting to view Carson's ten-year poetic withdrawal after the publication of his well-received first book, *The New Estate*, in 1976,[10] as a result of his personal search, in the cunning of a stay-at-home silence, for a way of registering in his own writing the full shock of the challenge to recognised modes and forms represented by the realities of post-1968 Northern Ireland, and more particularly post-1968 Belfast. Carson's work is inextricably meshed into the city in which he has spent his entire life. A resolutely urban poet, even when he strays into the Irish *rus* it is a squalidly depleted one: the Donegal-derelict rather that the Derry-lush of early Heaney or the Armagh-deciduous of Muldoon. His Northern postmodernism has its origin here: he is, pre-eminently, the poet of Belfast in its contemporary disintegration. A response to that city in this time has necessitated the construction of his radically *sui generis* forms. In rejecting the metanarrative of myth, Carson constructs a narrative poetry of his own: *The Irish for No* and, since then, *Belfast Confetti*[11] are powerfully original contributions to the genre of the 'new narrative' in contemporary British and Irish poetry. Carson's narratives are not the clipped, staccato abruptions of Tom Paulin or the 'deconstructed' sonnets of Paul Muldoon, with their inbuilt interruptions in the flow of narrative current. Carson's is an exfoliating narrative of turnings and returnings, digressions and parentheses, lapses and dissolvings, the haphazard and the circuitous. In this essay I want to try to define its contours, suggesting ways in which an alignment of it with some theories of the postmodern may be analytically useful and culturally suggestive. I do this with some tentativeness, however, since the 'postmodern' is notoriously resistant to agreed definition and use of the term can appear merely modish. I should not, therefore, wish to press the word upon the poems with too great a diagnostic rigour; but to read the most knowledgeable synthesising interpreters of the postmodern is to recognise a discourse, and a range of categories, appropriate to the striking originality of Carson's poems.[12]

## 2

The Irish language has no word for no; there is no Irish for no. In the poem 'The Irish for No', it is made plain that there is, nevertheless, an Ulster English for no: *Ulster Says No* is scrawled in huge letters on the side of a power-block. The presence of the other language of Irish can be glimpsed several times through the English of *The Irish for No*; and the book's title, with its signals of alterity, impossibility and negativity, is profoundly appropriate to its poems. Carson's poems are difficult to describe in any very available prosodic terms, but formally they may be said to join together two widely divergent kinds of structure: the very long line which Carson derives primarily from the American poet C.K. Williams, and the oral forms of Irish traditional story-telling and even Irish traditional music.[13] The book is scrupulous in acknowledging "John Campbell of Mullaghbawn whose storytelling suggested some of the narrative procedures of some of these poems"; and in letters to me Carson has illuminatingly developed his conception of an experimentally individuated prosody developed from an intertwining of kinds of otherness:

> Storytelling is there; the line breaks are points of suspense, where you want to see what happens next. The length of line is a story-teller's deliberate fast-paced gabble. It's also based around *haiku's* seventeen syllables, and the intention is to have a kind of *haiku* clarity within the line—stumbling-blocks of word-clusters, piling up adjectives, etc. And it's not unlike Irish (séan-nos) singing. The traditional dance form known as a reel is there too—the line and rhythm of a reel is always in my ear, the way you extend notes beyond ostensible bar lines, or cut them short: going against the form all the time, but observing it; knowing that it's always there, 'in back', as they say in the States. It's supposed to tease the reader a little, or to keep him on the edge of the seat. I hope the humour of this comes across.[14]

Some of this is probably a bit fanciful, but it manifestly registers an affiliation based on passionate knowledge and affection. Although born in Belfast, Carson's first language is Irish, and he has, for a number of years, been Traditional Arts Officer for the Arts Council of Northern Ireland, a job which has involved the playing, collection and taping of Irish stories and music; he himself plays the flute and has published a guide to Irish traditional music.[15] He insists that this work for a long time made the writing of poetry seem, by comparison, "remote, alien, artificial, unattached to ordinary speech. The music, singing and yarn-spinning seemed much more vital". Playing the oral against the literary, the long lines of his poems have something of the sustained, improvisatory panache of the Irish story-teller or *seanachie*, always aping the movement of the speaking voice in self-involved but audience-aware address, repetitive, self-corrective, elliptical; while also, in their sustained syntactical ebb and flow, maintaining a control of uncommonly sophisticated writerly resourcefulness. With an ear attuned to the oral energies of Irish speech and song, and an intelligence alert to a range of recent American models (Ashbery is also there), Carson is enabled to construct an astonishingly fertile poetic resource, one which allows him the possibility of writing a poetry of the Northern Irish present fraught with the urgency and terror of its moment but vigilantly resistant to the potentially seductive and glamourising modes offered by a modern literary tradition.

The sinuous shapeliness of the line in *The Irish for No* is echoed in the shapeliness of the book's structure. It has three sections, the first and last of which each contain four separate long narratives; the central section contains sixteen short poems on Belfast employing a similar long line but containing a regular nine lines, divided into two stanzas of five and four lines respectively. In the Wake Forest and Bloodaxe editions—but not in the original Gallery Press edition—the whole is prefaced by a further short poem of this kind called 'Turn Again'. The book therefore combines a high degree of well-shaped formality with the apparently wanderingly digressive thread of its actual narrative structures, as indeed its individual poems do too. The suavely sophisticated playing of control against licence is the crucial element in their delicate manipulation of tone. These are shapes which can accommodate the blackly humorous, the wry, the witty, the intensely nostalgic, the murderously brutal, the near-slapstick, all in the same poem-space. They can, as it were, hesitate across their line-breaks between such variant tones, moving always with a buoyancy whose apparent confidence may at any moment collapse into a chasm of poignancy, regret, misgiving or hopelessness.

In 'Dresden', for instance, which is probably the finest single poem in the book, the variations are orchestrated with a consummate poetic tact which is also a kind of moral and political tact. It is a poem which, inventing a postmodern form for itself, also invents a quite new register for the very neo-classical virtue of poetic 'decorum'. It opens with a good joke about the dubious naming of its main protagonist:

> Horse Boyle was called Horse Boyle because of his brother
>     Mule;
> Though why Mule was called Mule is anybody's guess.

Anybody's guess is nobody's certainty, least of all this insouciant but interestedly sympathetic narrator's: so the joke about how Horse second-handedly derived his name is also an indication of narrative undecidability, a sort of *mise-en-abime* opening as the poem itself opens. But Horse's second-hand name, and perhaps the way his narrative is conveyed to us by a proxy (or second-hand) narrator, are an appropriate introduction and response to the way Horse's tale is a tale of, in the end, second-handness and subjection, like the tales of many of the characters in *The Irish for No*. This narrative initiated by a joke stays a humorous narrative, just about, but grows in tonal complexity, as it grows in social implication, during its recounting. It accommodates the almost stage-Irish, Flann O'Brien-like farce of Horse's tale of Flynn, who carries a bomb on a bus across the border for the IRA and immediately confesses to a policeman who boards the bus only because his bicycle has a puncture. This is a tale, however, whose farce is transformed into something altogether other when, during his consequent seven years' imprisonment, Flynn learns to speak "the best of Irish"; "He had thirteen words for a cow in heat; / A word for the third thwart in a boat, the wake of a boat on the ebb tide": the pathetically confined spirit of Irish nationalism meets the beautiful, antique redundancies of the Irish tongue. The narrative also includes the much less attractive Irishry of Horse's story of the schoolmaster McGinty, which anatomises the stonily mean-spirited and ill-natured parish of Carrowkeel, "so mean and crabbed . . . men were known to eat their dinner from a drawer. / Which they'd slide shut the minute you'd walk in", where the line-break reveals excellent comic timing. Such tales-within-the-tale accumulate towards a revelation of the nature and kind not only of the individual, Horse Boyle, but of the depleted and demeaning social, cultural and political context in which he survives resourcefully.

The full revelation comes only at the end of the poem, where the reason for its title becomes clear at last (this is probably a matter of some frustrating delay for the first-time reader, eagerly nosing forward into the narrative for some way of attaching it to such a significant name: titles too may play their part in the narrative recessiveness of these poems). In his youth Horse has, in another representatively Irish mode of subjection, been an emigrant to England and been so bored by his work in Manchester ("Something to do with scrap") that he enlists in the RAF during the war, flying as a rear gunner over Dresden. The poem releases its epiphanic climax as Horse remembers this mission which "broke his heart":

> As he remembered it, long afterwards, he could hear, or almost
>     hear
> Between the rapid desultory thunderclaps, a thousand tinkling

echoes—
All across the map of Dresden, store-rooms full of china
    shivered, teetered
And collapsed, an avalanche of porcelain, slushing and
    cascading: cherubs,
Shepherdesses, figurines of Hope and Peace and Victory,
    delicate bone fragments.
He recalled in particular a figure from his childhood, a
    milkmaid
Standing on the mantelpiece. Each night as they knelt down
    for the rosary,
His eyes would wander up to where she seemed to beckon to
    him, smiling,
Offering him, eternally, her pitcher of milk, her mouth of rose
    and cream.

This is itself heartbreaking poetry, as the *kitsch* statue remembered from Horse's childhood serves as his sad, quasi-religious benediction for the diminishments of his own life, and for those of the Irish and European history he has lived through. Its femininity is an erotic substitute for the Marian-virginal piety of the rosary, an eroticism in which the 'eternal' promise and solace is a sexual, not a religious one. Beckoning, smiling and offering him her pitcher and her mouth, she is set over against the apparently quite womanless and sexless, and probably alcoholic, world Horse shares with his brother. The end of the poem lets us know that Horse eventually dropped her, "reaching up to hold her yet again", and that her remains (the hand and pitcher) now share a biscuit tin with pencils, snuff, tobacco, his war medals and a "broken rosary". Compacted in his memory into Horse's experience of bombing Dresden, she acts as a kind of radiant but forever lost metonym for all the lives broken there along with the china; those "delicate bone fragments" are the remains of human bodies as well as of expensive porcelain.

    The "thousand tinkling echoes" of the breaking china which Horse imagines he can hear over Dresden may also metonymically summarise or include all those other noises which this poem so prominently contains: the collapsing "baroque pyramids of empty baked bean tins" which surround ("good as a watchdog") the caravan which Horse shares with Mule; the tinkling of the shopbell which this noise recalls to the poem's unnamed narrator; the "grate and scrape" of a spade digging into the miserably poor ground of Carrick, which reminds Horse of the noise of digging a tip of broken delph and crockery and of the squeaking of chalk on a blackboard. Those noises—mnemonic, associative, setting the memory on edge in the way the teeth are set on edge by squeaking chalk—chime together into the peculiar atonal harmony of 'Dresden'. Sounding together, they draw the narrative's different stories together too, making out of Horse Boyle's life not only a tale but an emblem of diminishment and depredation. Permanently shattered by the act to which he was led by his own subjection, the act of placing others under the ultimate subjection of death by bombing in Dresden, Horse is a mule too, doing for England to beautiful, strategically insignificant Dresden what poor farcical Flynn would do to England for his idea of Ireland and for the IRA. For all its noises of lighter timbre, the noise that this poem called 'Dresden' really echoes with is the noise of exploding bombs, those almost oxymoronic "rapid desultory thunderclaps".

Despite all the deadpan humour in Carson's narrative poems, and the grace and delicacy of their procedures, they almost always reveal, even if only in the end—like 'Dresden'—stories of such depredation. Their characters and narrators are the rundown, the supernumerary, the pathetic. They are mentally ill or subnormal, like the Johnny Mickey of 'Judgement', who is on his way into the care of "two attendants", and like the Uncle John of 'Asylum' with his "babbling, stammering" tale; they are the loonies, winos, down-and-outs, tinkers and murder victims of the working-class Belfast of Part II. The subjects of their own narratives, they are subjected by the narratives of history and politics into which they are written. In the passage from 'Dresden' which I quote above, Carson's trope for this imprisoning narrative of history is the map: Horse in his bomber-plane imagines the china breaking "all across the map of Dresden". Human lives are being broken because they happen where they are target points on an already written chart: peoples' lives are taken out of their hands by the alien mapmakers and mapreaders of their destinies.

The map is prominently a figure for such entrapment throughout *The Irish for No*, inheriting a significance from its prominent role in a colonial history. The prefatory poem, 'Turn Again', initiates the trope in its opening line, referring to a map of a Belfast which does not exist, citing a collapsed bridge, non-existent streets, jails which "cannot be shown for security reasons":

> The linen backing is falling apart—the Falls Road hangs by a
> thread.
> When someone asks me where I live, I remember where I

used to live.
Someone asks me for directions, and I think again. I turn into
A side-street to try to throw off my shadow, and history is
    changed.

Everywhere in Carson metaphor and figure tend to be themselves
dense with a social and cultural history: here the 'linen' backs the
Belfast map since Belfast's economic development through the late
eighteenth and nineteenth centuries was largely dependent on the
linen trade. In 'Turn Again' the figure of the map follows Belfast's
social history into the present moment, however, with its implications
of disintegration, directionlessness and pursuit. The 'other' Belfast
represented by the non–existent map remains a haunting shadow, the
ghost of a never-realised possibility. The nature of the exclusion is
plain when the meticulously itemised street names of Belfast map
their Irish streets with British imperial names (Raglan, Inkerman,
Odessa and so on); and the map as trope of cultural and political
inscription, as imprisoning maze and labyrinth, is made explicit in
'Smithfield Market', where the burnt-out old market of Belfast
harbours a secret, unidentifiable beast:

Since everything went up in smoke, no entrances, no exits.
But as the charred beams hissed and flickered, I glimpsed a
    map of Belfast
In the ruins: obliterated streets, the faint impression of a key.
Something many-toothed, elaborate, stirred briefly in the labyrinth.

The city as labyrinth is a staple modern and postmodern figure; but
Carson renders it here with an almost Gothic *frisson* by raising the
ghost of the labyrinth's original inhabitant. In a complex and darkly
witty conceit, the "key" to this burning map has many teeth, like a
house key, but they are teeth which may bite, like the teeth of a
mythical wild beast or Minotaur, fed on human flesh in the Cretan
labyrinth. The key to the map of Belfast may offer not a way out but
only a way further in to the ungovernable source of its own
conflagration. Always out-of-date (as explosions and demolitions eat
away the city's fabric) and even when burning, the map of Belfast
harbours within itself the most minatory of possibilities. Bombs, like
minotaurs, feed on human flesh.
    If human subjects are dispersed along the labyrinthine grid of a
map in *The Irish for No*, however, suffering the history they are plotted

into, they are also markedly dispersed into other kinds of inscription in the volume too: in particular, into brand name, advertising slogan and list. The book contains a remarkable number of brand names, often themselves occurring in lists. The following is my own selective listing, from the book's twenty-four poems (I italicise where Carson does): Gold Leaf, the *Dundalk Democrat*, Gold Label, Cointreau, Blue Grass, Calvin Klein's *Obsession*, Andy Warhol (a brand name of a kind, after all), Brylcreem, *Phoenix* beer, Guerlain's *Sous le Vent*, Saravel's *White Christmas*, Corday's *Voyage à Paris, Rhythm*, Boots' *Buttermilk and Clover* soap, Saracen, Kremlin-2 mesh, Makrolon face-shields, Sellotape, Blu-Tack, *Contact, Men Only*, Portakabins, Telstar Taxis, Durex, Drawbridge British Wine, Black & Decker, Jabberwocks, Angels' Wings, Widows' Kisses, Corpse Revivers, *Pampers*, HP Sauce, Heinz Baked Beans, Crosse & Blackwell's Cock-a-Leekie, Ford Zephyr, Audi Quattro, Red Heart Stout, Park Drive cigarettes, Dunville's whisky, *Guinness, Peter Pan loaf*, Harp, Paddy whiskies, Lucozade, Polaroids, baby Power's. Brand names can be affectionately evocative of particular times and places (as they are in those most quintessentially English poets, John Betjeman and Craig Raine, for instance), and Carson is a superb poet of evocation, of the moods and atmospheres conjured by retrospect and recall. The brand names label the moment, freeze the frame of history, nowhere more vividly than in 'Patchwork', where somebody buys a bottle of Lucozade in a pub:

> the baby
> Version, not the ones you get in hospital, wrapped in crackling see-through
> Cellophane. You remember how you held it to the light, and light shone through?
> The opposite of Polaroids, really, the world filmed in dazzling sunshine:
> A quite unremarkable day of mist and drizzle.

When the word 'Lucozade' is used, who does not remember such bedridden transformations of reality, the *ersatz* orange dazzle of the Lucozade cellophane harmonising with your drugged or fevered state? But who would anticipate seeing them realised with such inventiveness and particularity in a brief digression in a poem preoccupied with other matters entirely? Carson is full of such moments where the almost forgotten and the almost inconsequential are given their accurate names.

But brand names may also appear eerily dominating when used in such profusion, suggesting the ways in which human subjects are subject to, precisely, the manipulative manoeuvres of the market place. If that market place is the streets of Belfast (and it is, after all, Smithfield *market* which has gone up in smoke), then the agents of domination and control may hide themselves in the glitter of packaging and product as easily as they may reveal themselves in the obviousness of military surveillance. In streets patrolled by armoured personnel carriers branding themselves 'Saracen, Kremlin-2 mesh' all other brand names are likely to seem less innocent too, more malevolently or ironically elements in a system of signification which is also a system of subjugation; human beings, wandering in the interstices of such names, may also seem all too easily commodifiable. In *The Irish for No* named commodities have a habit of refusing their proper function, rebelling against the uses for which they are advertised. A dirty magazine called *Contact*, when read by a lonely British soldier in his Belfast barracks, reminds us that soldiers make 'contact' with the enemy as well as with sexual partners and, indeed, that in Belfast they do the former where they dare not do the latter. Durex is used for making bombs as well as for making love. A Black & Decker drill may be used for the novel DIY job of putting terrified suicidal holes in your own head; and when you have become the half-forgotten facts of someone's cocktail-bar reminiscence, the names of the cocktails (Widows' Kisses, Corpse Revivers) will grotesquely ironise your death and the consequences for your family. If you are Horse Boyle, Heinz Baked Bean tins will be the only watchdog you can afford, but you will need a watchdog.

The itemisations in the volume are also, however, manifestly Carson's attempt to keep a tally of Belfast as it disappears: and in this, brand names join street names and other kinds of list, some of them intense little mnemonic poems-within-poems (the itemisation of smells at the opening of 'Calvin Klein's *Obsession*', for instance). Such an act of poetic reclamation may be an act of love, but it may also be preparatory to an act of vengeance, as the end of 'Slate Street School', the final shorter poem of Part II, makes plain. The poet remembers returning to his primary school at the beginning of a new term and chanting once again the mnemonic lists of rote-learning: distances, weights and measures, the multiplication tables. When the Belfast snow begins to fall, an anonymous voice (the teacher's, a priest's or some religious manual's?) makes the snowflakes an opportunity for catechetical instruction:

> *These are the countless souls of purgatory, whose numbers*
>   *constantly diminish*
> *And increase: each flake as it brushes to the ground is yet another*
>   *soul released.*
> And I am the avenging Archangel, stooping over mills and factories
>   and barracks.
> I will bury the dark city of Belfast forever under snow: inches,
>   feet, yards, chains, miles.

The prophetic, Blakean savagery of the denunciation is a note struck only this once in the book; but it is given its licence and authentication by the accumulation of the tally kept by the rest of the volume. That tally indicates that Slate Street School has made a poet: mnemonic itemisations chanted in rhythm may be the origin of those others chanted in these poems by the man who here remembers the child he was. But the Belfast classroom is also the origin of a tally of the depredations that must be not merely remembered but avenged. 'Avenging' is a dangerous adjective to use in a poem about Belfast, though it goes without saying that no serious poem about Belfast can afford to ignore the palpably motivating effect of the emotions generated by the desire for retribution. 'Slate Street School' confronts such emotions within the child/poet himself, but retains a probity in relation to them. The lines originate in pity, implying that the city of Belfast is the true purgatory for its "countless souls" longing for release, and thereby giving *The Irish for No* probably its single most memorable figure of entrapment, significantly but understatedly drawn from religious instruction. The poet/angel/avenger then promises to exact vengeance not on faction or person, not on organisation or tribe or side, but on the city itself, making the poem for once (from a depth of quite unironised anger) not a retrieval system but a grave: calling up, itemising, evoking with a view to burying in language what has become insupportable in place, eradicating in its own linguistic space those sites of repression and subjugation, "mills and factories and barracks", the chosen ground of Carson's imagination, as the labyrinth of the Falls Road was the given ground of his childhood.

## 3

When Carson reviewed Seamus Heaney's *Sweeney Astray* (his translation of the early medieval Irish poem *Buile Suibhne*) in the

*Honest Ulsterman* in 1984, he noted the way that narrative poem seems always written over, or written into, by Sweeney's prophesied death:

> He is the chronicle of a death foretold; he is living out the knowledge of a
> prophecy. The intricate circularity of purpose is mirrored in the rule of
> the Irish verse forms, that they must begin and end on the same word;
> the effect, at times, is like taking one step forward and two steps back.[16]

The effect of repeated readings of the poem on Carson is, as a result, to make his mind feel "a bit like Sweeney's, reeling and frantic". This is the effect of some of Carson's own poems on the reader too, it seems to me; and the simile used of the forms of *Sweeney Astray* ("one step forward and two steps back") occurs also in 'Calvin Klein's *Obsession*'.[17] The poem's erotic reverie free-floats over a love affair in early adolescence, remembered in tandem with a pop song of the time:

> It was April, a time
> Of fits and starts; fresh leaves blustered at the window, strips
>     and fronds
> Of fish and water-lilies sloughed off round my feet. A Frank
>     Ifield song
> From 1963, I think, kept coming back to me: *I remember you—*
>     *you're the one*
> *Who made my dreams come true—just a few—kisses ago.* I'm taking
> One step forward, two steps back, trying to establish what it
>     was about her
> That made me fall in love with her, if that's what it was . . .

Carson is a poet who writes his own characteristic signature into the self-reflexivity of contemporary narrative by letting the reflexes cluster and collide almost exhilaratedly; and this is a characteristically self-reflexive passage. The time of fits and starts is the time of the poem as well as the time of the year, as its memories stagger forwards and backwards in the discontinuities and intermittences of personal voluntary and involuntary memory; the song remembered and associated with a remembered love affair is a song about a remembered love affair; as soon as "love" is mentioned, it is placed under suspicion, scrutinised by the undermining scepticism of a past conditional. The passage, that is to say, is itself a demonstration of moving in the stately, obsessive and slightly absurd pavanne of "one step forward, two steps back".

Movement by digression, the characteristic movement of all the longer poems in the book, is the movement of one step forward, two steps back too: these poems get not exactly forward but back in upon themselves. In their own intricate circularity of purpose they too plot prophecies of foretelling and pre-figuring and maps of dislocation, erasure and derangement: the title of one poem, 'Serial', and its vertiginous realisation of the impression of *déja vu*, may be regarded as paradigmatic. This is as true of the poems of the personal and creative life as it is of the more outwardly turned and social poems. Indeed, it is 'Calvin Klein's *Obsession*' which gives this structure an implicit figure for itself when Carson remembers Boots' *Buttermilk and Clover* soap "Slipping and slipping from my grasp, clunking softly downwards through. The greying water; I have drowsed off into something else." The narrative of past time in this poem, its *recherche du temps perdu*, is a slow, expansive drowse through the processes of memory and sensation provoked by the Proustian mnemonic spurs of taste and smell. His glass of beer reminds him of the Ulster brewery, which reminds him of the perfume *Blue Grass*, which reminds him of the fur worn by an early girlfriend, which reminds him of candy apples, which remind him of buying snuff for his grandmother: and so on, in a gradual drift of apparently free association. The drift, however, is in fact cunningly plotted into a wistful, rueful account of the haunting of one's present by one's past, the temptations to sentimentality and nostalgia, and the tricks and turns of a fiction-alising memory. The drowsing digressions, the artful somnam-bulisms of 'Calvin Klein's *Obsession*', point ultimately into another black hole or *mise-en-abime*: in its final line, memory and perhaps language itself are conjured in all their recessive duplicity, as products without origin and names without substance, when they disappear into a suspicious association with a perfume manufacturer's dream of the ultimately skilful piece of marketing: "*Or maybe it's the name you buy, and not the thing itself*".

That line is a kind of pseudo-quotation: it represents the drifting into consciousness of a suddenly new appropriateness for the cliché that 'you're only paying for the name'. This kind of citation is typical of *The Irish for No* whose intertexts are frequently, as here, the texts of popular culture, Irish ballad, advertising and street-maps. Early on in 'Calvin Klein's *Obsession*', however, Carson quotes (or actually slightly misquotes) Edward Thomas's 'Old Man': "*I sniff and sniff again, and try to think of what it is I am remembering.*" "I think that's how it goes", he says, "like Andy Warhol's calendar of per-fumes . . .", and he is immediately into the next association. In that casual, imprecise and almost languid "I think that's how it goes" (which could as appropriately be said of, say, a Frank Ifield song), there is a marked lack of respect for the products of high art. Where Heaney is sometimes almost reverential and entranced in his literary allusiveness and Muldoon is, for all the slyness and obliquity with which he manages it, endlessly and insouciantly allusive to the texts of high literary culture (along with many other kinds of text too, of course), Carson's literary allusions are notably not a major feature of the nevertheless extremely sophisticated play of his poems. And when he is allusive, he is almost uninterpretably so, not pointed or ironic or context-creating or self-displaying in any of the recognised ways. The poem in which this is at its clearest is 'Whatever Sleep It Is'; and, as this is also the poem in *The Irish for No* most manifestly itself about the processes of creativity, I want to discuss it in some detail.

The poem is a painter's account of the process of making an apparently relatively representational canvas, a process of continuous erasure and substitution. The problematic leg of a spy or a pilot is changed into a flight of stairs, which then 'leads to' a skylight; the skylight is eventually given a broken pane, and the painter imagines that it has been broken by the character just painted out. This character is in love with a woman quickly painted in, behind a rather corny Chianti bottle with a candle. Then, suddenly, the painting's final narrative realises itself, although perhaps only as imaginative possibility rather than canvas actuality since, as in several of Carson's most stunning effects, the syntax is fluidly irresolvable, and there is a slippage between the tenor and vehicle of metaphor. The erased character ("Mr Natural, / As we'll call him": he who is anything but natural, this abandoned product of imaginative artifice) turns out to be an angel, and the painting—apparently without the painter's conscious decision or manipulation—becomes a kind of contemporary Annunciation:

> I see it is an angel, not a man, who has
> Descended, looking faintly puzzled at the poor response of the
>     girl
> To whatever important announcement he has just made. She
>     is, in fact, asleep,
> Oblivious also to the clink and hum of the electric milk float
> Which has just pulled up outside. And the milkman looks up,
>     momentarily
> Amazed at curtains, wings, gusting from the attic window. He
>     rubs his eyes;
> He is still drowsy with these six days out of seven. Tomorrow

yawns ahead
With routine promises; tomorrow, after all, he will be free.

The milkman's amazement apes the reader's at the successive metamorphoses of this painting (and this poem). An allegory of its own process of creation or construction, of the one-step-forward, two-steps-back kind of accident, trial and error that make all paintings and poems, this poem noses out its own narrative in a ritual of self-cancellation, discovering itself only—in the memorable Derridean phrase—by "letting go of the pen", just as this painting's narrative discovers itself in the series of controlled accidents produced by letting go of the brush.[18] To paint an Annunciation, of all things, *by accident*, and only *faut-de-mieux*, seems a destabilisingly postmodern recognition of the artist's or poet's lack of rational control over the processes of his or her own creativity. This angel has indeed descended—come down—a long way in the world since the orthodox angels of Biblical tradition and the imaginative angels of modern literary tradition: more Wim Wenders's *Wings of Desire* than Rilke's *Duino Elegies* or Wallace Stevens's 'Angel Surrounded by Paysans'. And yet this coming down, this bathos, is a kind of epiphany too, if not for this sleeping Virgin then at least for the milkman, rapt from his routine.

This is what appears to happen in 'Whatever Sleep It Is'; this seems to me the story that takes shape within the story this painterly narrator tells us. It is a story, however, that seems to happen virtually independently of the poem's nevertheless heavily foregrounded allusiveness. The poem's title is a phrase from one of Robert Frost's best-known poems, 'After Apple-Picking', which is cited again, along with an almost arch literary joke, towards the conclusion. The woman in the painting has "a bowl of apples at her elbow":

> Meanwhile Mr Natural,
> As we'll call him, has climbed on to the roof, and, with his feet lodged
> In the guttering, is staring through the hole at her. *The pane of glass*
> *I skimmed this morning from the drinking-trough*, he whispers to himself,
> *Melted, and I let it fall and break.* Early frost: the stars are blazing
> Now like snowflakes—stem end and blossom end
>
> Swelling and dimming over the black Alp of the roof.

The presence of Frost's poem seems peculiarly supernumerary, like the presence of Keats's 'Ode to a Nightingale' and Heaney's *Door into the Dark* in 'The Irish for No', and like Edward Thomas's 'Old Man' in 'Calvin Klein's *Obsession*'. Apparently instances of frail but poised coincidence rather than of the more vibrant energy and tension usually evident in complex and sophisticated intertextuality, they have their clear local point but lack defining context. In the Carson poems, that is to say, the allusions seem themselves parenthetical, digressive, in no sense an inevitable element of the structure, suspended in an air of almost irretrievable connections ("I think that's how it goes . . ."). They seem therefore not easily recuperable by the will to interpret and explain. What is the point of the Frost poem here? To frame the narrative? To ironise the possibility of 'naturalness' in a work of art? To suggest to the reader who knows the anxiety of Frost's poem that this poem of Carson's is the 'trouble' that must disturb an artist's sleep? Or that paintings and poems are, always, the forms given to dreams? Or that they offer a world transformed in the way it might seem if looked at through a pane of ice? To act merely as decoration? Simply to provide the opportunity, in the 'early frost' joke, for a moment of pawky self-congratulation for the literate reader? Or to make that joke, in its possibly preening self-regard, the vehicle for a criticism of exactly such opportunities afforded by allusion in modern poetry, a poetry written and read almost exclusively by people trained in the English departments of institutions of higher education? Or just to supply the chance for that lovely, glancing and zany comparison of Frost's apples to the painting's stars?

All of these things, perhaps, but none of them of necessity. The poem does not explore or explicate the allusion in a way that would allow readerly certainty: it retains an heuristic secrecy and patience. It is as if the literary reference takes its place as just another element in the poem's patchwork fabric, as just another piece happening to be to hand, but one which makes 'Whatever Sleep It Is' the tracing of an acknowledgement, a deference as well as a difference. Given that apple-trees are in question here, it may not be beside the point to adduce Derrida's phrase for Mallarmé's *Mimique*: "grafted onto the efflorescence of another text".[19] The graft gets by on its own, however, independent of origin: this allusion appears actually to lighten the burden of what the writer must drag behind him, asserting no system of hierarchy or patrimony. In this it manifestly divorces itself from the sanctity of any Eliotic concept of tradition and from the impassioned anguish (and rhetorical gusto) of any Bloomian struggle and swerve. As such, it might well be regarded as the turning to profit of a genuinely postmodern sense of the intertextual one in which hierarchy is emptied into equivalence.

The way Carson uses literature may imply that literature is almost what his poems aspire not to be. Tall tales, ballads, songs, fiddle tunes and flute tunes, reportage and annotation: these seem much more what they would wish to be, given the chance. Literature is too full for them. If the poems of *The Irish for No* are full, they are full of holes too, emptying themselves out into gap, fissure and the other story that they always seem aware they might be telling. The painting in 'Whatever Sleep It Is' has "everything as full of holes as a Swiss cheese"; in 'Snowball', "Like a fish-net stocking, everything is full of holes"; and their own interpretative holes, their irresolvable abysms and aporias, are the register of a scepticism, even a guilt, about the relationship between poem or 'story' and the matter it must handle in contemporary Belfast which is probably their profoundest principle of form. It is a scepticism, it should be said, given a more than merely figurative authority by Carson's long poetic silence but it finds its most perfect figure in *The Irish for No* at the end of 'Snowball', where a postman is at work in the Tomb St. GPO in Belfast at Christmas time:

> Arse-about-face, night-shift and the Christmas rush, perfume oozing from
> Crushed packets—*Blue Grass, Obsession*—and, once, in a forgotten pigeon-hole,
> I woke up to this card stamped 9 August 1910: *Meet me usual place and time*
> *Tomorrow—What I have to tell you might not wait—Yours—*
> *Forever—B.*

A card in a hole in a Tomb: a very dead letter indeed, undelivered for decades, its written urgency and desire ironically poignant and finite where they wished to be eternally enduring; this seems the aptest of emblems for the well-directed but misgiving *The Irish for No* (a book written, as some poems in *The New Estate* and *Belfast Confetti* make clear, by a postman's son). The emblem has its interesting correspondences with Jacques Derrida's fascination with the post card in his extraordinary book *The Post Card: From Socrates to Freud and Beyond*,[20] and his sense there that, once committed to the post, there is always the risk that the letter will be lost or disseminated. Those oozing perfumes too, which reappear from 'Calvin Klein's *Obsession*', perhaps also figure a scepticism about how much can be made to cohere in any organisation of poetic language, a consciousness of how much may ooze and slip and spill. This is a very long way from the claims implicit in mythical methods: more disillusioned, more jaded, later. If such scepticism has its affinities with postmodern theory, its formal expression in Carson's narratives is also peculiarly appropriate to a poetry of the contemporary fate of Northern Ireland. Narratives wander duplicitously or digressively, taking wrong turnings, turning again; language may well not mean at all what it seems to say, or may be read quite differently from how it is written; messages may not be delivered for eighty years. If you take one step forward you may well take two steps back. But there is no Irish for no.

## NOTES

1.  Ciaran Carson, 'Escaped from the Massacre?', *Honest Ulsterman*, 50, Winter 1975, pp. 183–6.
2.  See Neil Corcoran, *Seamus Heaney* (London: Faber & Faber, 1986), Chapter IV.
3.  See Edna Longley, ' "Inner Emigré" or "Artful Voyeur"? Seamus Heaney's *North*' in *The Art of Seamus Heaney* (Bridgend: Seren Books, 1982) and Paul Muldoon, *The Faber Book of Contemporary Irish Poetry* (London: Faber & Faber, 1986).
4.  Heaney to Harriet Cooke, 1973, cited *Seamus Heaney*, p. 95. Terence Brown has written excellently on the fate of the 'well-made poem' in Northern Ireland in 'A Northern Renaissance: Poets from the North of Ireland 1965-1980' in his *Ireland's Literature: Selected Essays* (Mullingar: The Lilliput Press, 1988).
5.  *The Irish for No* exists in three separate editions: Dublin: Gallery Press, 1987; Winston-Salem: Wake Forest University Press, 1987; Newcastle upon Tyne: Bloodaxe Books, 1988.
6.  See, for instance, Muldoon's 'The More a Man Has the More a Man Wants' in *Quoof* (London: Faber and Faber, 1983), p. 49, for a parodistic moment conflating Heaney's version of *Sweeney Astray* and his poem 'Broagh' from *Wintering Out*; and Paulin's 'And Where Do You Stand on the National Question?' in *Liberty Tree* (London: Faber & Faber, 1983), p. 68.
7.  T.S. Eliot, 'Ulysses, Order and Myth' (1923), reprinted in Richard Ellmann and Charles Feidelson jnr., *The Modern Tradition* (New York: Oxford University Press, 1965), pp. 679–81.
8.  Fredric Jameson, Introduction to Jean-François Lyotard, *The Postmodern Condition: A Report on Knowledge* (Manchester: Manchester University Press, 1984), p. xxiv.
9.  *The Postmodern Condition*, p. 41.
10. *The New Estate* (Belfast: Blackstaff Press, 1976), subsequently published in an enlarged version as *The New Estate and Other Poems* (Loughcrew: Gallery Press, 1988). That edition incorporates poems from a pamphlet publication, *The Lost Explorer* (Belfast: Ulsterman Publications, 1978).

11. *Belfast Confetti* (Loughcrew: Gallery Press, 1989 and Newcastle upon Tyne: Bloodaxe Books, 1990).
12. I have found the following particularly illuminating: Steven Connor, *Postmodernist Culture* (Oxford: Blackwell, 1989); Linda Hutcheon, *A Poetics of Postmodernism* (London: Routledge, 1988); Richard Kearney, *The Wake of Imagination: Ideas of Creativity in Western Culture* (London: Hutchinson, 1988); and Brian McHale, *Postmodernist Fiction* (London: Methuen, 1987).
13. Reviewing two books by Williams, he writes: "I hereby acknowledge a debt". See 'Against Oblivion', *The Irish Review*, no. 6, Spring 1989, pp. 113–16. It is worth pointing out that, in addition to his experimentation with the long line, Williams also characteristically makes use of American urban working-class material.
14. Quotations in these paragraphs are from Ciaran Carson's letters to me of 5 May and 19 October 1989.
15. *The Pocket Guide to Irish Traditional Music* (Belfast: Appletree Press, 1986).
16. Ciaran Carson, 'Sweeneys Ancient and Modern', *Honest Ulsterman*, no. 76, Autumn 1984, pp. 73–9. A revised and expanded version of the review appears in Tony Curtis (ed.), *The Art of Seamus Heaney*, 2nd ed. (Bridgend: Poetry Wales Press, 1985; Chester Springs: Dufour Editions.)
17. It also occurs in the poems 'Ambition' and 'Narrative in Black and White' in *Belfast Confetti*.
18. See Jacques Derrida, *Dissemination* (Chicago: The University of Chicago Press, 1981), p. 274. I am reminded by the poem of the work-processes described by the Irish painter Louis le Brocquy when making his ink-paintings for *The Gododdin* (Dublin: Dolmen Editions, 1977). Labouring under the apparent disadvantage of a right hand immobilised in plaster, he made the images with his other hand: "images emerge not by imposition on my part but, as it were, automatically jerked into coherence by a series of vaguely directed accidents, discovered rather than executed". The images are, nevertheless, recognisably representational. See Dorothy Walker, *Louis le Brocquy* (Dublin: Ward River Press, 1981), p. 111. It is notable how frequently a painterly vocabulary features in *Belfast Confetti*: see particularly 'Queen's Gambit' and 'All the Better to See You With'.
19. *Dissemination*, p. 202.
20. Chicago: University of Chicago Press, 1987.

**John Kerrigan**
Ulster Ovids

# Ulster Ovids

Towards the end of Brian Friel's *Translations*, as friction between locals and English soldiers flares into violence, the hedge-school master Hugh staggers in from a wake. He has just been told that the headship of the new National School will not be going to him after all but to a certain Bartley Timlin, who has recommended himself by his knowledge of bacon-curing:

> HUGH: Ha-ha-ha-ha-ha! The Cork bacon-curer! *Barbarus hic ego sum quia non intelligor ulli*—James?
> JIMMY: Ovid.
> HUGH: *Procede.*
> JIMMY: 'I am a barbarian in this place because I am not understood by anyone'.[1]

Given the destruction raging around him, Hugh's appeal to *Tristia* (V. x. 37) is bound to seem indulgent, the tipsy self-dramatisation of an alienated intellectual. Yet the play expects us to register more than disappointed vanity. Hugh's failure to get the headship stands for the replacement of indigenous schooling by a proto-Thatcherite system which prizes utility above knowledge, business above cultural aspiration. The demise of the hedge-school at Baile Beag in 1833 will lead, by a single movement, to a loss of popular Latinity and decline in living Irish. British audiences can misconstrue this, since for them Latin suggests stage pedantry (Hugh as Shakespeare's Holofernes) or educational privilege. In the Ireland shown by Friel, however, Latin was read and spoken at the lowest social levels. As one observer in 1824 reported, "A tattered Ovid

or Virgil may be found even in the hands of the common labourers."[2]
Instruction in Latin went back to the early monastic schools,
where the tongue of Eriugena and Aquinas belonged to "religious
education but was also particularly useful . . . as a lingua franca."[3]
After the Tudor and Jacobean plantations, Latin was the language in
which mass was secretly celebrated. It was the argot of an oppressed
faith, taught in hedge-schools by priests and masters harassed
under the penal laws.[4] Latin could express detachment from the
British *imperium*, linking its speakers to a holier Roman Empire.
For intellectuals it represented an allegiance to European Latinity
which by-passed much that was English. That Hugh composes
"verse . . . after the style of Ovid . . . in Latin", not "Gaelic" (pp.
41–2), does not prevent him standing in a vital relationship to national
culture. Indeed he claims to have written a book called 'The Pentaglot
Preceptor or Elementary Institute of the English, Greek, Hebrew,
Latin and Irish Languages'—invoking a work published by Patrick
Lynch, secretary of the Gaelic Society from 1815.

   Talk of Ireland and empire raises ghosts not easily laid. It sets up an
explosive paradigm, Big Island v. Little, which revisionist history is
still far from defusing. Yet *Translations* is not the only recent work in
which a colonial analysis of the North is at once clarified and
complicated by Latin. Seamus Heaney's 'Freedman', for example,
takes an epigraph from R.H. Barrow's *The Romans*: "slavery comes
nearest to its justification in the early Roman Empire: for a man from a
'backward' race might be brought within the pale of civilization,
educated . . . and turned into a useful member of society." Alert to
the complacency of this, Heaney explores both the privilege and
conditioning which education in British Ulster confers on a Catholic.
His poem begins with a free fluency which is yoked, nonetheless, to
the Latin diction which remains a hallmark of his high style:
"Subjugated yearly under arches,/Manumitted by parchments and
degrees . . .". By line 3, moreover, another Rome has emerged:

> My murex was the purple dye of lents
> On calendars all fast and abstinence.
>
> '*Memento homo quia pulvis es.*'
> I would kneel to be impressed by ashes,
> A silk friction, a light stipple of dust—
> I was under that thumb too like all my caste . . .

What might have been a Harrisonesque poem about the eleven plus
and social tension is given a territorial twist ("within the pale") by the

imperial connection, then ambiguated by resemblance or complicity
between the dominant and colonized order. The Cicero that young
Harrison slogs over is not in the tongue of his father's faith. Heaney's
lyric ends with a *non serviam* freighted with guilt—"Now they will say
I bite the hand that fed me"—because becoming a truly freed man
(whatever that might mean) would involve the rejection of more than
one Rome. One thing it might mean is shown in Paul, the half-mad
derelict of Frank McGuinness's *Carthaginians*. In lines which show
psychological damage as well as clear–sightedness he calls Derry

> A harbour. An empire. Part of a great empire.
> GRETA: British Empire?
> PAUL: That's dead. Roman Empire.
> GRETA: Catholic?
> PAUL: Roman. This city is not Rome, but it has been destroyed
> by Rome . . . I'm no slave. I am Carthaginian. This earth is
> mine, not Britain's, nor Rome's.[5]

Rejecting 'slavery' involves dismissing Rome or Rome, in ways which
do not sit easily (for all the ambiguities which are the truth of the
passage) with traditional Irish nationalism. The awkwardness is
typical of *Carthaginians*, and it is interesting that Field Day, which
commissioned the play, refused, for whatever reason, to produce it.
Beside the laminated complexity of such allegiance and resistance,
some 'colonial' situations are simpler. A writer like Derek Walcott, for
instance, has a "sound colonial education"[6] which equips him
confidently to imitate Propertius, chat with the ghost of Ovid and
ventriloquize a new *Tristia* (in 'The Hotel Normandie Pool'). Heaney
refers, oddly but self-revealingly, to Walcott's "imperious linguistic
gifts",[7] and there is indeed a scope and confidence in the black poet
which suggests that the energies of his empire-educated speech are
aligned with telling and naming. The virtue of Heaney's predicament
lies elsewhere, among anxieties of apartness (Paul's tragedy) and
entanglement. In *North*, the collection which includes 'Freedman',
this is most apparent in the famous closing passage, where talk of
"prismatic counselling" and "conducive voices" crystallizes round a
Latin allusion. Leaving Ulster for Wicklow, experiencing media and
other forms of 'Exposure', Heaney sees himself as an "inner émigré",
like Ovid at Tomis, culturally "within the pale" (near Dublin) yet
removed from the imperial centre. As "Mutter about let-downs and
erosions" whispers in his ears, he describes himself, with pride,

doubt and self-deprecation, "weighing and weighing/My responsible *tristia*."

For an Ulster Protestant, in rather different ways, the colonial problem can be negotiated through Rome. John Hewitt's account of the history of his province, 'The Colony', images the plantation in classical terms:

> First came the legions, then the colonists,
> provincials, landless citizens, and some
> camp-followers of restless generals . . .

The displaced Gaels become "barbarian tribesmen" in arms against "Caesar". The penal laws are rules that "forbade them,/for many years, to worship their strange idols." Moderatingly, however, an 'I' emerges with Ovidian traits. Hewitt hints at a fascination with indigenous imagery, expressing his grief for the ruin of Ireland's ancient forests by crossing native tree-myths with *Metamorphoses*:

> I could invent a legend of those trees,
> and how their creatures, dryads, hamadryads,
> fled from the copses, hid in thorny bushes,
> and grew a crooked and malignant folk,
> plotting and waiting for a bitter revenge . . .

As centuries pass, and "from other lands the legions ebb", the settlers at this border of empire lose touch with the violence of their origin. No longer "the raw levies" which usurped "the land", they become rootedly provincial, and "would" (which is not "should") "be strangers in the Capitol". Hewitt's is a memorable formulation of the stance found elsewhere in Protestant poetry: aware of imperial decline ("British Empire?/That's dead"), seeking peace from a legacy of war, not at ease in the province yet alienated from the centre. Significantly, when Derek Mahon writes a poem 'for John Hewitt', it elaborates those concerns. 'The Return' starts in Surrey, heart of expansive England and speaks of not feeling at home. "I have", Mahon says,

> often thought if I lived
> Long enough in this house
> I would turn into a tree
> Like somebody in Ovid
> —A small tree certainly
> But a tree nonetheless—

> Perhaps befriend the oak,
> The chestnut and the yew,
> Become a home for birds,
> A shelter for the nymphs,
> And gaze out over the downs
> As if I belonged here too . . .

Withdrawn at the centre (for if he "belonged", he would not so bizarrely imagine blending with place), Mahon finds in his 'Return' to Coleraine a still bleaker sense of exile. Hewitt's thornscape has been reduced to Beckettian futility. "There are no nymphs to be seen", only a single "Rooted . . . growth":

> Crone, crow, scarecrow,
> Its worn fingers scrabbling
> At a torn sky, it stands
> On the edge of everything . . .

> As if it belongs there.

The Ovidian poet whose detachment gave him the fancifulness to imagine metamorphosis in Surrey finds himself beside an Euxine sea burdened with a larger sense of exile. In this, 'The Return' is typical of what Mahon takes from Hewitt and his Protestant inheritance generally. The poem draws on a pattern of feeling evident in his many works about god- or godot-haunted localities, which resolve into frontier alienation.

When Walcott's Ovid summarizes his output, beside the swimming pool of the Hotel Normandie, it goes "from Metamorphoses to Tristia". The omission of his other works—including the poems on love which preceded *Metamorphoses* (*Amores*, *Heroides*, etc.) and the *Ibis* and *Ex Ponto* which followed *Tristia*—is not unusual. Ovid has become for us a poet of two phases: the sophisticated, pleasure-seeking Roman years, during which he wrote the cycle of transformations, then (from 8 to 17 A.D.) the period of exile at Tomis "weighing and weighing" the *Tristia*. The fact that Ovid was banished—strictly, 'relegated'—by Augustus for *carmen* as well as *error* (*Tristia* II.207) has helped link these different phases and made their relations tragic. For post-Romantic readers, the poet becomes a victim of his art. That Ovid neither anticipated nor with much dignity embraced his banishment has mattered less to Mandelstam, St-John

Perse and the other poets who have invoked his exile than the overall
shape of his fate. The pressure of commentary and creativity which
condensed Ovid's career in this way began before our own time, but it
has been powerful in the twentieth century. During the Victorian
period, indeed, Ovid's stock was in decline. The modernist writers
rediscovered him. Acutely conscious of the 'broken images' and
mythic 'fragments' which made up their culture—encyclopaedic
remnants of what might have once compelled belief—and as often as
not living in exile, they were drawn to both dimensions of his work.
The Ovid-quoting author of *The Waste Land* comes first to mind,
along with Pound, who owes much of the rationale of his early cantos
to *Metamorphoses*. Sister M. Bernetta Quinn has written astutely
about both in *The Metamorphic Tradition in Modern Poetry* (1955),
and she shows without difficulty that an Ovidian strain runs through
Williams, Wallace Stevens, Hart Crane, Randall Jarrell and (most
suggestively) Yeats. Thanks to her study, and to Charles Tomlinson's
*Poetry and Metamorphosis* (1983), there is no need to demonstrate the
presence of Ovid in modernist verse. This essay will make more recent
and more particular claims. Ulster writers from a Catholic background seem aware of Irish Latinity in ways which not only make
Ovid accessible but which bring his metamorphic imaginings into
fruitful relation with Gaelic. It is scarcely the influence of Ovid which
turns the hero of 'Sweeney Redivivus', the last section of *Station
Island*, into a bird; Heaney has found that character metamorphosing
in the *Buile Suibhne*. But a knowledge of Ovid does attune poet and
reader to Sweeney's role in a collection which begins with a fable from
*Metamorphoses*: "And me, me then like a fleet god gaining / Upon you
before you turned to a reed." Poets from the Protestant community,
by (heavily qualified) contrast, seem drawn to Ovid's civic and secular
elegance. Urbanity is the style, quite often, of their background.
Unlike Paul Muldoon, John Montague and Heaney, Tom Paulin and
Michael Longley are city boys, or at least suburban, by origin. Mahon
gravitated to London, and his 'Kensington Notebook' invokes a text
written in his district, Pound's *The Spirit of Romance*, which catches
this aspect of Ovid's appeal: "Ovid—urbane, sceptical, a Roman of
the city—writes . . . in a verse which has the clarity of French
scientific prose . . . His mind, trained to the system of empire,
demands the definite. The sceptical age hungers after the definite,
after something it can pretend to believe."[8] Further, and inevitably,
Ovid is a figure of exile. The cultural contrasts can, again, be
overstated. But for Catholic writers Ovid's *Tristia* relate to a history

of internal and foreign exile for reasons of faith and politics. Protestant authors, educated to feel the presence of the centre elsewhere, have still stronger grounds for empathy. The frontier alienations of Mahon do not occur in any old nowhere, but at the vulnerable limit of civility where Ovid's life also ends.

But why so much stress on Ovid, when those literate labourers in 1824 were also reading Virgil? Traditionally Virgil's career has been thought the epitome of creative endeavour. When Heaney translates the *Buile Suibhne* for Field Day, is he not producing a national epic to follow his bucolics and poems of digging and ploughing, from *Death of a Naturalist* to *Wintering Out*, rather as the *Aeneid* was preceded by the *Eclogues* and *Georgics*? Paul, in *Carthaginians*, quizzes, "Who wrote *The Aeneid*? An Irishman wrote it./That's your only clue" (p.17). Given what has been said about allegiance to Rome under the penal laws, did Hewitt's displaced people, "plotting and waiting for a bitter revenge", mark this passage in their Virgils?

> An age is ripening in revolving fate,
> When Troy shall overturn the Grecian state,
> And sweet revenge her conquering sons shall call,
> To crush the people that conspired her fall.

As it happens these lines from Dryden's translation are quoted by Tom Paulin in a review-article which, after cuffing Tomlinson's *Poetry and Metamorphosis*, praises Dryden's "healing initiative" in "national culture".[9] For Paulin, Dryden's *Aeneid* ("much more important than his translations from Ovid") shows the Jacobite poet seeking compromise with the Whig administration. Most scholars hold Tonson, Dryden's publisher, responsible for the more ingratiating gestures (such as redrawn illustrations which give Aeneas King Billy's hooked nose). But pedantic doubts cannot detract from the force of Paulin's claim that "healing" acts of translation are needed now, as in 1697, in Ireland as well as Britain. The United Irishman in Paulin finds Dryden's accommodation with William III analogous to another Catholic/Protestant rapprochement. In Friel's *Translations*, he points out, Hugh recalls making for Sligo in 1798 with a pike across his shoulder and the *Aeneid* in his pocket. "Everything seemed to find definition that spring—a congruence, a miraculous matching of hope and past and present and possibility. Striding across the fresh, green land. The rhythms of perception heightened . . ." This is, as Paulin says, an "inspiring speech"—the voice of Field Day rather than a nineteenth-century schoolmaster, but still moving for all that. Does it matter, however, that this *Aeneid* never saw action, because Hugh stopped off at a pub and got homesick for Donegal? Paulin seems unable to find, in twentieth-century Irish writing, signs of an emerging *Aeneid*. He cites *Ulysses*, but Homer is not Virgil.[10] To confirm the "recent interest in translating classical and European poetry into Irish English" he mentions Tibullus (as rendered by Longley) who is different again. Paulin's prime example of 'neoclassical' translation exploring "the theme of national identity" is Muldoon's version of the *Immram Mael Duin*. That this is "the most brilliant imitation to appear in these islands for many years" (a fair claim for 1984), but also, as Paulin admits, "Ovidian" in spirit, suggests that the modernist, metamorphic strain which fascinates Tomlinson might have more to do with the best in Irish writing than Paulin is willing to concede.

Part of the problem is that Paulin's appeal to Virgil implies a view of history in which national definition is a needed, if not necessary, outcome. Virgil presents the Augustan empire as time's violent but providential achievement, and, in a not so paradoxical way, this makes his vision compatible with Marx-influenced nationalism (compare the role of 'history' in Seamus Deane's *Celtic Revivals*) as well as with cultivated imperialism: Paulin's argument is at points oddly reminiscent of Eliot's 'What is a Classic?' Virgil, in a word, is closer to nineteenth-century evolutionary historicism than Ovid or, for that matter, Tibullus. Joseph Brodsky (with some exaggeration) writes: "The Roman elegiac poets of the end of the first century B.C.— especially Propertius and Ovid—openly mock their great contemporary Virgil and his *Aeneid* . . . it is Virgil's concept of linear movement, his linear model of existence, that the elegists find so exasperating in him."[11] Certainly modernist writers, fed up with the "imbecility" of empire and its rhetoric of historical triumphalism, were drawn to more elegists than Ovid. Pound accuses both "the British" and "the Roman Empire" of "infinite and ineffable imbecility" in his defence of *Homage to Sextus Propertius*[12]—that founding example of anti-imperialist paraphrase. When Walcott writes his 'Propertius Quartet', it is this vein that he draws on. And, despite Paulin's eloquence, the most inventive, 'healing' recent translations in Ireland return to that poetry of the private, the erotic, the whimsically mythic. Indeed, they sometimes imply that the Roman elegists did not go far enough in resisting nationalist/imperialist ideology. Michael Longley's 'Altera Cithera', for instance, begins with a paraphrase of

Propertius II.x.1–4 which refuses to translate the poet's promise that
he will abandon love-songs for songs of war (a tribute to Augustus),
turning it into a question: "A change of tune, then . . . or / The same
old songs . . . Unwashed by epic oceans / And dipped by love / In
lyric waters only?" Longley provides a clear answer, in Propertius'
name but—as the Poundian shift from the margin implies—not at first
in his voice:

> Given under our hand
> (With a ballpoint pen)
> After the Latin of Gaius
> Sextus Propertius,
> An old friend, the shadow
> Of his former self
> Who—and this I append
> Without his permission—

Loaded the dice before
He put them in his sling
And aimed at history,
Bringing to the ground
Like lovers Caesar,
Soldiers, politicians
And all the dreary
Epics of the muscle-bound.

As this fine passage proceeds, the poet takes courage, abandons his
gloss, and reclaims the left margin with its authority of statement.
Longley's extended syntax has a discreet strength which welds his
irregular trimeters into an active tribute to Propertius' David-like
powers. In an *Honest Ulsterman* interview, published 1985, Longley
spoke of "the marvellous mixture of complexity and flow you can
achieve in an inflected language", and said "That lovely mixture still
influences my fascination with what can be achieved through syntax,
the arrangement of a sentence."[13] The fruits of his Latin reading are
apparent here. But so is Longley's resistance to big 'history' and its
"dreary / Epics". He flings Propertius' dice (of chance and play) at the
great march of time, and brings an emperor down.

"It wasn't till I went to Trinity and discovered the Latin love
elegists", Longley says in his interview, "that I felt I'd come face to
face with an ancient ghost . . . especially Propertius, . . . who's peculiarly modern in his sensibility. And just a few years ago I discovered

Tibullus". "Ancient" but "modern": Longley's 'Peace', glanced at
by Paulin, translates Tibullus I.x into a poem with those same
contraries. Firm syntax sustains a verse which entertains both the
archaic ("yapping Cerberus") and up-to-date ("sexual neurosis")
without dissonance. Tibullus' theme suits Longley well, because it
moves from an opening grand question ("Who was responsible for the
very first arms deal . . .?"), through what "slaughter" means, to the
intimate "skirmishes, guerrilla tactics" of lovers quarrelling. The
poem devolves to a lived-in, thing-detailed milieu characteristic of
Latin elegy. Tibullus is unblinkered: he sees that there is always going
to be violence of some sort, but follows his humane bias towards
private life, where anger is bad enough yet can be resolved by erotic,
domestic harmony. (Longley's *Poems 1963–1983*, has a postscript
from Tibullus I.v.7–8 along similar lines: *parce tamen, per te furtivi
foedera lecti, / per venerem quaeso compositumque caput . . .*[14]) The
'Peace People' who asked Longley for a poem as part of their
campaign[15] might have been surprised by what he provided. But the
classical perspective in which he sets the Troubles lends depth and
hope of resolution. His changes from "ancient" to "modern" can, in
that way, be very effective. For example, where Tibullus urges his
Lares not to be ashamed that they are carved from an old log (*e stipite
factos*), Longley speaks of a "handmade statue / Carved out of bog
oak". He quietly reclaims, from the ominous "mother ground" of
Heaney's bogland—"Insatiable bride" (as 'Kinship' puts it)—a
harmless god who can be niched in a household "shrine":

> A man could worship there with bunches of early grapes,
> A wreath of whiskery wheat-ears, and then say Thank you
> With a wholemeal loaf delivered by him in person,
> His daughter carrying the unbroken honeycomb . . .

This lovely extract would be a shallow idyll were it not underwritten
by Latin. 'Worship"at the "shrine" seems both in and hopelessly out
of reach when it might be done in Latin. But why should it be out of
reach when grapes, wheat and honeycomb can be found in Ulster too?
Hope becomes tangible. Longley's long measures recall the flow of
Latin elegiacs, but his metrical variety sharpens the ear and "delivers" things (in "bunches", "whiskery") to the reader. The one
anachronistic touch here, "a wholemeal loaf" (for *liba*), wonderfully
revives the ordinary, with its semantic load of humility, nutrition,
fullness (". . . unbroken").

"I'm interested now in having a go at Ovid", Longley declares in his interview: "Derek Mahon and Paul Muldoon are both interested as well, [*laughs*] so I think I'd better get moving." This evidence of like-minded interest in the mid-'80s is useful. But anyone looking at Muldoon, in particular, is not going to be surprised. An obsession with change, in slow motion or freeze frame, goes back to his early books. *Mules* (1977) is full of figures caught between identities: 'The Bearded Woman, by Ribera', 'The Merman', 'The Centaurs'. You could say that this attention to the state of between-states had to do with the state where the poetry was written. But the politics of Ulster are only expressed obliquely. Leonard Barkan has pointed out that Ovid "dissolves great public facts into private stories"[16] and something similar happens in *Mules*. Its title-poem, for instance, starts with a line that bristles with provocation for those living in a mixed state: "Should they not have the best of both worlds?" It is useless to pretend that this question is only about cross-bred beasts, "neither one thing or the other", because it explicitly turns out to be concerned with a lot more. After turning to "private stories" about "Sam Parsons and my quick father", Muldoon offers this "both worlds" conceit about the birth of a foal "in the cowshed":

> We might yet claim that it sprang from earth
> Were it not for the afterbirth
> Trailed like some fine, silk parachute,
> That we would know from what heights it fell.

The Ovidian idea of autochthonous birth (Deucalion's stones, Cadmus and the serpent's teeth) is put aside for the still more delicious notion that mules fall to life from heaven. The poet has explained, on a Faber Poetry Cassette (1983), that this idea came to him after seeing newsreel footage of the Korean War in which mules were dropped, from cargo planes, by parachute. The relevance of civil war in another partitioned country to the breeding of mules in Ulster is covert, but you are not surprised to learn about it because the poet makes it clear that having told us a thing or two, he could tell us three or four. Part of the pleasure comes from the way these 'things' become stories by virtue of definition: Muldoon carries you across a clarifying simile ("like some fine, silk parachute"), and his very uninsistence ('some' not 'a') helps bring off the fable. Barkan writes that "Above all, the heritage of the *Metamorphoses* is a vision of the universe under the metaphor of *things* . . . Ovid's stories are visual or 'photogenic' because the power and drama are expressed in the objects themselves".[17] This is true of Muldoon's highly-imaged, martian style. But it is the truer because his persona, both forward and self-effacing ("We might yet claim . . . Were it not"), is never far away, observably drawing "stories" out of "objects". Contrast Longley, who writes in his 'Metamorphoses':

> A boulder locked in a cranny,
> A head without a face, she waits
> For rain to hollow out a font
> And fill her eye in, blink by blink.

This absorbed craftsmanship is unlike the craftiness of Muldoon, dedicatee of the book which includes it. Sight emerges from a pronounced, audible sense of the stanza accumulating to an end. "Blink by blink" is the drip of water, a measure of time, and the life of an eye coming to be seen if not to see. The syllabic metre conveys a containment of evolving irregularities. Muldoon would be in there with some pronoun, and looser lines, wondering about the event as process.

His signalled attention to change makes Muldoon a narrative poet even in short spans. But it is not until the long poems of *Why Brownlee Left* and *Quoof*—'Immram' and 'The More a Man Has the More a Man Wants'—that he produces equivalents of *Metamorphoses*. Plot-lines melt and diverge; we are distracted by embedded tales. As L.P. Wilkinson says of the "epyllia" in Ovid's long poem, "we lose the thread, forget the situation or who is speaking to whom."[18] There is a cascading lucidity of detail which recalls Ovid's fluid precision. Praising 'Immram', Tom Paulin notes that its 'Ovidian' features are associated with " 'discandying' qualities and melting hallucinations" which "owe much to the sinuous essence of Gaelic culture." *Quoof* begins with an epigraph from Rasmussen's *The Netsilik Eskimos* (if Muldoon can be believed) which seems to promise a different cultural backdrop. It describes an "old foster-mother" who "was a great shaman". She has the power to change sexes, to turn her genitals into a sled, and a lump of shit-stained snow into a dog to pull it. This Teiresian muse—the 'Bearded Woman' of *Mules* raised to a higher power—oversees *Quoof*'s stories. Yet the shape-shifting Eskimo magician does not preside over a poem in which the "melt-ing . . . sinuous" properties of Irish narrative are neglected. Muldoon seems familiar with Montague's assertion (1975), "An Irishman of

Gaelic background is, in a sense, a White Indian . . . The poet-king
Sweeney . . . might be a figure . . . from Haida legend."[19] The hero of
*Quoof*, who slips phonetically through many poems and takes centre-
stage in 'The More a Man Has . . .', does not boast the unmixed
Irishness of Heaney's hero Sweeney. His name flits around Golightly,
from 'Gallowglass' to 'English'. But his picaresque adventures recall
the windings of the *Buile Suibhne*. Indeed there seems a direct tribute
to Sweeney's farmyard scavenging when, outcast and on the run,
Gallogly sups from a footprint which "A milkmaid" has filled

> with beastlings for him to drink.
>
> In Ovid's conspicuously tongue-in-cheek
> account of an eyeball
> to eyeball
> between the goddess Leto
> and a shower of Lycian reed cutters
> who refuse her a cup of cloudy
> water
> from their churned-up lake,
> *Live then forever in that lake of yours,*
> she cries, and has them
> bubble
> and squeak
> and plonk themselves down as bullfrogs
> in their icy jissom.
>
> A country man kneels on his cap
> beside his neighbour's fresh
> grave-mud
> as Gallogly kneels to lap
> the primrose-yellow
> custard . . .

This is a complex passage, but one thing it has in mind is that Leto
transformed the reed-cutters for being quarrelsome and mean-
spirited. In a characteristic piece of false aetiology, Ovid (*Metamorphoses* VI.374-81) implies that bullfrogs croak grumpily and so
have their throats distended because they failed to show charity and
have been locked ever since in the consequences. *Sweeney Astray*
gives life on the run a deprived, desperate glamour which draws on
Irish traditions of guerilla heroism. Muldoon questions this with a

fable about reed-cutters who quarrel for the sake of it, unhappily ever after. Hence their muddy water slurs into the "fresh / grave-mud" of a neighbour, victim of those "neighbourly murders" that Heaney describes in 'Funeral Rites'.

Discussing Leto and why frogs quarrel, Wilkinson says: "Ovid likes to suggest thus the origin of the myths, as also the etymology of names—the bat (*vespertilio*) from his habit of flying at evening (*vespere*), the newt or lizard (*stellio*) from being spangled (*stellatus*) with spots."[20] Muldoon's pleasure in aetiological narrative goes with a playful recognition of the too ready persuasiveness of etymology. "Hash, hashish, *lo perfido assassin*"—fair enough; "*oregano, / orgone . . . organs . . . Arigna . . . Aragon*"—surely not.[21] Where Heaney "digs" down through what Hill calls "the vertical richness of language" ("etymology is history"),[22] Muldoon glissades. He subjects words to synchronous shock waves, delighting in what philologists call 'morphology'. He is not averse to the frisson of what Heaney has called, in a moment of self-criticism, "the auto-eroticism of an etymology",[23] but his typical stance is more analytic and surreal. Edna Longley writes well about Muldoon's "metamorphic . . . diction, and cultural co-ordinates",[24] pointing up, for instance, the mock-portent of place in 'The Right Arm': "Eglish . . . wedged between / *ecclesia* and *église*." This might be almost "English", or nearly Latin, or something else again—and certainly not "Anahorish". "Morphology", semantic change in relation to shifted elements within word-forms, is a ponderous description of Muldoon's subject. But there is no doubt that he increasingly asks us to notice how meanings are assembled. In *Meeting the British*, this leads to a glut of hyphenated compounds. A simple quasi-*haiku*, like the first four lines of 'The Earthquake', lightens its descriptive density by making you aware of the way its epithets are put together:

> The jacket of her chalk-stripe suit
> over a straight-backed chair,
>
> her tie's navy-blue
> rope-burn.

Exactness has the odd effect of reminding you of the observer, the palpable 'wedging' of adjectives points up the success of the act of description. At times, Muldoon's 'morphological' virtuosity has the superb pointlessness of change-ringing: "Gallogly, O Gallogly /

juggles / his name like an orange . . . and ogles / a moon". Compared with this, from 'The More a Man Has . . .', a poem by, say, Mahon aspires to the tacit inward cohesion of a Dutch still life. Instead of Magritte- or Dali-like quibbling in the medium you get a connectedness that seems mysteriously independent of language:

*Morphology*

Beans and foetuses,
brains and cauliflowers;
in a shaft of sunlight
a dust of stars.

This would not be so fully open to the world were it not for its internal harmonies, acoustic and syntactic, yet it musters those resources towards concealing artfulness. The *haiku*-effect recalls the (unwritten) "four-line poem / about the life of a leaf" that Mahon claims to have worked "years / on" in 'The Mayo Tao'. There he feels moved to express "an immanence in . . . things", and this vitalism elsewhere takes on specifically Ovidian overtones. In 'The Woods', for instance, "foxgloves and wood-anemones / looked up with tearful metamorphic eyes." Barkan observes that, in *Metamorphoses*, "the world is numinous . . . objects . . . contain some spark of life, of divinity, of poetic meaning, however inanimate and trivial they may seem on first glance", and he notes that Ovid's animism finds its logical outcome in the witty, speculative speech of Pythagoras which dominates the final book of his poem. For the philosopher, correspondences (beans as foetuses, souls) merge into a larger order, "metamorphoses dissolve into metamorphic nature".[25] As Mahon puts it in 'The Mute Phenomena': "Everything is susceptible, Pythagoras said so."

Mahon's concealment of art is an effect of his wanting poetry to be (as they say) a window onto things, whereas Muldoon delights in the way objects play through his consciousness with the effervescence of language. Logically enough, Mahon's linguistic self-consciousness is most apparent in a concrete poem called 'The Window', which uses "woodwoodwoodwood" and "windowwindowwindow" to box in the middle of the page with "wind" blown through it where excluding glass might be. Mahon has a number of poems in which he is the observer at a window. In this text words come forward in a concerted attempt to deliver an actual window onto the world. Though interesting, and indicative, 'The Window' is too much a work of poetics to have at stake what makes a good poem. By contrast, Muldoon's work thins in those texts which summon other linguistic consciousnesses but which, honourably, cannot accommodate their difference. '7 Middagh Street', the long poem which ends *Meeting the British*, is the clearest partial failure. It consists of a cycle of monologues spoken by Britten, MacNeice, Carson McCullers and others belonging to Auden's New York ménage on Thanksgiving Day 1940. But, in what is perhaps the best section, 'Salvador' tells us: "This lobster's not a lobster but the telephone / that rang for Neville Chamberlain." What is Dali doing in Middagh Street, and why does he sound like Muldoon? Sweeping objections cannot go deep, but they do encourage the reader to wonder whether the poem's metamorphoses are not, as often in Dali, easily won. Certainly '7 Middagh Street' develops the 'Ovidian' tactics of 'Immram' and 'The More a Man Has . . .'. In its opening lines, "Wystan" says,

> a blizzard off the Newfoundland coast
> had, as we slept, metamorphosed
>
> the *Champlain's* decks
> to a wedding cake . . .

and that vehicle then becomes his tenor. More obscure is the opening of MacNeice's monologue, as he takes over from 'Carson':

> two girls, I thought, two girls in silk kimonos.
>
> LOUIS
>
> Both beautiful, one a gazebo.
> When Hart Crane fell
> from the *Orizaba*
> it was into the *trou normand* of the well
>
> at Carrickfergus castle.
> All very Ovidian,
> as the ghostly
> *Healfdene*
>
> once remarked of both sorts of kipper
> we were forced to eat
> at supper
>
> every night in Reykjavik . . .

The transition springs a good joke, for by what metamorphic fancy or Muldoonish rhyme with "Lissadell" (and "fell") did Yeats call Eva Gore-Booth "a gazelle"? But then we are into the near-opacity of 'private stories'. You reach for a guidebook to Carrickfergus castle and *Letters from Iceland*, but hesitantly, because "the *trou normand*" and "as the ghostly / *Healfdene* // once remarked" have an elaborate bookish whimsy which promises a long way round to empty-handedness. Far from sounding like MacNeice, the monologue makes you hanker after his impurities—spat tangerine pips and so forth. Of course, the privacy of these stories is part of Muldoon's point, or scope. He is looking at a group of artists forced to weigh the claims of politics and patriotism (1940, World War II) against responsibility to their art. That this is a semi-autobiographical concern (variously signalled, and subsequently accented by Muldoon's emigration to America), makes it the more urgent and difficult for the workings of Auden's or MacNeice's intelligence to seem in some convincing way their own preserve while being disclosed. It is a sign of the uneven success of '7 Middagh Street' that those parts of it which have attracted most attention are concerned with public issues (e.g. "If Yeats had saved his pencil-lead / would certain men have stayed in bed?"). The more the privacy of 'Louis's' thoughtstream is signalled, by invoking parts of his experience which a reader will not take as 'MacNeice', the more they are likely to appear the fruits of Muldoon's assiduous reading and frivolity.

In '7 Middagh Street' everything turns into something else through the unrelenting lightness of fancy. Mahon takes the more thing-centred view of Pythagoras at the end of Ovid. Since, in a material universe (and increasingly manufactured world), everything actually has been something else, Mahon cannot understand why, for instance, "The ranged crockery" (in 'The Studio') does not

> freak and wail
> Remembering its dark origins, the frail
> Oilcloth, in a fury of recognitions,
> Disperse in a thousand directions . . .

When he addresses this theme directly, Mahon can seem merely adroit. 'Lives', for instance, dedicated to Seamus Heaney, describes how "I was a torc of gold" then "an oar . . . stuck in the shore . . . a stone in Tibet, // A tongue of bark", and so on, until "Now . . . I am / An anthropologist / With my own / Credit card, dictaphone". This saga of metempsychosis has the flatness of an oblique poet confronting squarely what most concerns him. Heaney gets inside transformation, as when Sweeney translated is translated to a bird:

> His brain convulsed,
> his mind split open.
> Vertigo, hysteria, lurchings
> and launchings came over him,
> he staggered and flapped desperately,
> he was revolted by the thought of known places
> and dreamed strange migrations . . . (Section 11)

Despite the "he" of this, as against Mahon's "I", the words used to draw Sweeney from the mental to the physical ("flapped" with panic and wings, "revolted" and swung violently round) tap into the reader's nervous system. In Heaney's prose source, intensity is drained by cataloguing—"darkness, and fury, and giddiness, and frenzy, and flight, unsteadiness, restlessness, and unquiet filled him"[26]—whereas his free verse, refusing to distance the subject as object, breaks the list by having Sweeney's grammatical position fluctuate with the push and tug of experience. The metamorphosis is rapid yet impressively gradual. Heaney has an empathy with natural process which gives his thought nature's speed, even when slow.[27] At the end of 'Sweeney Redivivus' he describes a rock formation which has the shape of "a drinking deer":

> For my book of changes
> I would meditate
> that stone-faced vigil
>
> until the long dumbfounded
> spirit broke cover . . .

And you believe that Heaney's *Metamorphoses* could emerge from that stag's emerging, partly because an aesthetic of patience is writ large across his work, but also because the Sweeney of the *Buile Suibhne*, Heaney's persona here, has imagined his own transformation into a stag (Section 40) and knows the rock's life from inside. Mahon's stance is different: a strong residual humanism puts his consciousness outside things. As that poem for John Hewitt, 'The Return', suggests, he experiences nature as other; trying to become a torc of gold or tongue of bark (even a mindless anthropologist) is an imaginative struggle, or mere conceit. Symptomatically, when Mahon thinks of being a bird, Sweeney-like, in 'The Dawn Chorus', it is a desperately remembered event, anticipated with more yearning than patience:

> Listening heart-broken to the dawn chorus,
> Clutching the certainty that once we flew,
> We yearn for that reality in this.
>
> Awaiting still our metamorphosis,
> We hoard the fragments of what once we knew . . .

Mahon's tenacious humanism combines with his sense of 'immanence' to produce a strangely Romantic devotion to the deities of stone and vegetation. "Who said the banished gods were gone for good?" is a typical line ('The Andean Flute'), repeated till the doubt seems empty. There is an affinity here with such nineteenth-century poets as Nerval, source of 'The Mute Phenomena', who writes in a sonnet which Mahon translates in *The Chimeras*, "They will come back, the archaic gods you mourn!" ('Delphica'). Mahon's version of *Les Chimères* ends, in the manner of *Metamorphoses*, with a poem called 'Pythagorean Lines'—a title which, uniquely in this volume, diverges from Nerval. In 'The Banished Gods', Mahon describes the places where his Romantic gods are waiting, far upstream or out at sea:

> It is here that the banished gods are in hiding,
> Here they sit out the centuries
> In stone, water
> And the hearts of trees,
> Lost in a reverie of their own natures—
>
> Of zero-growth economics and seasonal change
> In a world without cars, computers
> Or chemical skies,
> Where thought is a fondling of stones
> And wisdom a five-minute silence at moonrise.

The Green slant of this predates current fads and distinguishes Mahon's Romanticism from the sub-Wordsworthian strain which remains staple in much Irish poetry. Even Heaney, whose writing about farm life is too raw for some English readers (others neglect the divergence between their own, and Irish, views of 'nature'),[28] depicts a countryside unscathed by industry, pollution, farm technology. Such a vision of the four green fields is often achieved by ignoring the grimy reality of Belfast (and southern industry). Capitalism is British, Erin must be agricultural. Mahon is not culturally positioned to accept a De Valeran outlook, or idyll. Perhaps because he spent his first years in New York, Montague is the Northern Catholic writer most alert to the destruction of Irish landscape by the bulldozers of development. With Brooklyn and Garvaghey for contrast, and with later departures and returns to Ireland underlining the ratcheted advance of change, he is able to write about the Tyrone of his boyhood with a sense of the passing of more than one child's way of life. There are republican energies in Montague's feeling for "the rough field", a desire to recover home ground. Potential links between green nationalism and Green politics—which might strengthen in the 1990s[29]—begin to emerge in his work. Even an irenic poem like 'The Errigal Road', which describes a visit to "my old Protestant neighbour . . . Eagleson", associates British army "Helicopters overhead, hovering locusts" with ecological decline: "Soon all our shared landscape will be effaced, / a quick stubble of pine recovering most". Yet Montague increasingly views such losses in global terms. He praises poets like Ted Hughes, Wendell Berry and the Snyder of *Earth House Hold*.[30] For readers committed to political analysis, his fear for the habitat sometimes overshadows history. Seamus Deane says of 'Balance Sheet', which itemizes the environmental 'Loss' and 'Gain' of building the new Omagh Road, "This is ecology, not poetry . . . Poetry and history . . . are both annulled here and replaced by nothing more than a tract."[31] Developing related doubts: Montague's nature poetry can look dubious because it reverts to archaic politics for the sake of suggesting magnitude. In his last book, *Mount Eagle*, a salmon is "Great river king . . . Prince of ocean", 'Peninsula' celebrates "Dame Nature's self– / delighting richness", and so on. Compared with this, Mahon's powers of earth are democrats: dryads, nereids, minor gods of locale and difference. Ovid encourages Mahon to shun the misleading holism of Montague's ecology.

Another contrast is already evident. Montague regrets the impact of industrial culture on the countryside. Mahon, Belfast and London centred, has gone through and beyond that shock: he is a post-industrial poet awaiting nature's re-emergence. He anticipates, "after / The twilight of cities", the gods' "return" to "a world of waste" ('The Golden Bough'). Beautiful lines on the last page of *Poems 1962–1978* imagine "The day the girl among the trees / Strides through our wrecked technologies". This sense of imminent collapse puts Mahon at odds with the myth of progress which is almost our secular faith. Like Ovid's Pythagoras undoing Augustan history, he challenges the assumption, common to both capitalism and socialism, that an empire of technological development will bring peace and prosperity to the world. Not that he contemplates the end of industry without dread. He has written of "the Northern poet, surrounded . . . by the Greek gifts of modern industry and what Ferlinghetti called the 'hollering monsters of the imagination of disaster' ".[32] The likeliest disaster is nuclear, and Mahon's writing is haunted—especially of late—by "the big bang" (e.g. 'Mt Gabriel'). If he inclines to pastoralism, it is of the kind which flourishes in post-apocalypse movies, where small groups of survivors work the land. Typical of these films is low-tech culture in which the trash of a previous epoch is integrated into a new life. Mahon's attitude to rubbish, in the same way, has a touch of the *bricoleur*. Although he declares "The fruits of industrialism are ruination and waste, ugliness",[33] his developed view differs from the simple hostility of most Greens. For one thing—as you would expect from 'The Studio'—his dislike of trash on the landscape is modified by satisfaction at seeing things revert to nature. "The grime of an ephemeral / Culture . . . The refuse of an era" that he speaks of in 'One of these Nights' has an allure not least because it shows that "era" choking up in "a world of waste". Every cycle can be recycled; so, in 'Entropy', there is a gleam of transcendence when "The roads at evening glitter / with ditched bicycles". Clearly there is a link between "waste" and what lies near the heart of Mahon's sensibility: "My interest is in a sort of secular numen."[34] In 'The Mute Phenonema' we are told: "Already in a lost hub-cap is conceived / The ideal society which will replace our own". Like the bric-a-brac assembled by early-'50s Picasso into strange beasts which display what they are made of, trash in Mahon is stuff en route to new meanings, in metamorphosis. The poet takes some pleasure in 'The Apotheosis of Tins', in what that poem calls "the terminal democracy / of hatbox and crab". Mahon is a beachcomber, a connoisseur of lists and detritus (e.g. 'Deaths'), and this can extend to his tolerance for people out of place, social litter. Sweeney seems especially Irish to Heaney because "the green spirit of the hedges embodied in [him] had first been embodied for me in the persons of a family of tinkers, also called Sweeney, who used to camp in the ditchbacks along the road to the first school I attended" (Introduction, p. ix). In 'Gipsies' Mahon registers a rather different sympathy, which comes from the shared trash-living of bourgeois and traveller:

> I listen to the wind
> and file receipts. The heap
> of scrap metal in my
> garden grows daily.

Indeed the larger-than-human existence of Sweeney finds a curiously answering elevation in Mahon's 'The Death of Marilyn Monroe', where the movie idol is a "Goddess" because "she was . . . queen among the trash". But by this stage a reversal is apparent in Mahon's Green logic. For this most aesthetical of Northern poets, the spheres of possibility and transcendence grounded in art are involved with a rubbishy disorder which the artist also recoils from.

Some light is shed here by Michael Thompson's *Rubbish Theory: The Creation and Destruction of Value* (1979). The ingenious sociologist argues that objects pass from the class of consumer transients—to which "terminal democracy" tends to reduce all products—into the class of durables (where art-objects belong) by passing through a category of "rubbish" which it is in the interests of society (if you think art-values have a function) to make occult. Without a period in which, say, bakelite radios, treadle sewing-machines and, currently, Moody Blues records become invisible (literally in box-rooms, but also in attics of the mind), they cannot be sifted and transformed into the stuff of heritage. Various sorts of Victorian tat are now framed and sold as durables—the remains of empire become antique—but this would not have been possible without a period of neglect which purged their value as transients. That Mahon finds an aura around rubbish not only because it shows things reverting to nature but because it represents aesthetic value in the making is apparent from several poems. 'A Garage in Co. Cork', for instance, describes a place left by economic migrants:

> Where did they go? South Boston? Cricklewood?
> Somebody somewhere thinks of this as home,
> Remembering the old pumps where they stood,
> Antique now, squirting juice into a chrome
> Lagonda or a dung-caked tractor while
> A cloud swam on a cloud-reflecting tile.

The nimbus of value-gain which surrounds the transition from wreck to heritage is finely caught by the ambiguous "Antique now", while the name "Lagonda" musically suggests the deep-sprung luxury of a car which at some point in the collective consciousness turned from 'old' to 'vintage'. Mahon the aesthete comes into focus. For him, the fact that rubbish rewards our attention because it metamorphoses, with delectable ungainliness, back to nature is complicated by a sense that its value is shaped in ways which parallel the processes of poetry:

> Left to itself, the functional will cast
> A death-bed glow of picturesque abandon.
> The intact antiquities of the recent past,
> Dropped from the retail catalogues, return
> To the materials that gave rise to them
> And shine with a late sacramental gleam.

> A god who spent the night here once rewarded
> Natural courtesy with eternal life—
> Changing to petrol pumps, that they be spared
> For ever there, an old man and his wife.
> The virgin who escaped his dark design
> Sanctions the townland from her prickly shrine.

This inimitably makes wit from portentousness. The fastidious harmony of "intact antiquities" and "retail catalogues" verges on self-parody, whispering 'Mahon'. Rhyme-words like "cast" or "abandon" mark points of formal achievement by politely pausing for their quibbles to be noticed. Initial terms similarly earn their prominence. Where Muldoon's joke about mules falling to birth from heaven is led by the mind's (and cinematic) eye, Mahon exploits the trochaic aplomb of "Dropped" to elicit 'born' (as foals are "Dropped") as well as 'left out of', 'let fall'. The pleasures of ambiguity are audible, and depend on respect for order—a classical quality enhanced by the decorum of what is described: "Natural courtesy . . . that they be spared . . . Sanctions the townland". There is an affinity with seventeenth-century writers like Marvell (a connection still more apparent when Mahon writes octosyllabic couplets), not least in the impression of faintly misplaced sophistication, of a stylist underemployed by his material though not his theme. Certainly Mahon has a 'metaphysical' interest in illuminating large issues with conceits that start from homely objects. As in 'The Garden' or 'Upon Appleton House', moreover, the poet's inventiveness is felt to rival the way such objects revalue themselves. Here Mahon's self-regarding style comes into its own, since it allows him smoothly to modulate into the allusion to Ovid. The "sacramental gleam" which haloes things that "return / To" nature, which lights up transients as they become "antiquities", is seen to be matched by the mock-transcendence of art as Mahon translates trash, fabulously meta-morphoses the wrecked petrol-pump and shrub.

Mahon's title puts us in 'Co. Cork,' yet his penultimate stanza begins, "We might be anywhere . . .". A few pages earlier in *The Hunt By Night*, 'A Lighthouse in Maine' starts: "It might be anywhere . . .". Clearly places are more important than where they are. At times this tension relaxes into the benign internationalism of poems like 'The Globe in North Carolina': "The earth spins to my finger-tips and / Pauses beneath my outstretched hand . . .". More often an underlying dislocation, estrangement, is declared. Mahon seeks the handhold of places on 'The Globe', but it keeps rolling from his grasp—like something in *The Myth of Sisyphus*. Since his generation was nurtured on Sartre and Camus, it is not surprising that the alienation of a poet who feels at home neither in leafy Surrey nor Coleraine should find expression in such terms. "I would call myself an existentialist", he has said, "an open-minded existentialist."[35] Mahon's *Antarctica* ends with a tribute to the author of *L'Etranger*; and he admits the link with his colonial background when he says of James Simmons and Longley: "*Mutatis mutandis*, their relationship, as men of goodwill, to the indigenous Catholic-Irish culture is not unlike that of Camus to the Algerian Muslims".[36] Almost invariably when Mahon writes about place, there is an ontological subplot concerned with man's desire to belong in the world, cross-cut with colonial anxiety. In 'Going Home', for instance, he describes the shadowlife of Hull shiftworkers, ferried across the Humber like so many souls over the Styx. These commuters would have plenty to worry about in a poem by Larkin or Dunn (to whom the poem is dedicated); but Mahon gives them a generalised existential appli-cation—"For ours is the afterlife / Of the unjudgeable, / Of the desolate and free"—and has them walk under "The sort of sky / That broke the hearts / Of the foundered legionaries." Up near Hadrian's wall, the Roman empire reasserts itself, defining the place as ineffably removed, a bleak frontier. 'Going Home' is determined to exclude any Larkinesque sense that, despite its grottiness, Hull might be where people belong:

> A sunken barge rots
> In the mud beach
> As if finally to discredit

> A residual poetry of
> Leavetaking and homecoming,
> Of work and sentiment . . .

The scene is characteristic. Mahon's passion for windows is only out-stripped by his fondness for desolate shorelines. The view from a window permits a lofty perspective; on the beach, where "the terminal democracy / of hatbox and crab" leaves its litter for the poet to sift through, the outlook is onto nowhere. At least since Ovid's *Tristia*, shorefronts have represented that despairing frontier of mind from which exile poetry speaks. Mahon's recurrent word "terminal", though, draws in borders of every sort, including the temporal. For the limits of empire are historical as well as geographical. Mahon's creative plight is enriched by the fact that, even if he felt at home in the home counties, what they stand for now is not what his "colonial education" claimed. In 'Brighton Beach', the poet visits not only a shoreline, but a town where empire retires to, just lingers; and he finds the place entangled with the thought that places have no location:

> the spirit of empire
> Fugitive as always.
> Now, in this rancorous peace,
> Should come the spirit of place.
>
> Too late, though, for already
> Places as such are dead
> Or nearly . . .

The problem is not just of being provincial at the centre, colonist at the margin. It is that the centre does not hold, and that with it vanishes the *genius loci* which empire helped destroy by turning locality into a measure of each place's relation (London/Derry) to the capital, capitol.

The contours of loyalty and emotion are very different for a Catholic nationalist. In 'Exile's Return', Seamus Deane describes what it means to leave America and come back to a violent province

> condensed
> Out of ocean, malingering far
> West of Eden, its truest colour
> Nettle-green. Here the heart begins.

The gap between Mahon's title, 'The Return', and Deane's is great because of the tradition the latter invokes. Erin has buried its dead in South Boston, Cricklewood, and places further afield. As a returning exile, Deane can represent, almost too easily, the fate and hope of "a dispersed people". The phrase is Heaney's ('From the Land of the Unspoken'), and he adds: "When or why our exile began . . . we cannot tell". Indubitably the story goes back centuries. Montague, observing that "our countrymen have a long habit of exile", finds it "significant that the first two poets whose names are recorded in our literary history (after the mythical Amergin, the bard of the Milesians) were both exiles."[37] Such a weighty and articulate past can be disabling: it fosters bland piety, or that manipulation of received feeling which Kinsella fears when he writes, in 'Baggot Street Deserta':

> We fly into our risk, the spurious.
>
> Versing, like an exile, makes
> A virtuoso of the heart . . .

Where might he find "the spurious"? Kinsella's exclusion of Brian Coffey from his *New Oxford Book of Irish Verse* suggests dissatisfaction with the kind of epistemological miniature which that poet has, virtuosically, refined from exile:

> But in mind
> the dead centre
> like like yawning
>
> yawning away
> in shadows
> straight and still
>
> Nothing that flickers
> for sidelong glances
> Nothing   Period . . .

'How Far from Daybreak' typifies a minimalism which leaves the reader uncertain whether what must be taken to the poetry is metaphysically necessary or a compensation for creative thinness. Coffey's verse at its best details a Beckettian scrupulousness which strips exile of glamour and makes that experience, in a complex sense, mundane.[38] But it is not yet clear how securely his verse can be recognised 'at its best'. There is an equal, though opposite, danger. Kinsella admits of a comment of his own ("Ireland is a necessary burden, a place I must keep coming back to . . ."), "I detect the voice of an exile there, a certain hysteria."[39] "The spurious" might be the product of derived and inflated emotions. Perhaps inevitably, after Coffey, Denis Devlin comes to mind—working in translation, too, where received ideas are of the essence:

> Doors open on the sands, doors open on exile . . .
>   I have chosen a place glaring and null as the bone-heap of the
>       seasons,
>   And, on all the shores of the world, the ghost of the god in smoke
>       abandons his bed of asbestos . . .

Devlin's relentless magniloquence, in this rendering of St-John Perse's *L'Exil*, like Coffey's delicacy (as, e.g. 'Missouri Sequence' shows), draws on integrally Irish structures of feeling about exile. Except that Ireland is not integral. Next to Derry is another country. Villages straddle the border, and roads wind back and forth across it. Few Southern poets work out in depth (Kinsella is an exception) how this maims or enables them. But it gives Northern views of space, as in Deane's journey from exile ("Now it is the tinder of border towns, / Greened ruins, locked headlands . . ."), a definite organisation and texture. Predictably enough, partition in Muldoon is a tricksy line running down the middle of Golightly's lane ('The Boundary Commission'). It makes him "wonder which side, if any, he should be on", and the brilliantly casual "if any" (less than one, more than two?) could not be so liberating without the tragic history which is read from geography by writers like Montague and Heaney. In their work partition spreads a crazed network which separates fields and streets ('The Other Side', 'A New Siege') and can divide the mind. Anxiety about, or perverse delight in, partition correlates with larger feelings about expatriation. Montague—whose book-title *Forms of Exile* is revealingly plural—concedes that the "habit of exile" comes "most often through necessity, but also through curiosity".[40] Muldoon, happily curious, continues his refabling of Irish myths of space by suggesting, in recent transatlantic work, that his new found land is home from home: "I was browsing through Nora Chadwick's *The Celts* / Somewhere near Belfast, Maine . . .". Characteristically he rhymes "*Celts*" with "two colts" (the poem's title) and—why not, indeed?—"gaults". Ovid among the gaults is no more estranged in exile than at home in Golightly's lane. As Muldoon shows in 'Tea', Ovid's philosopher and pious Rome are as ready to hand in the States as in Belfast, Ulster:

> I was rooting through tea-chest after tea-chest
> as they drifted in along Key West
>
> when I chanced on 'Pythagoras in America':
> the book had fallen open at a bookmark
>
> of tea; a tassel
> of black watered silk from a Missal . . .

What exile liberates into suave invention here could not more sharply contrast with the verse that Heaney, half-expatriated, has written from Boston. Ireland in *The Haw Lantern* is divided and ruled, culturally unrealised. Heaney's Catholic geography leads the émigré mind back to lines of separation across a land and some levels of imagination. The bird-hero of *Sweeney Astray* is thus an 'exile' within Ireland (like his redivived equivalent in 'On the Road'), and "exiled from myself" (Sections 13, 27). Edna Longley is right to say, "when Heaney too deliberately tries for the tone of 'responsible *tristia*', he loses his real touch",[41] but the danger is there in part because the estrangement Heaney inherits has an expressive power which distance, if anything, amplifies and which licences emotional automatism. Certainly, alluding to Ovid at the end of 'Exposure', Heaney not only draws on the traditional energies of exile poetry but highlights that inner expatriation which specially belongs to Northern Catholics in an incomplete state. Undertones of victimisation, flight from British authority, covert operation, ally him with a vital fraction of his community, even while he asserts his isolation as artist.

It is a layered allusion. Heaney recalls Ovid as—and partly because—Mandelstam had done in the magnificent title-poem of *Tristia*, published in 1922. There is a suggestion in 'Exposure' that the Revolutionary civil war in Russia, which Mandelstam escaped to write his poem, be compared with another war of 1922, in Ireland, a war which seemed in the early '70s to be flaring up again. One review published by Heaney in 1974 cites Mandelstam on Ovid to help define the former's inclusiveness;[42] and the longer chain of identification is confirmed by a piece in *The Government of the Tongue* which praises Mandelstam's "metamorphic excitements" and talks of him being led "to identify himself increasingly with outcasts and exiles".[43] Heaney's sojourn in America has encouraged him "increasingly" to affiliate with such exiles as Dante and Milosz, as well as with displaced Irish writers like O'Rathaille. This has seemed to claim a range and significance for Heaney's poetry which, because of his high Romantic stance in many texts, asks to be taken *ad hominem*. There is a touch of grandiose bathos which Muldoon—to contrast him again—would never hazard. The younger poet plays on parallels between MacNeice's career and his own (Ulster, the BBC, New York). But MacNeice is not a poet of Dante's magnitude, and, whatever his moral courage, he was not required by events to become an exemplary figure like Mandelstam. In any case, Muldoon's game with MacNeice is an extension of parodic method into those aspects of his own life which, as life-story or life style, matter in poems that are heavily ironised. Further, while Heaney writes criticism which encourages us to see him as an Irish Dante, an Ulster Mandelstam, Muldoon remains aloof. There are dangers in Edna Longley's yoking of the younger poet and Mac-Neice,[44] in that weaker critics might not challenge the perspective through which she so illuminatingly and (it follows) narrowingly construes these unlike poets, but her formidable and vigilant essays raise opinion so near to knowledge that Muldoon is provided with assumptions in his readership for glancing at and from. In criticism as in verse, it would seem, Muldoon creates situations in which the forward youth need not appear. Heaney's use of the exile motif, by contrast, bites off a great deal to chew. A poet like Mandelstam was relegated to get him out of the public mind. Heaney is open to sniping about his exile getting too much 'Exposure'. But then, media coverage was not a difficulty which dissident writers had to negotiate in Stalinist Russia.

The matter is clarified by returning to Mahon, whose metaphysical version of exile poetry is less politically applicable. His continual reference of places to everywhere and nowhere, his universalising the predicament of Hull shiftworkers or Cork emigrants, takes the edge off the political question—or, if what has been claimed is valid, was never an edge to the same issue. Mahon creates or reinvents figures who can represent aspects of everyman not because they are elevated like Cuchulain or enlarged like HCE but because the localities and times they inhabit stretch out so blankly from the "terminal" point where poems are spoken that specificity fades. The relations between

Mahon's voice and that of a persona like Tithonus are clear yet
unremarkable, not through a failure of projection but because
sheerness of time and unplace around the character inhibits the
emergence of those analogies (dependent on difference) which strike,
say, readers of Sweeney-Heaney's poem about the medieval poet-king
of Ulster. Mahon and his Tithonus are alike through blankness of
circumstance, inheriting a quotidian vacuousness from the systems of
dying stars which wheel about them, and us. Some such note of
sublimity needs striking in any adequate description because Mahon
uses Romàntic rhetoric to realise emptiness. As in Jaccottet (whom he
has translated),[45] there is an austere amplitude to his diction which
dissolves the particular in light. And if, in the foreground of his
poems, an estranged figure strikes us as having individual traits, that
persona will command more attention than Mahon so that the poet—
unlike Heaney-Mandelstam, or the elusively obtrusive Muldoon—
can be seen, but unnoticed, getting on with the impersonal job of
scanning his classical numbers. Such as, for instance, this speaker:

> What coarse god
> Was the gear-box in the rain
> Beside the road?
>
> What nereid the unsinkable
> Hair conditioner
> Knocking the icy rocks?

It is, of course, 'Ovid in Tomis' from *The Hunt by Night*. In this
most direct invocation of the Latin Ulsterman, Mahon takes us into a
landscape of late industrialism which might be contemporary Belfast
— the cluttered scene of Ciaran Carson's poems, or some of Frank
Ormsby's—but can be general. 'Tomis', ousted by 'Constanza', is no
longer in the atlas, its empire dead. Place in the poem is neither here
nor there, except in so far as it defines a fading edge. History exerts its
pressure, not in ways which invite decoding and action, but to explain
the elegiac lassitude which is our substitute, Mahon implies, for
philosophy. This poem, enriched by an identification with Ovid
which deepens in *Antarctica* (where *Amores* I.v and II.xi are
translated), is the creative corollary of those passages in Mahon where
a frontier sense emerges from discernibly Protestant sources. But its
success depends on far more than the emotive force-field of politics.
Ovid's intelligence belongs to the centre, even though he has been

internally exiled to Tomis; and he personifies the wit in Mahon which stems from misplaced sophistication. "Imagine Byron banished / To Botany Bay / Or Wilde to Dawson City", Ovid says, "And you have some idea / How it is for me". In this way, the imagination which produced the *Metamorphoses* at Rome keeps reasserting itself. Ovid speaks of his "own transformation / Into a stone"—a quip of typically laconic cleverness, since it touches on the statue long since, but not yet in the poem, erected to the poet at Constanza. Likewise he describes "The pathos" of the delta, where Syrinx lives again in reeds which do not simply pass through the changes of fable but "keen" for "the certain future" in which "She and her kind" will be pulped and made "the cording / Of motor-car tyres". It is a triumphant bringing together of Mahon's Pythagorean wit, where shifts of matter are metamorphic jokes, and his own Ovidian storying. In the end the scope of the poem is larger than anything in Heaney (or Muldoon) because of its attention to the "infinity" which inheres in changeable things—"The cry at the heart / Of the artichoke, / The gaiety of atoms." Perhaps Mahon also provides a view of poetry which, for all his indirection, tells us more than bardic gesturing about the tacit fertility of that estrangement from language which is the burden of so much recent verse. With a turn towards reticence and self-doubt which contributes greatly to its beauty, 'Ovid in Tomis' ends where this essay must also stop, with fables and changes unwritten, and a sense of exile registered in no way that blunts its pain:

> Better to contemplate
> The blank page
> And leave it blank . . .
>
> Woven of wood-nymphs,
> It speaks volumes
> No one will ever write.
>
> I incline my head
> To its candour
> And weep for our exile.

NOTES
1. London: Faber & Faber, 1981, p. 64.
2. Quoted by W.B. Stanford, *Ireland and the Classical Tradition* (Dublin: Allen Figgis, 1976), p. 25.

3.  Stanford, *Ireland and the Classical Tradition*, p. 26.
4.  e.g. P.J. Dowling, *The Hedge Schools of Ireland*, rev. edn. (Cork: Mercier Press, 1968), pp. 37–41, 56–7.
5.  *Carthaginians and Baglady* (London: Faber & Faber, 1988), p. 17.
6.  'The Schooner *Flight*' (I, 'Adois, Carenage'), in *Collected Poems* (London: Faber & Faber, 1986), pp. 345–61, p. 346.
7.  *The Government of the Tongue* (London: Faber & Faber, 1988), p. 26.
8.  Published 1910; rev. edn (London: Peter Owen, 1952), p. 15.
9.  'In the Beginning was the Aeneid: On Translation', rpt. in *Ireland and the English Crisis* (Newcastle: Bloodaxe Books, 1984), pp. 205–16.
10. Homeric allusion in Northern poetry (e.g. Heaney's 'Whatever You Say Say Nothing' III, Muldoon's 'Making the Move'), translation (Michael Longley's 'The Butchers') and, generally, paraphrase from Greek (e.g. Paulin's *The Riot Act*) is matter for another essay.
11. *Less than One: Selected Essays* (Harmondsworth: Penguin Books, 1987), pp. 399–402.
12. See J.P. Sullivan's instructive account of this letter, from 1917, in *Ezra Pound and Sextus Propertius: A Study in Creative Translation* (London: Faber & Faber, 1965), pp. 26–7.
13. Number 78, 13–31.
14. "Yet spare me, by the bonds of our stealthy union, I entreat thee, by our love and the head that has lain by mine" (tr. J.P. Postgate, Loeb edn).
15. See Alan J. Peacock, 'Prolegomena to Michael Longley's Peace Poem', *Eire–Ireland* 23 (1988), 60–74, p. 64.
16. *The Gods Made Flesh: Metamorphosis and the Pursuit of Paganism* (New Haven: Yale University Press, 1986), p. 85.
17. *The Gods Made Flesh*, p. 88.
18. *Ovid Recalled* (Cambridge: Cambridge University Press, 1955), p. 147.
19. Note to *A Slow Dance*, rpt. in *The Figure in the Cave and Other Essays* (Dublin: Lilliput Press, 1989), pp. 52–3, p. 52.
20. *Ovid Recalled*, p. 162.
21. 'The More a Man Has the More a Man Wants', 'Sushi'.
22. 'Under Judgement', interview with Blake Morrison, *New Statesman*, 8 February 1980, 212–14, p. 214; *Viewpoints: Poets in Conversation with John Haffenden* (London: Faber & Faber, 1981), p. 88.
23. 'The Redress of Poetry', abridged from his inaugural lecture as Professor of Poetry at Oxford University, *TLS*, 22–9 December 1989, p. 1413.
24. 'Poetry and Politics in Northern Ireland' in *Poetry in the Wars* (Newcastle: Bloodaxe Books, 1986), pp. 185–210, 210.
25. *The Gods Made Flesh*, pp. 89, 79.
26. *Buile Suibhne (The Frenzy of Suibhne)*, ed. J.G. O'Keefe, Irish Texts Society (London: David Nutt, 1913), p. 15; introducing *Sweeney Astray* (p. vii), Heaney acknowledges his debt.
27. It seems right that one of the finest metamorphic poems recently written in Ireland, though not Ulster, Paul Durcan's 'The Rape of Europa (after Titian)', should be dedicated 'To Seamus and Marie'.
28. See Michael Viney, 'Woodcock for a Farthing: The Irish Experience of Nature', *The Irish Review* 1 (1986), pp. 58–64.
29. For stirrings see the articles by Steve Dawe in *Green Line* 68 (New Year, 1989), pp. 9–11, and under 'The Greening of Northern Ireland?', 'Ending the Longest Little War', *Econews* 46 (August, 1989), pp. 7–8.

30. e.g., 'John Montague on Ted Hughes: Poet of Earth and Magic', *The Irish Times*, 4 November 1989 [*Weekend*], p. 9; *The Figure in the Cave*, p. 13.

31. *Celtic Revivals: Essays in Modern Irish Literature 1880–1980* (London: Faber & Faber, 1985), p. 152.

32. 'Poetry in Northern Ireland', in *Twentieth-Century Studies* 4 (1970), 89–93, p. 90.

33. Terence Brown, ' An Interview with Derek Mahon', *Poetry Ireland Review* 14 (1985), 11–19, p. 13.

34. 'An Interview with Derek Mahon', p. 16.

35. 'An Interview with Derek Mahon', p. 15.

36. 'Poetry in Northern Ireland', p. 92.

37. 'The Impact of International Modern Poetry on Irish Writing', *The Figure in the Cave*, pp. 208–20, pp. 208–9.

38. cf. Stan Smith, 'On Other Grounds: The Poetry of Brian Coffey', in Douglas Dunn, ed., *Two Decades of Irish Writing: A Critical Survey* (Cheadle: Carcanet Press, 1975), pp. 59–80.

39. *Viewpoints*, p. 105 (discussing a Radio Eireann broadcast, 1974).

40. 'The Impact of International Modern Poetry', p. 208. Cf. Mary McCarthy's distinctions: 'A Guide to Exiles, Expatriates, and Internal Emigrés', *New York Review of Books*, 9 March 1972, pp. 4–8.

41. 'Old Pewter' (review of *Station Island*), *Honest Ulsterman* 77 (1984), pp. 54–58, 55.

42. Rpt., from *Hibernia*, in *Preoccupations: Selected Prose 1968–1978* (London: Faber & Faber, 1980), pp. 217–20, p. 218.

43. 'Osip and Nadezhda Mandelstam', pp. 71–88, pp. 75, 87.

44. e.g., the closing pages of 'Poetry and Politics in Northern Ireland', '"Varieties of Parable": Louis MacNeice and Paul Muldoon', *Poetry in the Wars*, pp. 185–210, 211–43.

45. *Selected Poems*, in the Penguin International Poets series (Harmondsworth: Penguin Books, 1988).

# Select Bibliography

## 1. Individual Writers: Texts and Criticism

**John Montague**

*Forms of Exile*, Dublin: Dolmen Press, 1958
*Poisoned Lands*, London: MacGibbon and Kee, 1961; new edition Dublin: Dolmen Press, 1977
*A Chosen Light*, MacGibbon and Kee, 1967
*Tides*, Dolmen Press, 1970
*The Rough Field*, Dolmen Press, 1972; reprinted Loughcrew: Gallery Press and Newcastle upon Tyne: Bloodaxe Books, 1989 [with Montague's annotation]
*A Slow Dance*, Dolmen Press and Oxford University Press, 1975
*The Great Cloak*, Dolmen Press and Oxford University Press, 1978
*Selected Poems*, Dolmen Press and Oxford University Press, 1982
*The Dead Kingdom*, Dolmen Press; Oxford University Press; and Belfast: Blackstaff Press, 1984
*Mount Eagle*, Loughcrew: Gallery Press, 1988
*New Selected Poems*, Gallery Press and Bloodaxe Books, 1989
*The Figure in the Cave and Other Essays* (ed. Antoinette Quinn), Dublin: Lilliput Press, 1989
*Death of a Chieftain*, MacGibbon and Kee, 1964 [short stories]
*The Lost Notebook*, Cork: Mercier Press, 1987 [short stories]
*The Faber Book of Irish Verse* (ed.), London: Faber & Faber, 1974
'Global Regionalism: Interview with John Montague', *Literary Review: An International Journal of Contemporary Writing*, no. 22 (1979), pp. 153–74

See also:
Frazier, Adrian, 'John Montague's Language of the Tribe', *Canadian Journal of Irish Studies*, vol.9 no.2 (1983), pp. 57–75.

*Irish University Review*, John Montague Special Issue, vol.19 no.1 (Spring 1989)

Kersnowski, Frank, *John Montague*, Lewisburg: Bucknell University Press, 1975

Martin, Graham, 'John Montague, Seamus Heaney, and the Irish Past' in Boris Ford (ed.), *New Pelican Guide to English Literature: The Present*, Harmondsworth: Penguin, 1983, pp. 380–94

Redshaw, Thomas Dillon, 'That Surviving Sign: John Montague's *The Bread God*', *Eire-Ireland*, vol. 17 no.2 (Summer 1982), pp. 56–91

Redshaw, Thomas Dillon, 'The Bounding Line: John Montague's *A New Siege*', *Canadian Journal of Irish Studies*, vol.13 no.1 (June 1987), pp. 75–105

Redshaw, Thomas Dillon (ed.), *Hillfield: Poems and Memoirs for John Montague on the Occasion of his Sixtieth Birthday*, Dublin: Gallery Press, 1989

## Seamus Heaney

*Death of a Naturalist*, London: Faber & Faber, 1966

*Door into the Dark*, Faber & Faber, 1969

*Wintering Out*, Faber & Faber, 1972

*North*, Faber & Faber, 1975

*Field Work*, Faber & Faber, 1979

*Selected Poems 1965–1975*, Faber & Faber, 1980

*Sweeney Astray*, Derry: Field Day, 1983; Faber & Faber, 1984

*Station Island*, Faber & Faber, 1984

*The Haw Lantern*, Faber & Faber, 1987

*New Selected Poems 1968–1987*, Faber & Faber, 1990

*Seeing Things*, Faber & Faber, 1991

*The Cure at Troy*, Faber & Faber, 1990 [play, version of Sophocles' *Philoctetus*]

*Preoccupations: Selected Prose 1968–1978*, Faber & Faber, 1980

*Among Schoolchildren*, Belfast: John Malone Memorial Committee, 1983

*Place and Displacement: Recent Poetry of Northern Ireland*, Grasmere: Trustees of Dove Cottage, 1984

*The Government of the Tongue*, Faber & Faber, 1988

*The Place of Writing*, Atlanta: Scholars Press, 1989 [the text of his Richard Ellmann lectures at Emory University, this includes 'The Pre-Natal Mountain: Vision and Irony in Recent Irish Poetry']

*The Redress of Poetry*, Oxford: Clarendon Press, 1990 [inaugural lecture as Oxford Professor of Poetry]

See also:

*Agenda*, Seamus Heaney Fiftieth Birthday Issue, vol.27 no.1, Spring 1989

Andrews, Elmer, *The Poetry of Seamus Heaney: All the Realms of Whisper*, London and Basingstoke: Macmillan, 1988

Bloom, Harold (ed.), *Seamus Heaney: Modern Critical Views*, New Haven: Chelsea House, 1986

Corcoran, Neil, *Seamus Heaney*, London: Faber & Faber, 1986

Curtis, Tony (ed.), *The Art of Seamus Heaney* (revised ed.), Bridgend: Poetry Wales Press, 1985; Chester Springs: Dufour Editions

Foster, Thomas C., *Seamus Heaney*, Boston: Twayne, 1989

Kelly, H.A., 'Heaney's Sweeney: The Poet as Version-Maker', *Philological Quarterly*, vol.65 no.3 (Summer 1986), pp. 293–310

Morrison, Blake, *Seamus Heaney*, London: Methuen, 1982

Tamplin, Ronald, *Seamus Heaney*, Milton Keynes: Open University Press, 1989

## Michael Longley

*No Continuing City*, London and Basingstoke: Macmillan, 1969; Chester Springs: Dufour Editions

*An Exploded View*, London: Victor Gollancz, 1973

*Man Lying on a Wall*, London: Victor Gollancz, 1976

*The Echo Gate*, London: Secker and Warburg, 1979

*Poems 1963–1986*, Edinburgh: Salamander Press and Dublin: Gallery Press, 1985; reissued Harmondsworth: Penguin Books, 1986

*Gorse Fires*, London: Secker & Warburg, 1991

See also:

Corcoran, Neil, 'Last Words: Michael Longley's Elegies', *Poetry Wales*, vol.24 no.2 (1989), pp. 16–18

Peacock, Alan J., 'Prolegomena to Michael Longley's Peace Poem', *Eire-Ireland* no.23 (1988), pp. 60–74

## Derek Mahon

*Night-Crossing*, Oxford: Oxford University Press, 1968

*Lives*, Oxford University Press, 1972
*The Snow Party*, Oxford University Press, 1975
*Poems 1962–1978*, Oxford University Press, 1979
*The Hunt by Night*, Oxford University Press, 1982
*The Chimeras* [a version of 'Les Chimeres' by Gérard de Nerval], Dublin: Gallery Press, 1982
*Antarctica*, Gallery Press, 1985
*Selected Poems*, London and Loughcrew: Viking/Gallery, 1991
*High Time* [a version of Moliere's *L'Ecole des Maris*], Gallery Press, 1985
*The School for Wives* [a version of Moliere's *L'Ecole des Femmes*], Gallery Press, 1986
Philippe Jacottet, *Selected Poems* (translated, with introduction), Harmondsworth: Penguin Books, 1988
'Poetry in Northern Ireland', *Twentieth Century Studies*, no.4 (1970), 89–93
*The Penguin Book of Contemporary Irish Poetry* (ed., with Peter Fallon), Harmondsworth: Penguin Books, 1990

See also:
Brown, Terence, 'An Interview with Derek Mahon', *Poetry Ireland Review*, no.14 (1985), pp. 11–19
Constable, John, 'Derek Mahon's Development', *Agenda*, vol.22 nos.3–4 (Autumn/Winter 1984–5), pp. 107–18
Duytschaever, Joris, 'History in the Poetry of Derek Mahon', in Duytschaever, Joris and Leernout, Geert (eds.), *History and Violence in Anglo-Irish Literature*, Amsterdam: Rodopi, 1988, pp. 97–110
Frazier, Adrian, 'Proper Portion: Derek Mahon's *The Hunt by Night*', *Eire-Ireland*, vol.18 no.4 (Winter 1983), pp. 136–43
Riordan, Maurice, 'An Urbane Perspective: The Poetry of Derek Mahon', in Maurice Harmon, (ed.), *The Irish Writer and the City*, Gerrard's Cross: Colin Smythe, 1984, pp. 167–79
Waterman, Andrew, 'Somewhere, Out There, Beyond: The Poetry of Seamus Heaney and Derek Mahon', *PN Review*, vol.8 no.1 (21), pp. 39–47

## Paul Muldoon

*Knowing My Place*, Belfast: Ulsterman Publications, 1971

*New Weather*, London: Faber & Faber, 1973
*Mules*, Faber & Faber, 1977
*Why Brownlee Left*, Faber & Faber, 1980
*Quoof*, Faber & Faber, 1983
*The Wishbone*, Dublin: Gallery Press, 1984
*Selected Poems 1968–1983*, Faber & Faber, 1986
*Meeting the British*, Faber & Faber, 1987
*Madoc—A Mystery*, Faber & Faber, 1990
*The Faber Book of Contemporary Irish Verse* (ed.), Faber & Faber, 1986

See also:
Donaghy, Michael, 'A Conversation with Paul Muldoon', *Chicago Review*, vol.35 no.1 (1985), pp. 76–85
Goodby, John, 'Armageddon, Armagh-geddon: Language and Crisis in the Poetry of Paul Muldoon', in Bramsback, Birgit and Croghan, Martin (eds.), *Anglo-Irish and Irish Literature: Aspects of Language and Culture*, Uppsala: Uppsala Univ. Press, 1988, II, pp. 229–36
Wilson, William A., 'Paul Muldoon and the Poetics of Sexual Difference', *Contemporary Literature*, vol.28 no.3 (Fall 1987), pp. 317–31

## Tom Paulin

*A State of Justice*, London: Faber & Faber, 1977
*The Strange Museum*, Faber & Faber, 1980
*The Book of Juniper* (with drawings by Noel Connor), Newcastle upon Tyne: Bloodaxe Books, 1981
*Liberty Tree*, Faber & Faber, 1983
*Fivemiletown*, Faber & Faber, 1987
*The Riot Act: A version of Sophocles' 'Antigone'*, Faber & Faber, 1985
*The Hillsborough Script: A Dramatic Satire*, Faber & Faber, 1987
*Seize the Fire: A Version of Aeschylus's 'Prometheus Bound'*, Faber & Faber, 1990
*The Faber Book of Political Verse* (ed.), Faber & Faber, 1986
*The Faber Book of Vernacular Verse* (ed.), Faber & Faber, 1990
*Thomas Hardy: The Poetry of Perception*, London and Basingstoke: Macmillan, 1975
*Ireland and the English Crisis*, Newcastle upon Tyne: Bloodaxe Books, 1984 [a collection of Paulin's essays and reviews]

See also:
Frazier, Adrian, 'Juniper, Otherwise Known: Poems by Paulin and Muldoon', *Eire-Ireland*, vol.19 no.1 (Spring 1984), pp. 123–33

## Medbh McGuckian

*Single Ladies*, Budleigh Salterton: Interim Press, 1980
*The Flower Master*, Oxford: Oxford University Press, 1982
*Venus and the Rain*, Oxford University Press, 1984
*On Ballycastle Beach*, Oxford University Press, 1988

See also:
Sellers, Susan (ed.), *Delighting the Heart: A Notebook by Women Writers* (London: The Women's Press, 1989), containing five essays by McGuckian
Wills, Clair, 'The Perfect Mother: Authority in the Poetry of Medbh McGuckian', *Text and Context* no.3 (Autumn 1988), pp. 91–111

## Ciaran Carson

*The New Estate*, Belfast: Blackstaff Press, 1976; new, enlarged edition issued as *The New Estate and Other Poems*, Loughcrew: Gallery Press, 1988
*The Lost Explorer*, Belfast: Ulsterman Publications, 1978
*The Irish for No*, Dublin: Gallery Press, 1987; Newcastle upon Tyne: Bloodaxe Books, 1988
*Belfast Confetti*, Dublin: Gallery Press, 1989; Newcastle upon Tyne: Bloodaxe Books, 1990
*The Pocket Guide to Irish Traditional Music*, Belfast: Appletree Press, 1986
'Escaped from the Massacre?', *Honest Ulsterman*, 50 (Winter 1975), pp. 183–6
'*Sweeney Astray*: Escaping from Limbo', in Curtis (ed.), *The Art of Seamus Heaney* [see above], pp. 141–8
'Against Oblivion', *The Irish Review*, no.6 (Spring 1989), pp. 113–6
'Ciaran Carson interviewed by Randy Brandes', *The Irish Review*, no.8 (Spring 1990), pp. 77–90

## 2. General Criticism

Brown, Terence, *Northern Voices: Poets from Ulster*, Dublin: Gill and Macmillan, 1975

Brown, Terence, *Ireland's Literature*, Gigginstown: Lilliput Press, 1988 [includes 'A Northern Renaissance: Poets from the North of Ireland, 1965–1980']

Brown, Terence and Grene, Nicholas (eds.), *Tradition and Influence in Anglo-Irish Poetry*, London and Basingstoke: Macmillan, 1989 [includes Brendan Kennelly's 'Derek Mahon's Humane Perspective' and Edna Longley's 'Poetic Forms and Social Malformations']

Connolly, Peter (ed.), *Literature and the Changing Ireland*, Gerrard's Cross: Colin Smythe, 1982 [includes D.E.S. Maxwell's 'Semantic Scruples: A Rhetoric for Politics in the North']

Dawe, Gerald and Longley, Edna (eds.), *Across a Roaring Hill: The Protestant Imagination in Modern Ireland*, Belfast: Blackstaff, 1985 [includes Dawe's 'Icon and Lares: Derek Mahon and Michael Longley']

Deane, Seamus, *A Short History of Irish Literature*, London: Hutchinson, 1986

Deane, Seamus, *Celtic Revivals*, London: Faber & Faber, 1985 [includes essays on Montague, Mahon and Heaney]

Donoghue, Denis, *We Irish*, Brighton: Harvester Press, 1986

Dunn, Douglas (ed.), *Two Decades of Irish Writing*, Manchester: Carcanet, 1975; Chester Springs: Dufour Editions

*Etudes Anglaises*, vol.38 no.2 (April/June 1985) [an issue devoted to contemporary British poetry, it includes Damian Grant's 'The Voice of History in British Poetry, 1970–1984' which compares Heaney, Mahon, Tony Harrison and James Fenton]

Field Day Theatre Company (eds.), *Ireland's Field Day*, London: Hutchinson, 1985 [a collection of the first six Field Day pamphlets, this includes Seamus Heaney's *An Open Letter*]

Garratt, Robert F., *Modern Irish Poetry: Tradition and Continuity from Yeats to Heaney*, Berkeley and London: University of California Press, 1986; revised ed., 1989

Haffenden, John, *Viewpoints: Poets in Conversation*, London: Faber and Faber, 1981 [includes interviews with Heaney, Muldoon and Paulin]

Harmon, Maurice (ed.), *The Irish Writer and the City*, Gerrard's Cross: Colin Smythe, 1984 [includes Gerald Dawe's 'The Permanent City: The Younger Irish Poets']

Hederman, M.P. and Kearney, Richard, *The Crane Bag Book of Irish Studies*, Gerrard's Cross: Colin Smythe, 1983 [a reprinting in its entirety of the journal which acted as a forum of debate for many of the issues informing the work of these writers]

Hyland, Paul and Sammells, Neil (eds.), *Irish Writing: Exile and Subversion*, London and Basingstoke: Macmillan, 1991 [includes Neil Corcoran's 'Strange Letters: Reading and Writing in Contemporary Irish Poetry']

Johnston, Dillon, *Irish Poetry After Joyce*, Notre Dame: University of Notre Dame Press and Mountrath: Dolmen Press, 1985

Kearney, Richard, *Transitions: Narratives in Modern Irish Culture*, Manchester: Manchester University Press, 1987 [includes an Heideggerian reading of Heaney]

Kenneally, Michael (ed.), *Cultural Contexts and Literary Idioms in Contemporary Irish Literature*, Gerrard's Cross: Colin Smythe, 1988 [includes relevant essays by Anthony Bradley, Edna Longley, Michael Toolan, John Wilson Foster, Dillon Johnston, Gerald Dawe, Arthur E. McGuinness and Anthony Roche]

Longley, Edna, *Poetry in the Wars*, Newcastle upon Tyne: Bloodaxe Books, 1986 [includes individual essays on Heaney, Mahon and Muldoon and the long polemical essay 'Poetry and Politics in Northern Ireland']

Morrison, Blake and Motion, Andrew (eds.), *The Penguin Book of Contemporary British Poetry*, Harmondsworth: Penguin Books, 1982 [the introduction offers one account of the significance of Northern Irish poetry in the history of 'British' writing]

Ormsby, Frank, *Northern Windows: An Anthology of Ulster Autobiography*, Belfast: Blackstaff, 1987 [includes Michael Longley's 'Tu'penny Stung']

*Poets from the North of Ireland* (new edition), Belfast: Blackstaff Press, 1990 [an anthology of 27 poets with a lengthy introduction by the editor.]

Robinson, Alan, *Instabilities in Contemporary British Poetry*, London and Basingstoke: Macmillan, 1988 [includes chapters on Heaney and Paulin and comments on McGuckian]

Sekine, Masaru (ed.), *Irish Writers and Society at Large*, Gerrard's Cross: Colin Smythe, 1985 [includes George Watson's 'The Narrow Ground: Northern Poets and the Northern Ireland Crisis']

*Yearbook of English Studies: British Poetry Since 1945 Special Number*, vol.17 (1987) [includes essays by John Haffenden and Neil Corcoran on Heaney; by Arthur E. McGuinness on Mahon; and by Blake Morrison and Edward Larrissy making substantial reference to some Northern poets]

# Index

# Notes on Contributors

Born in Cork in 1948, Neil Corcoran is a Senior Lecturer in the Department of English Literature at Sheffield University. His publications include a study of David Jones, *The Song of Deeds: A Study of 'The Anathemata' of David Jones* (1982), and *Seamus Heaney* (1986) and he contributes regular reviews to such periodicals as the *Times Literary Supplement* and the *London Review of Books*. He is currently completing a study of modern poetry.

Gerald Dawe is a Belfast-born poet and critic. He has lived in Galway since 1974 and divides his time between his home there and Dublin where he teaches at Trinity College Dublin. His publications include *The Lundys Letter* (1985) and, with Edna Longley, *Across a Roaring Hill: The Protestant Imagination in Modern Ireland* (1985). A new and revised edition of his anthology *The Younger Irish Poets* will appear in 1991 and also a new poetry collection, *Sunday School*.

Stan Smith is Professor and Head of English at Dundee University and co-director of the Auden Concordance Project there. He is the author of many articles on modern literature and his books include *Inviolable Voice: History and Twentieth-Century Poetry* (1982); *W.H. Auden* (1985); *Edward Thomas* (1986); *W.B. Yeats: A Critical Introduction* (1990). He is also General Editor, with Raman Selden, of the *Longman Critical Reader* series.

Peter McDonald is Fellow and Lecturer in English at Pembroke College, Cambridge. He is the author of *Louis MacNeice: The Poet in his Contexts* (1991) and a volume of poems, *Biting the Wax* (1989).

Hugh Haughton was born in Cork and teaches in the Department of English and Related Literature at the University of York.

Clair Wills is a lecturer in English at the University of Essex, having previously taught at Queen's College, Oxford.

Richard Brown teaches English Literature at the University of Leeds. He is the author of *James Joyce and Sexuality*.

Bernard O'Donoghue was born in Cork in 1945 and lectures in English at Magdalen College, Oxford. He is the author of a number of books on Medieval Literature, and has published three collections of poetry, most recently *Immaturities*.

Thomas Docherty teaches Theory and English in University College, Dublin. His books include *John Donne, Undone* (1986) and *After Theory* (1989). He is presently preparing a study called *Critical Philosophy* on postmodern criticism and culture.

John Kerrigan is a Fellow of St John's College, Cambridge and University Lecturer in English. He is the author of numerous essays on renaissance poetry and drama, editor of Shakespeare's *Sonnets and 'A Lover's Complaint'* (1986) and reviewer of new verse, notably in the *London Review of Books*.